Inspiring Women

of the

WOMEN'S

Jill S. Tietjen, Jillaine Newman, Merrill C. Amos, Editors

Printed by The Jacobs Press, Auburn, New York

National Women's Hall of Fame books may be purchased for education, business or sales promotional use. For information, please contact National Women's Hall of Fame, 76 Fall Street, P.O. Box 335, Seneca Falls, NY 13148, 315-568-8060, admin@greatwomen.org

Book Design by Marsha Costello

SECOND EDITION

Tietjen, Jill S. (1954 -   )
Inspiring Women of the National Women's Hall of Fame/ Jill S. Tietjen, Jillaine Newman, Merrill C. Amos National Women's Hall of Fame – 2nd edition

ISBN-10: 0986 179108
ISBN-13: 978-0-986 1791-0-5

1. Women – United States – History I. Jillaine Newman II. Merrill C. Amos III. Title

The National Women's Hall of Fame

In 1969, the women and men of Seneca Falls created the National Women's Hall of Fame, believing that the contributions of American women deserved a permanent home in the small village where the fight for women's rights began. The Hall is currently housed in the heart of the downtown Historic District.

The National Women's Hall of Fame is the nation's oldest membership organization dedicated to recognizing and celebrating the achievements of great American women. This esteemed group grows with each Induction Ceremony and as women continue to influence and shape the arts, athletics, business, education, government, humanities, philanthropy and science.

Through 2015, 266 women have been inducted into the National Women's Hall of Fame. These great women serve as an inspiration thus the Hall's mission:

"Showcasing Great Women . . . Inspiring All!"

National Women's Hall of Fame
76 Fall Street
P.O. Box 335
Seneca Falls, NY 13148
315-568-8060
womenofthehall.org

Table of Contents

Induction Year: 2000

𝓕aye Glenn Abdellah, Ed.D.

1919–

Dr. Abdellah, pioneer nursing researcher, helped transform nursing theory, nursing care and nursing education. After receiving her nursing certificate from the Ann May School of Nursing and her Bachelor's, Master's, and Doctoral degrees in Education from Columbia University, Dr. Abdellah embarked on her distinguished career in health care. She was the first nurse officer to receive the rank of a two-star rear admiral. Her more than 150 publications, including her seminal works, *Better Nursing Care Through Nursing Research* and *Patient-Centered Approaches to Nursing*, changed the focus of nursing theory from a disease-centered to a patient-centered approach and moved nursing practice beyond the patient to include care of families and the elderly. Her Patient Assessment of Care Evaluation method to evaluate health care is now the standard for the nation. Her development of the first tested coronary care unit has saved thousands of lives.

As the first nurse and the first woman to serve as Deputy Surgeon General, Dr. Abdellah developed educational materials in many key areas of public health, including AIDS, the mentally handicapped, violence, hospice care, smoking cessation, alcoholism, and drug addiction.

Dr. Abdellah, after teaching at several prestigious universities, founded the Graduate School of Nursing at the Uniformed Services University of the Health Sciences and served as the school's first dean. Beyond the classroom, Dr. Abdellah presents workshops around the world on nursing research and nursing care.

Dr. Abdellah's work has been recognized with almost 90 professional and academic honors, including the prestigious Allied Signal Award for her pioneering research in aging. She is also the recipient of eleven honorary degrees.

As a leader in health care, she has helped transform the practice of nursing and raised its standards by introducing scientific research into nursing and patient care. Her leadership, her publications, and her accomplishments have set a new standard for nursing and for women in the health care field.

*B*ella Abzug
1920–1998

Bella Abzug always championed women's rights, human rights, equality, peace and social justice.

Abzug worked as an attorney in civil rights and labor law, working often without pay to represent the poor, minorities and those attacked by forces of repression. In 1970 she won the Democratic primary in New York's 19th District, and in 1971 took her seat in the U.S. House of Representatives. Wearing her trademark wide-brimmed hat, she landed running, introducing legislation calling for an end to the Vietnam War, banning discrimination against women seeking credit, gay rights, reproductive freedom, and more. She helped found the National Women's Political Caucus, and introduced legislation creating Women's Equality Day. Abzug ran unsuccessfully for the U.S. Senate in 1976.

She continued her advocacy, playing a major role in the 1977 National Women's Conference and serving for a time as President Carter's chair of the National Advisory Commission on Women. At the time of her death she headed the Women's Environment & Development Organization, part of Women USA, and worked to improve the environment.

$\mathscr{A}$bigail Adams
1744–1818

Wife of one president and mother of another, Abigail Adams was more than a family helpmate. Insightful, witty, and intensely concerned with politics, she shared and shaped her husband John's political thought and career. Because of his service to the nation in war and diplomacy, they spent more than half their married life apart, but they communicated closely. In early 1776 she was caring for their four young children alone, but she wrote him to urge daring and boldness.

In her famous "Remember the Ladies" letter, Abigail Adams proposed that women should claim their share of liberty.

She objected specifically to the legal codes under which married women could not own property. But she was ahead of her time; later generations of women would have to struggle to change such laws.

She said "I desire you would remember the ladies and be more generous and favorable to them than your ancestors. Do not put such unlimited power into the hands of the husbands. Remember, all men would be tyrants if they could,. If particular care is not paid to the ladies, we are determined to fomet a rebellion, and will not hold ourselves bound by any laws in which we have no voice or representation."

Jane Addams
1860–1935

Jane Addams was one of the first generation of American women to attend college. After graduation, unmarried, she struggled to find a career and a purpose. Finally in London she discovered Toynbee Hall and the cause to which she would devote her life: the settlement house, a special facility established to help the poor.. In 1889 she and a college friend moved into the slums of Chicago. They called their dilapidated old mansion Hull House.

Soon a nationwide settlement house movement sprang up. Jane Addams spoke and wrote widely about settlement work. Her vivid stories made the plight of the poor heartbreakingly immediate.

She prodded America to respond to the terrible ills of industrial development: child labor, infant mortality, urban crowding and unsanitary conditions, unsafe workplaces, juvenile delinquency, unemployment, and poverty wages.

Her pacifism during World War I caused Jane Addams's reputation to suffer. In the hysterical intolerance of the "Red Scare" she was branded "the most dangerous woman in America" by self-appointed superpatriots. But her accomplishments could not be denied. Calmer times brought renewed recognition, capped by the Nobel Peace Prize in 1931.

The Honorable
Madeleine Korbel Albright
1937–

Madeleine Korbel Albright, sworn in as the 64th United States Secretary of State in 1997 after unanimous confirmation by the U.S. Senate, became the first female Secretary of State and the highest ranking woman in the United States government. As Secretary of State and as U.S. representative to the United Nations before that, she has created policies and institutions to help guide the world into a new century of peace and prosperity.

Concentrating on a bipartisan approach to U.S. foreign policy, she has attempted to create a consensus on the need for U.S. leadership and engagement in the world. Among her achievements were ratification of the Chemical Weapons Convention and progress toward stability in Eastern and Central Europe.

Albright has dedicated her life to international study. After receiving her B.A. at Wellesley College, she studied international relations at Johns Hopkins University before earning her M.A. and Ph.D. at Columbia University. Before her appointment as Secretary of State, she had a diverse career. Albright was Sen. Edward Muskie's Chief Legislative Assistant; a Woodrow Wilson fellow; president of the Center for National Policy, a nonprofit research organization; and Research Professor of International Affairs and Director of the Women in Foreign Service Program at Georgetown University's School of Foreign Service. During President Clinton's first term, Albright served as the United States' Permanent Representative to the United Nations and a member of Clinton's National Security Council.

As a refugee whose family fled Czechoslovakia, first from the Nazis and later from the Communists, Albright represents the highest ideals and aspirations of immigrants who come to America seeking to make major contributions to our society. As a leader in international relations, she has helped change the course of history and, in so doing, has also set a new standard for American women and for women around the world.

After leaving the Secretary of State post in 2001, she has authored several bestsellers, launched a private investment fund, and provides global strategy consulting. In 2012, she received the Presidential Medal of Freedom.

$\mathcal{T}$enley Albright, M.D.

1935–

Tenley Albright is the first American woman to win a world figure skating championship and is the first winner of figure skating's "triple crown", capturing the World, North American, and United States ladies figure skating titles in a single year. In 1956, she became the first American woman to win an Olympic gold medal in figure skating. She has served on the International Olympic Committee and as a member of the United States Olympic Committee, becoming the first woman to serve as one of its officers. Dr. Albright has also been named one of the "100 Greatest Female Athletes" by *Sports Illustrated* magazine.

Diagnosed with polio in 1946 at age ten, when treatments for polio were not well developed, she was hospitalized and had to remain inactive for several months. Upon release from the hospital she returned to the ice and won her first skating title four months later. At the age of 16, Dr. Albright won the first of five consecutive United States singles titles and in the same year won a silver medal at the 1952 Olympics. Her gold medal came four years later at the Winter Olympics in Cortina D'Ampezzo, Italy.

Dr. Albright began a major in pre-medical studies at Radcliffe College in 1953, practicing her skating in the early morning hours before her classes. She took a leave of absence for one year from Radcliffe in 1955 to pursue her second world championship. After three years of study she left Radcliffe in 1956. She returned to her studies in 1957, entering Harvard Medical School as one of only five women in a class of 135, completing her M.D. in 1961.

A successful surgeon and leader in blood plasma research, today Dr. Albright is a faculty member and lecturer in general surgery at Harvard Medical School and also serves as the Director of the MIT Collaborative Initiatives. She has served on multiple corporate boards, received numerous awards and honors, and acted as a delegate to the World Health Assembly where she was involved in international polio eradication efforts.

$\mathcal{L}$ouisa May Alcott
1832–1888

A prolific author of books for American girls, Louisa May Alcott is best remembered for *Little Women*, one of the 270 published works by the Pennsylvania-born woman. This endearing novel captured forever the period's ideals and values of middle class domestic life. The book has appeared continuously in print since its first serial publication in 1868-70.

The popular novel drew largely upon her personal experiences. The second of four daughters, Alcott began her writing to support her perpetually impoverished family. Her strong and loving mother was a significant force in her life. "I think she is a very brave, good woman," Alcott wrote of her mother. "And my dream is to have a lovely, quiet home for her, with no debts or troubles to burden her."

Beginning with the publication of the poem *Sunlight* under a pseudonym in 1851, Alcott poured forth a variety of thrillers, poems, potboilers and an occasional juvenile tale. In 1867, she became editor of a children's magazine, *Merry's Museum*. At the urging of her publisher there, Alcott undertook the writing of *Little Women*. The novel, like her other works, was formed largely in her mind before she took pen to paper. The entire novel was written in two six-weeks periods.

In 1879, Alcott was the first woman to register in Concord when Massachusetts gave women school, tax and bond suffrage. Eventually she persuaded her publisher to publish Harriett Hanson Robinson's Massachusetts in the Woman Suffrage Movement in 1881. In her final novel, *Jo's Boys* (1886), Alcott made arguments for women's rights and other reforms. She said, "I can remember when anti-slavery was in just the same state that suffrage is now, and take more pride in the very small help we Alcotts could give than in all the books I ever wrote…."

Florence Ellinwood Allen, J.D.
1884–1966

Florence Ellinwood Allen opened doors in the legal profession previously closed to women.

A tireless worker for women's suffrage, international peace, and many reform causes related to women, children and families, Allen was born in Salt Lake City, Utah, in 1884 to a family engaged in community activism. They emphasized education. She received a bachelor's degree in music from Western Reserve University in Ohio, traveled to Germany to study music and then returned to Cleveland where she taught and wrote music criticism for the *Cleveland Plain Dealer*. She decided to study law and was graduated *cum laude* from New York University Law School in 1913.

When Florence Allen returned to Ohio to establish her own law office, she gained admittance to the Ohio Bar, campaigned for women's suffrage, became active in the Cleveland Women's City Club and the YWCA, helped establish the Cleveland Business Women's Club, and volunteered at the Cleveland Legal Aid Society. In 1919, she was appointed Assistant Prosecutor for Cuyahoga County and became the first woman in the country to hold such a position. From this time forward, her life became a catalog of legal firsts and breakthroughs for women and the law. As soon as the 19th amendment was ratified, Florence Allen ran for Common Pleas Court Judge in Cuyahoga County and became the first woman elected to a judgeship in the United States, winning by the largest popular vote ever given a candidate for the bench in that county.

In 1922, Judge Allen became the first woman to sit on a state supreme court, defeating both the Democratic and Republican candidates. She was elected to a second Ohio Supreme Court term in 1928. In 1934, on her fiftieth birthday, she was appointed to the United States Court of Appeals for the Sixth Circuit, the first woman to sit on any Federal bench of general jurisdiction. She served 25 years with outstanding distinction, the author of many groundbreaking opinions. In 1959, she became Chief Judge and the first woman in the nation to become a Chief Judge on a Federal Court. Many in the profession regarded Florence Allen as one of the most distinguished jurists in the nation. She authored *This Constitution of Ours, To Do Justly and Challenges to the Citizen*.

$\mathcal{L}$inda G. Alvarado
1952–

Linda G. Alvarado has changed the 'male only' image of construction contractors across the United States and opened doors to increasing numbers of women and minorities to enter construction and non-traditional fields of endeavor. Alvarado is founder and sole owner of Alvarado Construction, a commercial and industrial general contracting/site management, and design/build firm in Denver, Colorado; President of Palo Alto, Inc. Restaurant Company; and co-owner of the Colorado Rockies baseball team.

Born in Albuquerque, New Mexico, Alvarado grew up poor in a hard-working family with six children. Working her way through college, she found that she enjoyed outside work as a day laborer, took computer scheduling and blueprint training and worked after graduation as a construction site manager. Undaunted by construction site harassment, she decided to form her own company in 1976. There were no special programs to support women and minority business start-ups. Banks turned her down. Her parents mortgaged their home and lent her $2,500.

On this foundation, Alvarado built one of the most successful construction firms in the country, moving from simple paving jobs to bus-stop shelters, to duplexes, 7-11s, fast-food restaurants, and then onto aquariums, parts of the Denver airport, the convention center, schools, and other complex undertakings.

Alvarado and her husband Robert founded Palo Alto Inc., a franchise-based company that built and operates over 150 fast food restaurants in the southwest. In the 1990s, Alvarado became part owner of a major league baseball franchise, the Colorado Rockies…"the first time any woman, as an entrepreneur earning her own money, was able to bring capital to a major league franchise," she has stated.

In recognition of her outstanding entrepreneurship, Alvarado, at age 27, was invited to serve on the Board of Norwest Bank, and today sits on major corporate Boards across the nation. She has received numerous recognition awards for business and philanthropic activities.

Dorothy H. Andersen, M.D.

1901–1963

Dorothy H. Andersen, pediatrician and pathologist, was the first scientist to identify the disease, cystic fibrosis. Her research and discovery in 1938 of this, at that time, fatal disease led the way to modern day advances in the treatment and management of the illness.

A graduate of Mount Holyoke College, 1922, and the Johns Hopkins University Medical School, 1926, Andersen overcame the prevailing discrimination against women in medicine and spent most of her professional career as a pathologist at Babies Hospital, Columbia-Presbyterian Medical Center in New York.

She continued her research on cystic fibrosis during the 1940s and was able to develop a simple, definitive diagnostic test for this genetic disorder. The test made it possible for pediatricians to immediately begin appropriate treatment, thereby greatly extending the lifespan of the cystic fibrosis patient. What had been a fatal disease in infancy became a treatable disorder, leading to the survival of young people with cystic fibrosis into adulthood.

During Work War II, Dr. Andersen developed a training program for surgeons pioneering in open-heart surgery. She was also recognized for her path breaking research work in nutrition.

Throughout her career she was deeply committed to professional equality and refused to pattern her life according to conventional ideas of what was suitable for women.

Marian Anderson
1897–1993

The great conductor Toscanini told her, "Yours is a voice such as one hears once in a hundred years." This brilliant contralto struggled out of a childhood of poverty in South Philadelphia, where she scrubbed steps and ran errands to earn a few pennies to help her mother. She sang joyfully in the church choir whose members raised the funds for her to attend music school. "We don't take colored," they told her coldly at the music school where she inquired. But she built a career anyway, scraping up money for lessons, and riding the black-only "Jim Crow" railroad cars to sing before black audiences. She became the first African-American singer to perform as a member of the Metropolitan Opera in New York City.

Like many black artists in the days of segregation, she had to go to Europe to gain recognition. The show business promoter Sol Hurok heard her in Paris and decided to bring her back to this country, ignoring those who told him, "You won't be able to give her away." Her famous concert at the Lincoln Memorial on Easter Sunday, 1939, demonstrated that her great talent could shatter the color line.

The first African-American to perform at the White House, Marian Anderson's career helped to make music one of the first fields in which Black Americans' achievements were given fair and full recognition. Her many honors and recognition include the Presidential Medal of Freedom and a Grammy Award for Lifetime Achievement.

Photo: Carl Van Vechten

Ethel Percy Andrus
1884–1967

Ethel Percy Andrus, founder of the National Retired Teachers Association and the American Association of Retired Persons, created two national organizations that provide support to older Americans to achieve independence, purpose and dignity.

An outstanding urban educator, Andrus discovered the plight of retired educators struggling to survive on meager pensions. She founded NRTA to use group strength to provide low-cost insurance programs and in 1956, the first health insurance program for educators over age 65. To meet the needs of all older Americans, Andrus founded AARP in 1958, becoming president and leading the organization's rapid growth by creating an array of programs to help mature Americans with many aspects of their lives, including second careers, health insurance, travel, and more. AARP became a powerful lobby for the needs of the aging, and Andrus, a respected expert on problems of the aging, advised government on programs and policies. She also founded and edited *Modern Maturity,* AARP's magazine, which has the nation's largest circulation. Andrus lived her philosophy, helping others use their strengths and abilities throughout life.

Maya Angelou
1928–2014

Maya Angelou, through her powerful writings, has inspired generations of women, African Americans and all people who struggle to overcome prejudice, discrimination and abuse.

Throughout her life, Angelou defied social norms. After being raped by her mother's boyfriend, she withdrew and was mute for five years. However, encouraged by her grandmother, who introduced her to literature, she gradually emerged as a talented artist.

Angelou was a Renaissance woman on many levels, treating life as a smorgasbord to be fully experienced then reporting it to inspire others to reach beyond damaging stereotypes. Her seven volumes of autobiography entail a remarkable life in the arts, diplomacy, travel, and activism.

In 1954, Angelou turned to acting before she started writing while also working as northern coordinator and fund raiser for the Southern Christian Leadership Conference. In the 1960s, Angelou began to focus on her writing and, in 1970, her first autobiographical work, *I Know Why the Caged Bird Sings*, became a best seller and was nominated for a National Book Award.

Angelou's writings have altered society for the better, bringing greater diversity into the theater and literature. Her autobiographical works provide powerful insights into the evolution of black women in the 20th century. In 1971, she became the first black woman to have a screenplay produced as a film – *Georgia, Georgia*. Her writings have brought her numerous awards and have been nominated for a Tony Award, an Emmy Award and a Pulitzer Prize.

Susan B. Anthony
1820–1906

Susan B. Anthony taught school in New Rochelle and Canajoharie, New York, and discovered that male teachers were paid several times her salary. She devoted her first reform efforts to anti-slavery and to temperance, the campaign to curb alcohol. But when she rose to speak in a temperance convention, she was told, "The sisters were not invited here to speak!" Anthony promptly enlisted in the cause of women's rights.

In a lifelong partnership with Elizabeth Cady Stanton, Anthony's organizational skill and selfless dedication built the women's rights movement. The ballot, she became increasingly to believe, was the necessary foundation for all other advances. When she and Stanton published a newspaper, they called it *The Revolution*. Its motto was "Men their rights and nothing more; women their rights and nothing less." In order to press a test case of her belief that women, as citizens, could not be denied the ballot, Anthony voted. She was tried, convicted and fined for voting illegally.

For over thirty years she traveled the country almost ceaselessly working for women's rights. In 1906, her health failing, Anthony addressed her last women's suffrage convention. Although she sensed that the cause would not be won in her lifetime, she looked out across the assembled women and told them, "Failure is impossible."

Virginia Apgar, M.D.
1909–1974

Virginia Apgar, brilliant physician and humanitarian, is best known for her development of the Apgar Score (1952), a system to determine whether a newborn infant needs special attention to stay alive. In most births at the time, attention was focused on mothers, not the newborns, which resulted in many infant deaths. This simple test, performed in the very first minutes of a baby's life, measures an infant's pulse, skin color, activity and respiration very quickly, enabling medical staff to intervene if help is needed. This simple but brilliantly conceived examination has saved countless newborn lives.

Apgar, one of the few women admitted to Columbia University College of Physicians and Surgeons in the 1930s, trained first in surgery, but shifted her work to anesthesiology, a new field that offered the opportunity to do ground-breaking work. She was soon named director of anesthesiology at Columbia, the first woman to head a department at the University. In 1949, after she built a major academic department in the discipline, she was named the first full professor of anesthesiology – the first woman to hold a full professorship in any discipline at Columbia University.

Apgar's career shifted again in 1959 when she became a senior executive with the National Foundation-March of Dimes, and spent her time working to generate public support and funds for research on birth defects. She was a spectacular fundraiser and educator of the public, and greatly increased both visibility and attention paid to the problems of birth defects.

In 1973, she became the first woman to receive the Gold Medal for Distinguished Achievement in Medicine from the College of Physicians and Surgeons, Columbia University. In 1994, Apgar was pictured on a U.S. postage stamp, as part of the Great Americans series.

Ella Baker
1903–1986

A major force in shaping the development of the Civil Rights Movement in America, Ella Baker was the premiere behind-the-scenes organizer, co-founder of the Southern Christian Leadership Conference (SCLC) headed by Martin Luther King, Jr., and an inspiring force behind the creation of the Student Non-Violent Coordinating Committee (SNCC).

Baker began her long affiliation with the National Association for the Advancement of Colored People organizer in 1938. She was hired in 1940 and traveled widely raising money and organizing local branches. In the late 1950s she helped create SCLC to fight racism; she served as executive director (as opposed to King's primary spokesperson role).

As students – black and white – became involved in the movement, Baker supported the idea of a student-run organization, and encouraged young people to found SNCC. SNCC organized many successful voter registration drives and other activities.

Baker was also an adviser to the creation of the Mississippi Democratic Freedom Party (MDFP), created to help overturn the all-white Democratic Party delegation to the party conventions.

$\mathscr{L}$ucille Ball
1911–1989

Born in Jamestown, NY, Lucille Desiree Ball left her hometown at the age of fifteen to study drama in New York City and began her entertainment career with stints as a model and Goldwyn Girl.

In 1951, Lucy and her husband, Desi Arnaz, launched a comedy television series, *I Love Lucy*, based on their own lives. The show pioneered technical aspects of a comedy show, using three cameras, a set, and a live audience. It also became the launching pad for the endearing comic talents of Ball.

Lucy went on to win four Emmy Awards for her work. Proving that her talents extended beyond the realm of comedy, the entrepreneur became the first female studio head in Hollywood. As president of Desilu Productions, she broke the glass ceiling for women executives in the film and television industry.

In 1986, Ball received a Kennedy Center Honor for her work and her shows live on in syndication even today.

Photo: Courtesy of Desilu, too, LLC

$\mathscr{A}$nn Bancroft
1955–

A lifelong athlete and educator whose love for the wilderness includes sharing it with others, Ann Bancroft is the first woman to travel across the ice to the North Pole (as the only female member of the Steger International Polar Expedition) in 1986.

One of the world's most respected polar explorers, Bancroft also was the first woman to travel east to west across Greenland on skis, leading the first American women's team (1992). She was team leader of the AWE (American Women's Expedition), a group of four women to have skied over 600 miles pulling heavy sleds to the South Pole (1993). In 2001, she became one of the first women to sail and ski across Antartica's landmass.

A teacher who triumphed over her own struggle with dyslexia, Bancroft also coached numerous sports. She is an instructor for Wilderness Inquiry, an organization that helps disabled and able-bodied individuals experience wilderness adventure. She has developed educational curricula for teachers from elementary school through college, in mathematics, science, geography, the environment and women in non-traditional roles.

Bancroft is committed to and involved with numerous health concerns, including multiple sclerosis, cerebral palsy and those with learning disabilities. Bancroft has also worked as an active volunteer for women's health research, literacy efforts and the Special Olympics. She is dedicated to inspiring women and girls worldwide to follow their dreams.

Clara Barton

1821–1912

Clara Barton taught school and worked as a clerk in the U.S. Patent Office. When she 40 years old, the outbreak of the Civil War launched her on her life's work. She began to assemble and distribute supplies to the Union soldiers. Knowing that nurses were urgently needed at the battlefield, she "broke the shackles and went into the field." At Cedar Mountain, Second Bull Run, Fairfax Court House, Fredrickburg, Antietam, and the Wilderness, she assisted the surgeons in stitching up wounds and in bloody amputations.

Her life long timidity disappeared. She was calm and resourceful, always turning up with food and medical supplies just when they were needed most.

Clara Barton gained national acclaim as "the angel of the battlefield," but she was also "everybody's old maid aunt," fussing over the men she called "my boys."

After the war she coordinated a national effort to locate soldiers who were missing in action. Barton threw herself into relief work in Europe and was impressed with the International Red Cross. She then lobbied for United States ratification of the Red Cross Treaty. She was the founder of the American Red Cross and served for many years as its president.

Eleanor K. Baum, Ph.D.
1940–

In 1984, Dr. Eleanor K. Baum became the first female engineer to be named dean of an engineering college in the United States, breaking many professional gender barriers along the way.

Dr. Baum's career as an engineer began at City College of New York where she was the only female in the 1959 engineering class. "I felt very conspicuous," she said, "but I was stubborn enough to stick it out." Later she earned both her masters degree and Ph.D. in electrical engineering from Polytechnic Institute of New York.

During this time she discovered what became a life-long passion, a love for teaching. She began her teaching career as an assistant professor at Pratt Institute in Brooklyn. Her subsequent appointment to chairperson of the electrical engineering department was an historic achievement.

In 1987, Dr. Baum moved her career across town to Cooper Union. As Dean of the Albert Nerken School of Engineering at Cooper Union in Manhattan and Executive Director of the Cooper Union Research Foundation, she spent over twenty years vigorously promoting engineering as a profession, particularly for women.

Recognizing the stereotypical image of the white male engineer, Dr. Baum worked to dispel such thinking by actively encouraging young women and minorities to pursue careers within the profession.

When she became dean at Cooper Union, 5% of the student body was female. Under Dr. Baum's leadership, that number increased to 40%. Dr. Baum is committed to recognizing the importance of positive engineering and female role models for high school and college students.

She belongs to several professional organizations that share those convictions. In 1995, she was elected president of the American Society for Engineering Education, another first for a woman. She is an active member of the Society of Women Engineers and has served as national president of the Accreditation Board for Engineering and Technology.

In 1996, Dr. Baum was inducted into the Women in Technology International Hall of Fame. A frequent writer and speaker on educational and engineering issues, she is the author of many professional articles; a director on several business, professional, and college advisory boards; holder of more than 20 awards and citations; and also, five honorary doctorates from major colleges and universities including Notre Dame University and Union College.

*R*uth Fulton Benedict, Ph.D.
1887–1948

Ruth Benedict was a pioneering anthropologist who became America's leading specialist in the field, best known for her "patterns of culture" theory. Her book by that name revolutionized anthropological study, igniting the work of the culture and personality movement within anthropology. She strengthened the bonds among the branches of social science: anthropology, sociology and psychology, and deepened public understanding of the impact of culture on human behavior and personality. She received her bachelor's degree from Vassar College and her PhD from Columbia University, where she was a student of Franz Boas and then was his assistant. She became the mentor of Margaret Mead. Ruth Benedict did her fieldwork in the American west among the Serrano, Zuni, Cochiti, Pima, and Mescalero Apache. Benedict's academic career, 1923-1948, was at Columbia University, where she was appointed full professor in the Faculty of Political Science in 1948, the first woman to achieve that status. She acted as Chair of the Anthropology Department from 1936-1939, edited the *Journal of American Folklore* from 1925-1940, and worked for the United States" war effort in the Office of War Information, 1943-1945. Regarded by many as America's first woman anthropologist, author of six books: including the path-breaking *Patterns of Culture* (1934), deemed one of the major works of intellectual history of the 20th century, "It marked a turning point in American culture between what we think of today as 19th and 20th century ideas." Benedict's concept of cultural configuration, the idea that a culture is not a random collection of traits, but a unique patterning or organization of these traits, has been a major contribution to the world's understanding of cultural diversity. Among her other works are: *Tales of the Cochiti Indians* (1931), *Zuni Mythology* (1935), and *The Chrysanthemum and the Sword* (1946), Ruth Benedict also wrote and published poetry under the name Anne Singleton. Benedict was an active anti-racism voice during the 1940s. Her book *Race: Science and Politics* (1940), refuted then current theories of racial superiority. The book was used for a teaching unit on race and racism, and a public affairs pamphlet co-authored with Gene Weltfish, that was in turn used as the foundation for a children's book, cartoon-movie and comic book. Ruth Benedict met the challenges of her time: barriers and undercompensation of women in academe, obstacles to women doing fieldwork, racial and cultural superiority assumptions in the social sciences, with superior work, incisive observation, methodological analysis, and wide-ranging intellectual brilliance. She met personal challenges in her married life and in being a hearing impaired researcher, accomplishing her fieldwork with assistance from interpreters and extraordinary dedication and initiative. Benedict believed "The purpose of anthropology is to make the world safe for human differences."

Mary McLeod Bethune
1875–1955

Mary Jane McLeod was born in South Carolina, the fifteenth of seventeen children. Scholarships enabled her to attend Scotia Seminary and Moody Bible Institute. Turned down when she applied to go to Africa as a missionary, she returned to the South. She met and married Albertus Bethune, and began to teach school.

In Daytona, Florida, in 1904 she scraped together $1.50 to begin a school with just five pupils. She called it the Daytona Literary and Industrial School for Training Negro Girls. A gifted teacher and leader, Mrs. Bethune ran her school with a combination of unshakable faith and remarkable organizational skills. She was a brilliant speaker and an astute fund raiser.

She expanded the school to a high school, then a junior college, and then a college. Today, her legacy is Bethune-Cookman University.

Continuing to direct the school, she turned her attention to the national scene, where she became a forceful and inspiring representative of her people. First through the National Council of Negro Women, then within Franklin Roosevelt's New Deal in the National Youth Administration, she worked to attack discrimination and increase opportunities for Blacks. Behind the scenes as a member of the "Black Cabinet," and in hundreds of public appearances, she strove to improve the status of her people.

Antoinette Blackwell
1825–1921

As the first woman minister of a recognized denomination (Congregational), Antoinette Brown Blackwell worked throughout her life to validate women's public role by challenging traditional barriers that restricted them.

Blackwell encountered traditional restraints on women's intellectual endeavors and social action when she was not permitted to participate in classroom discussions, attend graduation or be awarded a preacher's license when studying theology at Oberlin College in 1850 (the institution later awarded her honorary master's and doctoral degrees).

Following ordination, she served as a pastor in Wayne County, New York and later as a visiting pastor – serving as role model to other young women seeking a life's work in the ministry.

Blackwell married and had seven children. Throughout her life, she engaged in philosophical and scientific studies, publishing eight books and many essays. Blackwell was elected to the American Association for the Advancement of Science, and was a leader in the women's rights movement. She was one of the few movement pioneers who lived long enough to cast her ballot in 1920 when the suffrage Amendment was enacted.

Elizabeth Blackwell, M.D.
1821–1910

Elizabeth Blackwell, born in Britain, was the first woman awarded the M.D. degree. Many nineteeth-century physicians, including a few women, practiced without a degree, but Elizabeth Blackwell wished to attain full professional status. She was rejected by all the major medical schools in the nation because of her sex. Her application to Geneva Medical School (now Hobart & William Smith Colleges in Geneva, New York) was referred to the student body. They accepted with great hilarity in the belief that it was a spoof perpetrated by a rival school. Working with quiet determination, she turned aside the hostility of the professors, students, and townspeople. She earned her medical degree in 1849.

Blackwell completed her medical education in Europe, but faced additional difficulties in setting up her practice when she returned to New York. Barred from city hospitals, she founded her own infirmary. Eventually she founded a Women's Medical College to train other women physicians.

Blackwell's educational standards were higher than the all-male medical schools. Her courses emphasized the importance of proper sanitation and hygiene to prevent diseases. She later returned to Britain and spent the rest of her life there, working to expand medical opportunities for women as she had in America.

$\mathcal{E}$mily Blackwell, M.D.
1826–1910

Emily Blackwell directed the New York Infirmary for Women and Children and the Women's Medical College, providing rare advanced training for pioneering women physicians and medical services for women, by women.

Sister of Elizabeth Blackwell, America's first woman physician, Emily Blackwell also became a physician and collaborated with her sister to expand the New York Infirmary to include a medical college for women.

Blackwell was a brilliant organizer and manager, and for more than 30 years served as the institution's dean and professor of obstetrics and gynecology. Her high standards made the college probably the finest of its time for educating women in medicine.

In the years before women were routinely admitted to medical schools with men, 364 women physicians were well-prepared for medical practice because of Blackwell's management and medical skills, and challenged by her inspiring example.

Amelia Bloomer
1818–1894

"It was a needed instrument to spread abroad the truth of a new gospel to woman, and I could not withhold my hand to stay the work I had begun. I saw not the end from the beginning and dreamed where to my propositions to society would lead me," said Amelia Bloomer, describing her feelings as the first woman to own, operate and edit a newspaper for women.

Bloomer, a woman of modest means and little education, nevertheless felt driven to work against social injustice and inequity – and her personal convictions inspired countless other women to similar efforts.

Bloomer's newspaper, *The Lily*, began in 1849 in Seneca Falls, New York, where Bloomer lived after her marriage. The newspaper was initially focused on temperance, but under the guidance of Elizabeth Cady Stanton, a contributor to the newspaper, the focus soon became the broad issues of women's rights. An intriguing mix of contents ranging from recipes to moralist tracts, *The Lily* captivated readers from a broad spectrum of women and slowly educated them not only about the truth of women's inequities but in the possibilities of major social reform.

This first newspaper became a model for other suffrage periodicals that played a vital role in providing suffrage leaders and followers with a sense of community and continuity through the long years of the campaigns for the right to vote.

Bloomer was also known for her support for the outfit of tunic and full "pantelettes," initially worn by actress Fanny Kemble and others, including Stanton. Bloomer defended the attire in *The Lily*, and her articles were picked up in *The New York Tribune*. Soon the outfit was known as "The Bloomer Costume," even though Bloomer had no part in its creation. Ultimately Bloomer and other feminists abandoned the comfortable outfit, deciding that too much attention was centered on clothing instead of the issues at hand.

Bloomer remained a suffrage pioneer and writer throughout her life, leading suffrage campaigns in Nebraska and Iowa, as well as writing for a wide array of periodicals.

Nellie Bly
1864–1922

Nellie Bly was born Elizabeth Jane Cochran in 1864. In the 1880s and 1890s, as a reporter for Joseph Pulitzer's *New York World*, she was a pioneer in investigative reporting.

Before the "muckrakers" of the early 20th century publicized corruption and today's investigative reporters sought the "story behind the story," Bly was one of the first to "go behind the scenes" to expose the ills of society. At considerable personal risk, she had herself committed to a mental institution so she could study first-hand how the mentally ill were treated. As a result of her 'exposé', the care of the mentally ill was reformed. *The New York Journal* recognized her as the "best reporter in America."

After her husband's death in 1905, she took over his failing industries, introduced the steel barrel to the distilling process, and made the companies a huge success. For almost ten years, she ran two multi-million dollar companies. More importantly, she recognized the value of treating her workers well. Her plants were social experiments, with physical fitness programs, health care, and libraries to teach employees how to read.

Later trapped in Europe while World War I broke out, she covered the war as a reporter again. Bly was a model of achievement for women.

Louise Bourgeois
1911–2010

One of the world's most preeminent artists, Louise Bourgeois's career spanned over seven decades. Her varied and extensive body of work has been displayed in the collections of major museums worldwide.

Born in Paris, Louise's appreciation of art began in childhood, when she helped her parents in their tapestry restoration workshop. Her interests shifted in her late teens and at the age of twenty-one, she earned a degree in philosophy from the Sorbonne. A year later, however, she returned to her true passion – art. That led to further education at the Ecole du Louvre, Ecole des Beaux-Arts, Atelier Bissiere and Academie de la Grande Chaumiere.

In 1938, after marrying Robert Goldwater, Bourgeois moved to New York City and later became an American citizen. Once in New York, she continued to immerse herself in art and enrolled in the Art Students League. Through her work with paint, sculpture and textiles, Louise explored sexuality and relationships in terms of the figurative versus the abstract, femininity versus masculinity and beauty versus revulsion. Her work often explored childhood trauma and hidden trauma that follows through life. She is noted for linking sexuality, fragility, and insecurity.

The 1940s saw Louise turn her attention to sculpture. It was this work that would ultimately lead to her world-wide recognition as a leader in the field of confessional art. In 1949, Bourgeois debuted a sculptural exhibit considered to be the first art installation, a groundbreaking way for artists to present their work.

Bourgeois's acclaim grew throughout the 1970s, and in 1982, she became the first female artist to be given a retrospective at The Museum of Modern Art in New York. She is the only American of two women sculptors represented in the National Gallery of Art Sculpture Garden on the Mall in Washington, DC; there are fifteen men.

She received numerous awards for her work, including the National Medal of Arts (1997), La Biennale di Venezia's Golden Lion (1998), the Japan Art Association's Praemium Imperiale Award (1999) and the French Legion of Honor medal (2008).

Margaret Bourke-White
1904–1971

In the era before television and instant communication, the photographs of Margaret Bourke-White showed the American people the world – the despair and depression of the dustbowl, London during the Blitz, Stalin and the Kremlin, battles of World War II, the liberation of concentration camps, India and Ghandi, South Africa, the Korean War.

The first female documentary photographer to work with and be accredited by the U.S. armed forces, Bourke-White began her work as photographer while at Cornell University. After her graduation, she became enthralled with the machine age, photographing the industrial plants in Cleveland, and the Chrysler Building in New York City. She was one of the first photographers for *Fortune* magazine in 1929 and in 1935 she was one of the first photojournalists selected to work for *Life* magazine.

Her photographs of a dam under construction in New Deal, Montana and the towns nearby were the cover and lead articles of the first issue of *Life*. She said of her work, "My life and my career was not an accident. It was thoroughly thought out." Bourke-White remained with *Life* through the 1950s when illness curtailed her work.

Photo: Life Magazine

$\mathscr{L}$ydia Moss Bradley
1816–1908

Born in Indiana, Lydia Moss Bradley grew up on the frontier, educated in a log home before becoming a wealthy businesswoman, an entrepreneur and the founder of what eventually would become Bradley University.

As a pioneer in so many fields, Bradley experienced both success and tragedy. She and her husband, Tobias Bradley, had six children, but all succumbed to various frontier diseases.

In 1896, after becoming a millionaire through her various business activities, Bradley founded Bradley Polytechnic Institute in memory of her children. Originally organized as a four-year academy, Bradley University became a four-year college in 1920 and has continued to grow and distinguish itself ever since. Bradley University is today a fully accredited institution that supports undergraduate and graduate education in engineering, business, teacher education, nursing, physical therapy and the liberal arts.

Inspired by this goal of creating an institute that taught boys and girls together and that combined practical and classical education, Bradley became a leader in land development and agriculture. She was the first female member of an American national bank board in the United States when she joined the Board of Directors of Peoria's First National Bank. She gave the Society of St. Francis the use of a large estate for a hospital, which is now the OSF St. Francis Medical Center, one of the largest medical facilities in downstate Illinois.

In 1884, she built the Bradley Home for Aged Women to care for widowed and childless women. She donated the land and pushed the city fathers of Peoria to establish a park system, the first in Illinois.

yra Bradwell
1831–1894

When Myra Bradwell passed the Illinois Bar Exam with high honors in 1869, her path was set on her road to becoming one of America's first woman lawyers.

Bradwell began her legal career with the 1868 establishment of the *Chicago Legal News*, which carried information about laws, ordinances and court opinions admissible as evidence in court. Bradwell, publisher and editor, also used its pages and power to advocate for women's rights, speaking out for women's suffrage, and removal of property ownership rights by women. She was permitted to run her business by special charter allowing a married woman to do so.

In 1869 Bradwell helped created Chicago's first women's suffrage convention, and passed the Bar. Despite an appeal to the state Supreme Court, she was refused admission because of her gender. Progress was made when the Illinois legislature opened most professions to women, and Bradwell was admitted to the United States Supreme Court and Illinois Supreme Court in 1892, retroactive to her initial application in 1869.

Mary Breckinridge
1881–1965

Mary Breckinridge was the nation's foremost pioneer in the development of American midwifery and the provision of care to the nation's rural areas as founder of the Frontier Nursing Service.

Breckinridge, descendant of a distinguished family that included a U.S. vice president and a Congressman and diplomat, lost her first husband and two children to early death. She turned to nursing as an outlet for her energies, committed to "raise the status of childhood everywhere," as a memorial to her own lost children. She spent time as a public health nurse during World War I, and became convinced that the nurse-midwife concept could help children in rural America.

After additional nursing studies and midwifery training, she went to rural Kentucky and began work in 1925. In 1928, her service was named the Frontier Nursing Service, and was for several years entirely underwritten by Breckinridge's personal funds. Designed around a central hospital and one physician with many nursing outposts to compensate for the absence of reliable roads or transportation, the service featured nurses on horseback able to reach even the most remote areas in all kinds of weather. Within five years, FNS had reached more than 1,000 rural families in an area exceeding 700 square miles and staff members of FNS formed the organization that became the American Association of Nurse-Midwives. Breckinridge masterminded the fundraising and publicity necessary to keep the service growing. The Frontier School of Midwifery and Family Nursing, another part of FNS, trained hundreds of midwives.

The FNS hospital in Hyden, Kentucky is now named the Mary Breckinridge Hospital, and it operates today, with a new Women's Health Care Center, still fulfilling the mission that Breckinridge created in the 1920s. On her deathbed Breckinridge commented, "The glorious thing about it is that it has worked!"

Nancy Brinker
1946–

Nancy Brinker is regarded as the leader of the global breast cancer movement. In 1982, with a promise to her dying sister, Susan G. Komen, she founded Susan G. Komen Breast Cancer Foundation (now known as Susan G. Komen®). At that time breast cancer was not openly discussed, there were no 800- numbers, and few, if any, support groups. Treatment options and research funding streams were limited. In a few short years after its founding, the work of the foundation broke the silence around breast cancer and Susan G. Komen® is now the world's largest grassroots network of breast cancer survivors and activists fighting to save lives, empower people, ensure quality care for all and energize science to find cures.

Her creativity in awareness raising campaigns led to revolutionary program-ming. Since the first Susan G. Komen Race for the Cure® in 1983, the race has evolved into the world's largest and most successful education and fundraising event for breast cancer, with annual events in over 150 cities throughout the world. Through her model, she became a pioneer in the concept of cause-related marketing, allowing millions to participate through businesses that share the commitment to eradicate the disease. The founda-tion's advocacy work has increased legislation and greater government funding leading to major advances in breast cancer research.

A breast cancer survivor herself, Ms. Brinker's determination to create a world without breast cancer is matched by her passion to enlist every segment of society to participate in the battle. Her efforts have garnered her much recognition including the Presidential Medal of Freedom awarded by President Barack Obama, the Mary Woodard Lasker Award for Public Service, the Champions of Excellence Award from the Centers for Disease Control, Forbes Trailblazer Award, and the Anti-Defamation League Americanism Award, among many others.

She has also served in several significant government positions including U.S. Ambassador to the Republic of Hungary, U.S. Chief of Protocol, a lifetime member of the Council on Foreign Relations, and Goodwill Ambassador for Cancer Control for the United Nation's World Health Organization. Through opportunities afforded her in these positions, she continues to put cancer control at the top of the world health agenda.

$\mathcal{G}$wendolyn Brooks
1917–2000

"I am *interested* in telling my particular truth as I have seen it." Gwendolyn Brooks has seen her truth on the south side of Chicago where her parents moved when she was less than one year old. An introverted, shy child, she grew up reading the Harvard classics and the Black poet Paul Lawrence Dunbar. And she grew up writing. Her first poem was published when she was 14.

Graduating from Wilson Junior College during the Depression, she could only find work as a domestic worker and as secretary to a spiritual advisor. Later, she became publicity director of the youth organization of the NAACP in Chicago. She continued writing and by the end of the early 1940's her poetry was appearing in *Harpers*, *Poetry,* and *The Yale Review*. In 1945, her first volume of poetry *A Street in Bronzeville* was published. "I wrote about what I saw and heard on the street," she said of that book. In 1949, she published

Annie Allen, a series of poems that traces the progress to womanhood of a black girl. It was for this volume that she won the Pulitzer Prize in 1950.

In 1967, an established and respected poet, she attended a writer's conference at Fisk University where, she says, she rediscovered her blackness. Her subsequent poetry broke new ground for her, reflecting the change that occurred at Fisk. *The Mecca*, a book-length poem about a mother searching for her lost child in a Chicago housing project, shows this new direction. This volume was nominated for the National Book Award for poetry. Her other work includes children's books, an autobiography, and a collection of poetry about South Africa. Her work is collected in a single volume titled: *BLACKS*. She has been called a poet who has discovered the neglected miracles of everyday existence. For Brooks, it was all a matter of telling her truth.

Photo Bill Teague

Pearl S. Buck
1892–1973

Pearl Sydenstricker was the child of American missionaries. She grew up in China and was always "mentally bifocal", as she put it. Becoming a writer at an early age, she married John Buck, an American agricultural expert in China, and bore a daughter. Her family was caught up in the turmoil of modern China, and in 1927 she narrowly escaped with her life from an angry mob, leaving behind an early manuscript.

Her novel, *The Good Earth* (1931), rocketed her from obscurity to international fame. *The Good Earth* headed the best seller list for months, sold nearly two million copies, and was translated into thirty languages. It inspired a Broadway play and a Hollywood film, and was awarded the Pulitzer Prize. In 1938, having published several other novels, she won the Nobel Prize in literature.

Pearl Buck continued to be a remarkably productive writer. A born storyteller, she took plot and character ideas from two different cultures, and her writings shone with universal human appeal. Her over seventy books always sold well. She wrote a book about her father, her mother, and even, courageously, about her daughter's mental retardation. Late in life she turned more to philanthropy, especially to the cause of East-West understanding.

Betty Bumpers
1925–

Betty Flanagan Bumpers, former First Lady of Arkansas, has dedicated her life to issues affecting children's health, empowering women, and the cause of world peace. A former art teacher, Bumpers was educated at Iowa State, the University of Arkansas, and the Chicago Academy of Fine Arts.

When she became First Lady of Arkansas, the state had one of the lowest immunization rates in the nation. Mrs. Bumpers spearheaded a statewide immunization program for childhood vaccinations, and the state achieved one of the highest immunization rates in the country. The "Every Child By "74" project model that brought together the Arkansas League for Nursing, the State Health Department, the Arkansas National Guard, the State Nurses Association, the State Medical Society, and the Cooperative Extension Service of the University of Arkansas, faith-based organizations, and other volunteers, was so successful it was used by the Centers for Disease Control and Prevention for immunization programs across America. It continued into the next decade.

When Jimmy Carter became President, Mrs. Bumpers contacted him and explained the deficits in the country's immunization program, and urged him to work to improve the situation. At that time, only 17 states in the country required immunizations by school age. Mrs. Bumpers" and Mrs. Carter's advocacy led to the first federal initiative in comprehensive childhood immunization, launched in 1977. These efforts led to laws in every state requiring vaccinations before entry into school. The CDC says it is the most successful public health program they have ever had.

In 1991, responding to the 1989-1991 measles epidemic, Betty Bumpers and Rosalynn Carter founded *Every Child by Two* to ensure that all children in America are immunized on schedule by age two and that states develop immunization registries. Former Secretary of Health and Human Services Donna Shalala said, "from Arkansas to Washington, DC, to the far corners of the globe, Betty has been a guardian of children, protecting them from polio, from rubella and from many other invisible enemies."

In 1982, Mrs. Bumpers, concerned about the growing nuclear arms race, formed *Peace Links* to "effect a mindshift in the way people think" about peace and nuclear war. For twenty years *Peace Links*, which encompassed over 200 gubernatorial and congressional women and global women leaders, worked to educate communities about a new concept of national security, the value of cultural diversity, non-violent conflict resolution, global cooperation, citizen diplomacy, violence prevention and peace building. Through the National Peace Foundation, she continues to draw the world together into a unified community dedicated to peace.

*C*harlotte Anne Bunch
1944–

A pioneering strategist and organizer, Charlotte Bunch is one of the foremost advocates of international attention to women's issues, and the inclusion of gender and sexual orientation on global human rights agenda.

A 1966 Magna Cum Laude graduate of Duke University, Bunch became active on the national scene as a writer, lesbian activist and lecturer, particularly in movements for women's liberation and women's rights. She created and edited *Quest: A Feminist Journal* (1974), one of the first and the leading journals to promote analysis and policy making to improve women's status in society.

Expanding her activities into the international arena, Bunch built an international network of women, united by common concerns, and prepared by education and training for effective action. Through her speeches and organizing at international conferences, she served as a critical catalyst for action on women's issues. For example, her speech to Amnesty International in 1989 marked the beginning of that organization's efforts to address gender-specific human rights issues. Her leadership was crucial to the adoption by the 1993 U.N. Conference on Human Rights, in Vienna, of strong support for women, and at the 1995 U.N. Conference on Human Rights, in Beijing, for supporting woman's place in human rights advocacy.

In 1989, Bunch founded The Center for Women's Global Leadership at Douglass College, Rutgers University, where she remains as Founding Director and Senior Scholar. Through the Center, she served as a leader of national and international networking, advocacy and training, to advance women's well-being around the world.

St. Frances Xavier Cabrini
1850–1917

Maria Frances Cabrini knew early in life she would make religious work her life's vocation. Of her confirmation in 1857 she remarked, "…from that moment I was no longer of the earth…I knew the Holy Ghost had come to me."

As an expression of her religious motivation, Cabrini began teaching and working in orphanages, taking formal religious vows in 1877. Since no missionary order admitted women at the time, she then founded the Missionary Sisters of the Sacred Heart of Jesus in 1880. As superior, she saw the new order grow rapidly to seven convents in as many years. Pope Leo XIII wrote that he found her "a woman of marvelous intuition and of great sanctity."

In 1889, Mother Cabrini relocated to New York City at the direction of the Pope to minister to the growing numbers of impoverished immigrants, many of whom were Italian, in American cities.

For the next 25 years, she traveled throughout the Americas and Europe, founding convents, schools, orphanages and hospitals. With amazing speed, she opened institutions in Panama, Argentina, Brazil, Paris, Madrid, Turin and London. Ultimately, she directed 67 houses, staffed by 1,500 nuns who aided the poor, the illiterate, the unskilled and the sick.

In 1909, Mother Cabrini became a naturalized citizen, and in 1910 she was named superior general for life over the order she had founded. Pope Pius XII canonized her, the first American to become a Saint, in 1946. In 1950, the Pope named her "the patron saint to immigrants."

Mary Steichen Calderone, M.D.
1904–1998

Mary Steichen Calderone, physician, author and founder of SIECUS – the Sex Information and Education Council of the United States – has shown a generation of Americans the importance of early and honest sex education in families, churches, schools and communities.

After an education at Brearly School in New York, Vassar College and the University of Rochester Medical School, with graduate work in public health at Columbia University, Calderone served as physician to the public schools of Great Neck, New York, for several years before becoming medical director of Planned Parenthood Federation of America in 1953.

Her greatest achievement came as co-founder, in 1964, of SIECUS. Serving as its president from 1975 to 1982, Calderone and SIECUS fought to gain recognition of the idea that sexuality reflects the entire human character, not solely our gender-nature. Working to ensure that children receive a sound foundation in sex education at home and at school, Calderone has helped young people understand and appreciate their own sexuality. Her numerous books have taught thousands of confused and reluctant parents how to explain sex and sexuality to their children.

Calderone's work has been recognized through numerous awards including the Margaret Sanger Award from Planned Parenthood Federation of America, the Lifetime Achievement Award from the Schlesinger Library of Radcliffe/Harvard College, and the Award for Human Service from the Mental Health Association of New York.

Summarizing Calderone's contributions, *People* magazine wrote: "What Margaret Sanger did for birth control and Rachel Carson [did] for the environment, Calderone…has done for sex education. Her work, like theirs, has profoundly changed the quality of life in this century."

Annie Jump Cannon
1863–1941

Astronomer Annie Jump Cannon perfected the universal system of stellar classification still in use today, and compiled the largest accumulation of astronomical information ever assembled by an individual – the Draper Catalog.

Cannon was an assistant at the Harvard Observatory beginning in 1896, and working with Williamina Fleming, she undertook a continuation of the project of recording, classifying and cataloging all stars down to the ninth magnitude. The resulting classification system by temperature was her concept, and was universally adopted. More than a quarter of a million stars were so classified, and published as *The Draper Catalogue* in nine volumes, from 1918 to 1924.

Cannon became curator of astronomical photographs of the Observatory in 1911 and professor of astronomy in 1938. She published the *Draper Catalogue Extension* in two volumes (1925 and 1949), with thousands more stars catalogued. These works were of enormous value to the science of astronomy, and forever secured Cannon's place in scientific history.

Cannon was a women's suffrage advocate and a member of the National Women's Party.

Photo: Harvard College Observatory

*R*achel Carson
1907–1964

A shy young woman who loved books and nature equally well, Rachel Carson trained as a zoologist. She joined the Fish and Wildlife Service in Washington to work on their publications.

In 1951 she came to national prominence when her book, *The Sea Around Us*, topped the best seller list for 86 weeks. Her graceful prose opened up scientific knowledge about the oceans to the layperson. An earlier work, *Under the Sea Wind*, was reissued. When she studied marine life in Maine for her next book, *The Edge of the Sea*, she stayed for hours wading in icy tidal pools until she was so numb with cold she had to be carried out.

She was not by nature a crusader, but when aerial spraying of DDT killed the birds in a friend's bird sanctuary, she began to investigate the effects of pesticides on the chain of life. "The environment" and "ecology" have since become household words for Americans, but it all began with her *Silent Spring* in 1962.

Driven by the knowledge that the book was desperately needed, she pored over and combined the work of many individual researchers. She wrote of the heedless pesticide poisoning of our rivers and soils, warning that we might soon face a spring when no bird songs could be heard.

Rachel Carson had to weather a storm of controversy and abuse, and she did not live to see the eventual banning of DDT. But the environmentalist movement carries on the work she began, preserving our natural heritage for the future.

Rosalynn Smith Carter
1927–

Eleanor Rosalynn Smith Carter, First Lady of the United States from 1977-1981, significantly raised public awareness of mental health issues by serving as honorary chair of the Presidential Commission on Mental Health. The work of the Commission led to the passage of the Mental Health System Act of 1980.

Her founding and continued work on the "Every Child by Two" initiative has saved thousands of children's lives through immunization and spearheaded further public health immunization initiatives worldwide.

Mrs. Carter has demonstrated a life-long dedication to the concerns of women and children, the poor and the mentally ill: contributing her active presence and policy expertise to the Policy Advisory Board of the Atlanta Project, the Last Acts coalition to improve end-of-life care, Habitat for Humanity, Project Interconnections that provides housing for the homeless and mentally ill, and the Friendship Force.

Her books have aided thousands of people seeking assistance and guidance regarding mental health issues, care-giving and creating new paths in life. She is the recipient of numerous honors including the Presidential Medal of Freedom, the nation's highest civilian honor.

Photo: Rick Diamond

Mary Ann Shadd Cary
1823–1893

Mary Ann Shadd Cary, born in Wilmington, Delaware, the eldest of 13 children of free African-American parents, became a role model for women in education and law.

After receiving an education from Pennsylvania Quakers, Cary devoted the first part of her life to abolition, working with fugitive slaves, and becoming the first African-American woman in North America to edit a weekly newspaper – the *Provincial Freeman*, devoted to displaced Americans living in Canada. She then became a teacher, establishing or teaching in schools for African-Americans in Wilmington; West Chester, Pennsylvania; New York; Morristown, New Jersey; and Canada. She was also the first woman to speak at a national African-American convention.

During the Civil War, Cary helped recruit African-American soldiers for the Union Army. She then taught in Washington, D.C., public schools until, in 1869, she embarked on her second career, becoming the first woman to enter Howard University's law school. She was the first African-American woman to obtain a law degree and among the first women in the United States to do so.

She then fought alongside Susan B. Anthony and Elizabeth Cady Stanton for women's suffrage, testifying before the Judiciary Committee of the House of Representatives and becoming the first African-American woman to cast a vote in a national election. As an educator, an abolitionist, an editor, an attorney and a feminist, she dedicated her life to improving the quality of life for everyone – black and white, male and female.

Mary Cassatt
1844–1926

In the nineteenth century many young women of wealthy background dabbled in painting to while away their leisure hours. Mary Cassatt took it seriously. She came from a well-to-do family and lived in Europe for several years when she was a child.

When, at twenty-two, she declared she could learn no more in Philadelphia, her parents let her return to Europe. In Rome, Seville, Antwerp, and Paris, she studied the masters' techniques. She sharpened her skills by copying Corregio, Rubens, and Franz Hals. Cassatt was in Paris at that extraordinary moment when the Impressionists first overturned established artistic standards. They recognized in her a kindred spirit and a powerful talent, and she was invited to exhibit in the Impressionist shows. "I accepted with joy," she recalled. "I took leave of conventional art. I began to live."

She never married, and in 1877 her parents moved to Europe to join her, and for the next eighteen years she was obliged to devote some of her time to their care. Surrounded by bourgeois respectability, she painted what she saw: interiors, gardens, and portraits, especially of mothers and children.

Mary Cassatt was self-disciplined, intense, and outspoken. She never did commissioned portraits, accepted no pupils, and refused to paint "pot-boilers." Her influence on American art carried beyond her own work because she gave advice to American art collectors.

The famed Havemeyer collection, now part of the Metropolitan Museum of Art, began when Mary Cassatt convinced young Lousiane Havemeyer to spend all her schoolgirl allowance on a Degas pastel.

Willa Cather
1873–1947

As an adolescent, Willa Cather defied the norms for girls: she cut her hair short, wore trousers, and openly rebelled against the roles girls were supposed to play.

At the University of Nebraska at Lincoln, she edited the school magazine and published articles and play reviews in local papers. After graduating, she languished awhile in Red Cloud until she was offered a position editing *Home Monthly* in Pittsburgh. While editing that magazine, she wrote short stories to fill its pages. These stories, published in a collection called the *Troll Garden* in 1905, brought her to the attention of S.S. McClure. She became a member of the staff of *McClure's Magazine* and finally, its editor.

In 1912, after five years with *McClure's,* she left the magazine to have time for her own writing. She subsequently published her first five novels. These novels announced her themes of strong women, the fight against provincial life, and the dying of the pioneer tradition. This was the period of *O Pioneers* (1913), *Song of the Lark* (1915), *My Antonia* (1918), *One of Ours* (1922), and *A Lost Lady* (1922). She won the Pulitzer Prize for *One of Ours*.

After this prolific period, Cather entered a period of despair. It was a time, she said, when the world broke apart. Recovering from this difficult period, she wrote her greatest novels: *The Professor's House* (1925), *My Mortal Enemy* (1926), *Death Comes for the Archbishop* (1927), and *Shadows on the Rock* (1931). These works are the best example of her classic and restrained language and her lyrical evocation of nature.

There always seemed to exist a tension in Willa Cather's life and, thus, in her writing. She was drawn to the East coast, its mountains and cities. And, she was drawn to the plains and the vastness of Nebraska. She loved the romantic literature of France, yet her own writing style was one of classic restraint.

Most of her work is autobiographical in nature, yet before she died she ordered her letters burned so no one could have access to her. She had a large circle of friends, yet to write she needed the solitude of Nebraska or New Hampshire. Red Cloud, Nebraska, her home, both attracted and repelled her; it was also the source of her art.

Carrie Chapman Catt
1859–1947

Growing up on the Iowa frontier, young Carrie Lane was active and self-reliant. She worked to put herself through Iowa State College, and become a principal and school superintendent, which were unusual posts for a woman.

When she married Leo Chapman, she joined him to co-edit a newspaper, but their marriage was cut short by his sudden death. As a young widow, she took to the lecture platform and began to work for woman suffrage, first in Iowa and then nationally.

Her second husband, George Catt, agreed she should devote two months each spring and fall to suffrage. She became a dynamic speaker, and exhibited a great talent for organization. Under her leadership, the days of isolated efforts and lost causes would end. More than any other woman except Susan B. Anthony,

Carrie Chapman Catt was responsible for securing women's right to vote.

In 1915, on the heels of a remarkable effort in New York State, Catt became the head of the National American Woman Suffrage Association and put into effect a secret "winning plan". She led a push for an amendment to the federal constitution and at the same time continued campaigns in the states to increase the pressure and the numbers of suffrage states. A series of state victories followed in 1917 and 1918. They were only the prelude to a tough national ratification battle until Tennessee finally put the Nineteenth Amendment "over the top" in August 1920.

Carrie Chapman Catt also did international work for woman suffrage, repeatedly touring Europe and presiding in international suffrage groups.

Julia Child
1912–2004

Julia Child's forty years as America's leading chef began in Boston in 1963 on public television station WGBH. Invited to the studio to discuss her first book, *Mastering the Art of French Cooking*, she brought along eggs and utensils to make an on-the-air omelet for the television host. Her breezy manner, unique voice, and relaxed chatter made her an instant hit and launched her acclaimed television series, *The French Chef.*

Julia McWilliams grew up in a well-to-do family with a younger brother and sister, all three over six feet tall, which caused their mother to boast, "I gave birth to 18 feet of children." After graduating from Smith College in 1934 she worked in a series of positions in advertising and journalism. Following the outbreak of World War II, she took a position with the Office of Strategic Services, hoping to become a spy, but became instead a file clerk in Ceylon, now Sri Lanka.

After the war she married Paul Cushing Child, a diplomat with the foreign service. Her husband was soon posted to France and en route to Paris, he took her to the oldest restaurant in the country, La Couronne. This was her first experience with classical French cuisine and she fell in love. "The whole experience was an opening up of the soul and spirit for me …I was hooked, and for life, as it turned out." After this experience, Child became devoted to French cuisine. She enrolled in the famous Le Cordon Bleu cooking school and explored the markets and bistros of Paris to refine her techniques. In 1951, she opened a cooking school, L"Ecole des Trois Gourmandes, (The School of the Three Gourmandes) with two partners. This venture led to the comprehensive French cooking manual for the American public, *Mastering the Art of French Cooking*, considered at the time to be the best English language cookbook.

Soon after the publication, the couple moved from Paris to Cambridge, Massachusetts. *The French Chef* television series began in 1963 and went on to become an outstanding public television success. Child won a Peabody Award in 1965, followed by an Emmy the next year. She only accepted $50.00 a show, donating the rest of her salary to the television station. She starred in eight television cooking series and published 11 cookbooks. She was the first woman to be inducted into the Culinary Institute of America's Hall of Fame. In 1978, she founded the educational American Institute of Wine and Food in Napa, California.

An honorary doctorate from Harvard University, received in 1993, read in part, "A Harvard friend and neighbor who has filled the air with common sense and uncommon scents. Long may her souffle's rise." In 2001, Child received the coveted Legion of Honor from the French government, and in 2003 the Presidential Medal of Freedom from President George W. Bush. Her famous television kitchen was placed in the Smithsonian Institute in Washington, DC.

Lydia Maria Child
1802–1880

The youngest of seven children born to an abolitionist family, Lydia Maria Child spent her life advocating for the rights of slaves and women.

Given the title "The First Lady of the Republic" by admirers including abolitionist William Lloyd Garrison, Child's writings dispelled ideas that African-Americans were a lower class. Her book *An Appeal in Favor of that Class of Americans Called Africans*, advocated education for African Americans and has often been cited as the first anti-slavery publication. She joined the American Anti-Slavery Society and she and her husband edited the *National Anti-Slavery Standard* from 1841-1844. Child was also a founding member of the Massachusetts Women's Suffrage Association and authored *The History of the Conditions of Women in Various Ages and Nations*, a publication that went on to influence the next generation of suffragists.

In addition to her activist work, Child also founded the country's first children's magazine, *Juvenile Miscellany*, and wrote many volumes dedicated to domestic endeavors.

$\mathcal{S}$hirley Chisholm
1924–2005

Shirley Chisholm, the first African-American woman elected to the U.S. Congress, was a passionate and effective advocate for the needs of minorities, women and children and changed the nation's perception about the capabilities of women and African Americans.

A New York City educator and child care manager, Chisholm saw the problems of the poor every day, and in the 1950s this led her to run for and win a seat in the New York State Legislature. In 1968 she was elected to Congress from the new 12th District. There she supported improved employment and education programs, expansion of day care, income support and other programs to improve inner city life and opportunity. She advocated for the end of the military draft and reduced defense spending. In 1970, she published her first book, *Unbossed and Unbought*. She served in Congress until 1982 and in 1972 entered several Democratic presidential primaries, receiving 151 delegate votes for the presidential nomination. Her second book, *The Good Fight*, was published in 1973.

She continued to be recognized for her legislative prowess in those years when powerful committee assignments were not available to women and persons of color. Her legacy is alive at the Shirley Chisholm Center for Research on Women at Brooklyn College.

$\mathcal{T}$he Honorable
Hillary Rodham Clinton, J.D.
1947–

Hillary Rodham Clinton is the first First Lady to be elected to the United States Senate, the first female US Senator from New York State, and only the third woman to serve as Secretary of State.

Raised in Park Ridge, Illinois, Clinton was an outstanding student. Initially active in politics as a young Republican, she received her bachelor's with honors in Political Science, was valedictorian, and the first student in Wellesley history to deliver a commencement address. Deeply affected by the death of Rev. Martin Luther King, Jr., whom she had met in 1962, and by her experience attending the "Wellesley in Washington" program, she joined the Democratic Party.

Clinton received her juris doctorate from Yale Law School, where she served on the Board of the Yale Review of Law and Social Action and where she met Bill Clinton in 1974. Clinton joined the Rose Law Firm in 1976, specializing in intellectual property issues, and providing pro bono work in child advocacy cases.

As First Lady of Arkansas, she continued to practice law, and chaired the Arkansas Educational Standards Commission and the Rural Health Advisory Committee. As First Lady of the United States (1993 - 2001), she chaired the Task Force on National Health Care Reform that recommended the Clinton Health Care Plan. The controversy over her public role in leading health care policy reform was intense, but she continued as a staunch advocate of health care reform, women's and children's issues, arts, culture, and heritage promotion, throughout the Clinton Presidency. She is the author of Living History and It Takes a Village.

In November 2000, she was elected to the U.S. Senate representing New York. In 2007, Clinton entered the Democratic primary race for the 2008 Presidency by posting "I'm in. And I'm in to win." on her website. In June 2008, Clinton conceded the primary race to eventual winner Barack Obama, but not before putting "18,000,000 cracks in the glass ceiling." In December of that same year, President-elect Obama nominated Clinton to serve as Secretary of State, making her just the third woman to hold the Cabinet position. In 2015, Clinton is a candidate for the Democratic Party nomination for U.S. President.

Along with Eleanor Roosevelt, Clinton is credited with substantively redefining the role of First Lady and opening new pathways for women in political leadership.

Jacqueline Cochran
1906–1980

Jacqueline Cochran's life was about risk and about triumph. A successful businesswoman and director of the Women's Air Force Service Pilots in World War II, at the time of her death Cochran held more speed, altitude and distance records than any other pilot, female or male.

Orphaned early in life and with almost no formal education, Cochran learned to fly at age 22, and it became a lifetime passion. The first woman to win the Bendix Transcontinental Air Race (1938), she established a woman's altitude record (1939) and broke speed records, as well.

After the United States entered World War II, she became director of the Women's Air Force Service Pilots, teaching 1,200 women to fly transports and becoming the first woman to pilot a bomber across the North Atlantic.

She was awarded the Distinguished Service Medal in 1945, and was commissioned a lieutenant colonel in the Air Force Reserve. In 1953, Cochran became the first woman to break the sound barrier and published her book, *The Stars at Noon*. She became the Chair of the National Aeronautic Commission and was enshrined in the Aviation Hall of Fame in 1971, the first living woman so honored.

$\mathscr{M}$ildred Cohn, Ph.D.
1913–2009

A groundbreaking scientist in several important areas of biological study, Mildred Cohn pioneered research that helped form the scientific understanding of mechanisms of enzymatic reactions and the methods of studying them.

She was born in 1913 in New York City to Russian immigrant parents and was educated in the city's public schools. Cohn earned her bachelor of arts degree from Hunter College in 1931 and her Ph.D. in chemistry from Columbia University in 1937. It was at this point that Cohn shifted fields from physical to biological chemistry.

She served as the first female research associate in the laboratory of Vincent du Vigneaud at Cornell Medical College from 1938-1946. In 1946, Cohn moved to the biochemistry department of Washington University in St. Louis, where she introduced the use of isotopic oxygen 18 to study metabolic processes and enzyme mechanisms. She later applied nuclear magnetic resonance (NMR) and electron paramagnetic resonance (EPR) to investigate metabolism and metabolic intermediates.

In 1960, Cohn accepted an associate professorship at the University of Pennsylvania, and in 1961, became Professor of Biochemistry and Biophysics. She continued at the university until 1982. In 1971, Cohn chaired a faculty committee on *The Status of Women on the Faculty*. The report released by the committee lead to many positive changes for female professors and faculty members.

Following her retirement from the University of Pennsylvania, Cohn served as a senior member of the Fox Chase Cancer Center. She returned to research work at the University of Pennsylvania on a part time basis and continued until 1998.

Cohn published more than 150 scientific papers and received several awards for her pioneering work on magnetic resonance in biological systems. Most notably, Cohn received the National Medal of Science in 1982 in biological sciences for "pioneering the use of stable isotopic tracers and nuclear magnetic resonance spectroscopy in the study of the mechanisms of enzymatic catalysis." She was the first female biochemist to receive the National Medal of Science.

Bessie Coleman
1892–1926

The world's first African-American woman aviator, Bessie Coleman, earned her pilot's license in 1921 in France, two years before her more famous contemporary, Amelia Earhart.

Bessie Coleman, the tenth child in a family of thirteen, grew up in a large, single-parent family in rural Texas. She learned about aviation through childhood reading, finished high school and some teacher's college training, and moved to Chicago. There, she was mentored by two African-American philanthropists, Robert Abbott and Jesse Binga. Denied admission to American aviation schools because of her race and gender, she learned French and went to France. In 1921 she earned an international pilot's license from the highly respected Federation Aeronautique International.

She returned to the United States and spent the next five years touring the country, giving exhibition flights, barnstorming and parachuting at airports. Earning the nickname *Queen Bess*, she challenged the barriers of racial discrimination and refused to participate in segregated events. She planned to open an aviation school to teach other African Americans to fly and become an active part of the growing aviation industry.

Tragically, her life and dream ended in her untimely death on April 30, 1926 during an exhibition accident when she fell from the plane and died instantly. She left a substantial legacy because of her modeling a pathway for women and people of color in aviation, and her challenges to Jim Crow practices. Bessie Coleman is honored every year by African-American pilots dropping a wreath from the air over her gravesite.

*E*ileen Collins
1956–

Eileen Collins was launched into history when she became the first American woman to pilot a spacecraft. Of this trailblazing mission, Collins said, "This mission marks the first baby steps in international space cooperation."

Collins worked hard and overcame adversity every inch of the way on her journey to space. Her family struggled to make ends meet in upstate New York, and she put herself through community college and paid for flying lessons by working full time in a variety of jobs. Collins learned to fly when she was only 19: "I didn't spend money on clothes…I'd grown up watching gliders fly off Harris Hill (in Elmira, New York) and I'd always dreamed of flying." She graduated from Syracuse University with a bachelor's in mathematics and economics, and obtained a master's in operations research from Stanford University in 1986. She also holds a master's in space systems management from Webster University. From 1986 to 1989, Collins was a math instructor at the Air Force Academy. During that time, she was also a test pilot at Edwards Air Force base, flying 26 different aircraft in a single year.

In 1990, Collins was selected by NASA and became an astronaut in July 1991. Collins became the first woman to pilot a space shuttle, when *Discovery* completed an eight-day mission in February 1995. That mission included the first space rendezvous with the Russian space station *Mir*. Collins made history again in 1999, when she commanded the *Columbia*, for mission STS-93. Throughout her career, Collins has logged over 6,751 hours in 30 different types of aircraft.

Retired from NASA since 2006, Collins has received numerous awards including the Distinguished Flying Cross, Defense Meritorious Service Medal, French Legion of Honor, NASA Outstanding Leadership Medal, Free Spirit Award, and the National Space Trophy.

Collins is well aware of the pioneering nature of her work: "I want to do well because I know that I'm representing other women, other pilots, military pilots as well as civilian pilots who are hoping to come here to NASA and be pilots themselves for the space shuttle."

Ruth Colvin
1917–

Ruth Johnson Colvin saw a problem – pervasive adult illiteracy – and used formidable organizing skills and tenacity to help solve it through the creation of Literacy Volunteers of America, Inc.

Colvin learned the scope of illiteracy in 1962 when she discovered that more than 11,000 people in the upstate New York county where she lived could not read. Her life was transformed as she undertook the necessary training needed to help correct the situation.

She determined that traditional classroom methods would not work and instead focused on the development of community networks in which a climate was created that empowered adult learners in new ways. The organization developed tutor training programs, special materials, community support components and a model that involves people from all walks of life in a community. Former dropouts became tutors, as did bank presidents, educators and many others.

In 2002, Literacy Volunteers of America, Inc. merged with Laubach Literacy International to form ProLiteracy Worldwide. Of her sometimes daunting work, Colvin has said, "If you believe in your idea, you go from there. If you do it with love, it will work out."

During her more than over four decades of literacy work, Colvin has published nine books, and visited or worked in more than sixty countries. In 2006, she was awarded the Presidential Medal of Freedom.

Colvin traveled internationally for many years to share her knowledge, exemplifying the power of one individual to change the world for the better.

$\mathscr{R}$ita Rossi Colwell, Ph.D.
1934–

Rita Rossi Colwell is one of the most influential and visionary scientists of her generation. She is a microbiologist, marine expert and internationally recognized authority on cholera and infectious diseases.

Dr. Colwell has pioneered the expanding role of women and minorities in science from Bangladesh to America, and a dynamic understanding of complex systems, integrated data, and the multi-level interplay among the earth's systems.

In developing nations, Dr. Colwell used "high-tech analyses to produce extremely low-tech solutions." Researching the environmental aspects of cholera outbreaks with new tracking techniques, Colwell and her colleagues developed locally based, inexpensive filtration methods to remove the plankton associated with cholera bacteria that are responsible for high death rates in poverty-stricken countries. They taught women a simple, folded-sari-cloth filtration technique of water purification to reduce the incidence of cholera by 50%. The global impact on reduction of mortality from cholera infection is profound.

Dr. Colwell became the eleventh Director of the National Science Foundation in 1998, the first woman to become Director and the first biologist. At the NSF, she spearheaded the agency's emphases on K-12 science and mathematics education, increased the participation of women and minorities in science and engineering, and led the NSF through the greatest period of growth in its fifty-year history. Her policy approach strengthened core NSF activities and established support for major initiatives in Nanotechnology, Biocomplexity, Information Technology, Social, Behavioral and Economic Sciences, and the 21st Century Workforce.

A member of the National Academy of Sciences, Dr. Colwell has received numerous awards including the 2006 National Medal of Science for her work in studying oceans, climate and human health. She is the author or co-author of 17 books and more than 700 scientific publications, and produced the award-winning film Invisible Seas. In recognition of her work in the world's polar regions, the geological site in Antarctica, Colwell Massif, has been named in her honor.

Dr. Colwell currently chairs Canon U.S. Life Sciences and is distinguished university professor at the University of Maryland, College Park, and the Johns Hopkins University Bloomberg School of Public Health.

𝒥oan Ganz Cooney
1929–

Joan Ganz Cooney, as creator of *Sesame Street*, has benefited millions of young children.

After graduating from the University of Arizona, Cooney worked as a newspaper reporter. In 1954, she moved to New York City to write for television. In 1964, she received an award for her analysis of the antipoverty program in New York. That same year, after studying the use of television for preschool education and successfully soliciting over $8 million in funding, Cooney founded the Children's Television Workshop and created *Sesame Street*.

Debuting in 1969, *Sesame Street* won numerous awards and is still seen by millions of children around the world. In some places, *Sesame Street* provides preschool children with their only structured opportunity to develop learning skills. Not only has the program enhanced preschool children's understanding of the fundamentals of reading, but it has helped them appreciate the world and the variety of people in it.

Cooney's research on poverty, education, and on children's inquisitive nature, along with her creativity, led to this television program of unequaled success. Perhaps no other woman in the late 20th century has influenced the education of children as much as Joan Ganz Cooney.

$\mathscr{S}$t. Marianne Cope
1838–1918

Barbara Koob was born in Heppenheim, Germany. In 1839, her family immigrated to the United States and settled in Utica, NY. As soon as she completed school, she supported her family from 1853-1862. She then entered the Sisters of the Third Order of St. Francis in Syracuse, NY and became known as Sister Marianne. She held a variety of leadership positions in her religious community and at upstate New York schools.

In 1866, she helped found St. Elizabeth's Hospital in Utica, NY and in 1869 became the primary founder of St. Joseph's Hospital in Syracuse, NY: two hospitals that were among the first 50 hospitals founded in the United States. The St. Joseph's Hospital Charter stated: "In the admittance and treatment of patients, no distinction shall be made because of theological belief, nationality or color."

Saint Cope became the Administrator of St. Joseph's in 1870, a pioneering advocate for patients' rights, sanitation and hygiene. The College of Medicine of Syracuse University was moved from Geneva, NY to Syracuse because of the training opportunities available to doctors at St. Joseph's Hospital, and Mother Marianne admitted the medical students and initiated their clinical instruction.

In 1874, her policy was "the wishes of the patients with regard to their being brought before the medical students should be respected in every case." Responding to an appeal from the King and Queen of Hawaii, Saint Cope and six other Sisters of St. Francis arrived in Honolulu in late 1883. In four years, they transformed the Kakaako Branch Hospital for those with leprosy from an unsanitary institution plagued by vermin into a hospital compound with beautiful grounds and cottages, where people were treated with dignity.

In 1884, Saint Cope founded the Malulani Hospital, the first general hospital on Maui. The next year, she founded the Kapiolani Home in Honolulu for the healthy female children of persons with leprosy, most likely the first institution of its kind in the world. In 1888, she arrived at the remote settlement on Molokai's Kalaupapa peninsula, a desolate place where individuals of all ages challenged by leprosy had been abandoned by society. She established the Bishop Home for single women, providing a safe, affirming environment. Her influence spread to all of Kalaupapa, slowly transforming it from a place of abandonment and despair to a community of hope and dignity.

More than 130 years later, her philosophy of seeing value in every individual and promoting a "quality of life spirit", ensuring human rights and individual dignity, belonging and community, still resonates today. Her vision that those marginalized by society be afforded opportunities and access to health care, dignity and equal treatment, is manifested in the St. Joseph Hospital Center of Syracuse, St. Elizabeth's of Utica, in Hawaii's St. Francis Medical System "hospital without walls", and in the Kalaupapa National Historical Park.

Gerty Theresa Radnitz Cori, M.D.
1896–1957

Gerty Theresa Radnitz Cori, a pioneer in biochemistry, received international recognition for discovering, along with her husband, Carl, how glucose is converted into glycogen, a process dubbed the Cori Cycle.

Her research had a profound effect on the treatment of diabetes, allowing physicians to understand how the body stores glucose by converting it into glycogen stored energy, which can be used when the body's reserves run low.

In 1947, she and her husband, along with Bernardo A. Houssay, received the Nobel Prize for Physiology and Medicine for this discovery. Cori's later studies on enzymes and hormones further advanced research in the treatment of diabetes and contributed to our understanding that missing enzymes indicate defective genes. This laid the foundation for future studies of genetic defects in humans.

Cori received her M.D. at the German University of Prague in 1920 and came to the United States in the 1920s. Despite her significant research, she had to fight discrimination and nepotism rules.

Finally, in 1947, the same year she became the first American woman and the third worldwide to receive a Nobel Prize in the sciences as well as the first woman to be awarded the Prize in Physiology or Medicine, she was named a full professor of biochemistry at Washington University in St. Louis. In 1950, President Harry Truman appointed her to the Board of Directors of the National Science Foundation.

Jane Cunningham Croly
1829–1901

Journalist Jane Cunningham Croly – a pioneer in her profession – was also the founder and driving force behind the American club women's movement. She was the founder of the General Federation of Women's Clubs.

Croly, a working journalist in a male-dominated world of newspapers and magazines, was probably the nation's first syndicated woman's columnist. Her column, "Jennie June," went to an array of newspapers around the East and South. She became an editor at the *New York World* in 1862, and continued her column.

In 1868, when the New York Press Club refused admission to women to hear a special program by Charles Dickens, Croly founded Sorosis, a club for women.

Croly was a staunch believer in equal rights for women, although not an active suffragist, believing that the more important task was to lift women throughout all levels of society, and all reforms would evolve naturally. When she convened a national convention of women's clubs in 1889 (the General Federation of Women's Clubs was organized there), she set in motion the power of a vast, previously untapped and unorganized sisterhood of capable American women that would reshape American society.

Paulina Wright Davis
1813–1876

The work of Paulina Kellogg Wright Davis as a women's rights advocate, social reformer, educator, and author extended over forty years from the late 1830s to her death in 1876. Mrs. Wright began her work for women's rights, anti-slavery and temperance causes when she was only twenty and newly married to Francis Wright, a wealthy merchant from Utica, NY.

In the late 1830s, she met Elizabeth Cady Stanton and Ernestine Rose, with whom she joined in a petition to the New York legislature that eventually led to the passage of the Married Women's Property Act in 1848 that gave married women control of their own personal property and real estate.

Following the death of Francis Wright in 1845, Paulina Wright was left an independent and wealthy woman. She invested her time in studying the anatomy and physiology of women and then conducted a lecture series on female physiology and anatomy, unprecedented in her time, which is said to have encouraged some of her listeners to join the first generation of women physicians.

In 1849 she married Thomas Davis, a Rhode Island Congressman and went with him to Washington. In 1850, she was an organizer and then served as president of the First National Women's Rights Convention in Worcester, MA, which drew participants from nine states. She repeated this the next year at the Second National Women's Rights Convention, again in Worcester.

From 1853 to 1855, she edited and published a distinctively women's rights newspaper *The Una,* which expressed broad views of individual freedom. Post-Civil War, she helped found the New England Woman Suffrage Association. In 1871, she published *A History of the National Woman's Rights Movement.*

When a split occurred in the women's rights movement, she supported the National Woman Suffrage Association with Susan B. Anthony and Elizabeth Cady Stanton. At her funeral, Mrs. Stanton and Ms. Anthony eulogized Davis and urged others to follow her lifelong example of service to women.

Dorothy Day
1897–1980

Dorothy Day was a radical Catholic social change activist, widely considered one of the great Catholic lay leaders of the 20th century. Co-founder of the Catholic Worker movement and the publication that became its voice, she worked indefatigably to promote peace, social justice, non-violence, and direct aid to the poor and destitute.

Early in her life she was a journalist for *The Call* and *The Masses* and was arrested demonstrating for women's suffrage in 1917. With her conversion to Catholicism and initiation of the Catholic Worker, her activism manifested in Christian voluntary poverty and direct works of mercy. More than 100 Catholic Worker communities and Houses of Hospitality were founded across the U.S. and abroad. Then and now these houses offer food, clothing and shelter to those in need.

Day resolutely resisted war and war preparations inclusive of nuclear testing and armament for over half a century. Spear-heading the Catholic Worker, she led the movement in supporting peace, civil rights, worker rights and women's rights through prayer, publications, organizing, demonstrating, and educating.

Marian de Forest
1864–1935

Visionary Marian de Forest overcame childhood hardship to become a respected journalist and playwright, and major force in the progressive women's movement.

Upon graduating from Buffalo Seminary, de Forest became one of the first female reporters in Western New York State and quickly rose to become a drama critic and department editor.

In 1919, in Buffalo, NY, she founded Zonta (later Zonta International), a service organization of executives and professionals dedicated to improving the legal, political, economic, educational, health and professional status of women. Today, Zonta International has more than 30,000 members in 65 countries worldwide.

De Forest was also a strong proponent of the arts. As a leading playwright, she supported women's role in the theater and received numerous accolades, including induction into The Lyceum of London. De Forest's love of music led her to co-found the Buffalo Musical Foundation, bring the American Opera Company to Western New York, and play a prominent role in the formation of the Buffalo Philharmonic Orchestra.

*D*onna de Varona
1947–

At the age of thirteen, Donna de Varona became the youngest competitor at the 1960 Olympic Games. Within the next four years, she broke an unprecedented 18 world swimming records and won two Olympic Gold Medals.

By age seventeen, she was voted Most Outstanding Female Athlete in the world by both the Associated Press (AP) and the United Press International (UPI).

After attaining 37 national championships and two Olympic gold medals, she retired from competitive sports in 1965. That same year, de Varona became the first female sports broadcaster on network television and in so doing paved the way for future female athletes and journalists.

As an ABC Sports on-air analyst, commentator, host, writer and producer she earned an Emmy Award nomination for "Keepers of the Flame" a TV special on the Olympics, and received an Emmy for her story about a Special Olympian. She also won the Gracie Award two consecutive years for her Sporting News Radio show: "Donna de Varona on Sports".

De Varona is a founding member of the Women's Sports Foundation and its first President. She served five terms on the President's Council on Physical Fitness and Sports, and was a moving force in Congress' passage of the 1978 Amateur Sports Act and the 1972 landmark "Title IX" legislation.

Some of the many honors bestowed on her include: The International Swimming Hall of Fame Gold Medallion, The Olympia Award for her contribution to the Olympic Movement, The Olympic Order, which is the highest award given by the International Olympic Committee, honorary doctoral degrees, and many leadership awards.

In 2002-2003, she served on the U. S. Secretary of Education's Commission on Opportunity in Athletics. Her leadership in sports communication, and consistent advocacy for expanding women's opportunity in sports have had a wide and lasting impact across the nation and globe.

Karen DeCrow
1937–2014

A nationally recognized attorney, author and activist, Karen DeCrow is one of the most celebrated leaders of the women's movement.

Born in Chicago, and educated in its public school system, Karen DeCrow earned her bachelor's degree from Northwestern University, Medill School of Journalism, in 1959. Her literary career began after graduation, and she spent ten years as a writer and editor. During this time she also became active in the women's movement.

1967 saw Karen ascend to the presidency of the Syracuse, New York chapter of the National Organization for Women (NOW). From 1968 to 1974, she also served as a member of the National Board of Directors of NOW. In 1974, she was elected National President of NOW, serving in that capacity for two terms. During DeCrow's tenure as President of NOW, the organization embarked on important initiatives including achieving non-governmental status with the United Nations, supporting the first ordination of eleven Episcopal women, persuading the federal government to include sex discrimination in the Fair Housing Law, and instituting highly publicized and successful discrimination actions against Sears and AT&T. She was the last President of NOW to serve without pay or an office.

In 1969, DeCrow returned to college at Syracuse University, College of Law, graduating as the only female in the class of 1972. She devoted her legal career to cases promoting gender equality, eliminating age discrimination and protecting civil liberties. She was also a strong supporter of equal rights for men, evolving to support joint custody when parents divorce. DeCrow campaigned tirelessly for passage of the Equal Rights Amendment (ERA). During the 1970s and 1980s, she traveled throughout the United States (often at her own expense) to debate anti-feminist author, Phyllis Schlafly, on the ERA. She wrote numerous books and articles and is recognized as a noted lecturer worldwide for her expertise on topics including law, feminism, politics, civil rights, parental rights and the ERA. In 1970, she served as National Coordinator of the Women's Strike. In 1974, *Time* magazine named her as part of the 200 Future Leaders of America. In 1988, she co-founded World Women Watch.

Emma Smith DeVoe
1848–1927

Emma Snutg DeVoe, as a leading suffragist in the early twentieth century, not only successfully ran the campaign that enfranchised women in the State of Washington ten years before the national amendment was ratified, but also helped transform the face of politics in America.

While DeVoe supported woman's suffrage from her early childhood, her real impact came after she moved with her husband to Tacoma, Washington in 1905. She revitalized the near-defunct Washington Equal Suffrage Association and headed up the campaign that resulted in the approval, by a nearly 64 percent majority vote, of a constitutional amendment enfranchising Washington State women. A ladylike, polite, and tactful woman, DeVoe pioneered what she called the Washington plan of campaign. She advocated using "womanly" ways and one-on-one persuasion. She urged her fellow workers to see that women asked every voter in the state to support the suffrage amendment. Thus, DeVoe coupled the precinct method, introduced in Idaho's 1896 campaign, with her new idea of a statewide canvass to determine how every voter stood on the question of suffrage. She also used other mass techniques, such as penny postcards and posters. She avoided alienating potent forces, such as big business and the brewers, by urging supporters like labor and temperance organizations to support the movement quietly rather than aggressively. She told her workers to remain "good-natured and cheerful." And to prove that suffragists did not want to change women's traditional role as homemakers, she published a cookbook that she distributed throughout the state, the back of which had the words "Votes for Women."

After her victory in Washington, DeVoe campaigned in other states, advocating the Washington method rather than the more aggressive style of eastern suffragists who tended to imitate their British sisters with sit-ins and mass rallies. In addition, she organized the first national organization of voting women, the National Council of Women Voters, which studied issues to educate voters on a non-partisan basis. The organization's "Declaration of Principles" proclaimed a dedication to holding itself above partisan politics and sectarian affiliations and instead working for equality of opportunity for all, the protection of children, and the promotion of the family. DeVoe's council eventually merged with the National League of Women Voters.

As a suffragist, DeVoe not only brought new energy to the suffrage movement but also helped personalize politics and introduce the idea of voting the issues rather than the party.

Photo: Washington State Historical Society, Tacoma

Emily Dickinson
1830–1886

Emily Dickinson's father, Edward Dickinson, a pillar of the community in Amherst, Massachusetts, exerted great influence over his middle child, Emily.

She spent a year at Mount Holyoke Female Seminary. There her stubborn resistance to conversion during a religious revival marked her as one who did not fear to tread a lonely path.

Dickinson returned from Mount Holyoke to her father's house and remained there for the rest of her life. Busy about the house and garden, she began to write verse. The narrow boundaries of "woman's sphere" were deadly limitations for many women.

Somehow Dickinson found within herself the imaginative resources to exceed and shatter such boundaries. Although untaught and virtually unpublished during her lifetime, she became one of the greatest poets in the English language.

Sometimes Dickinson sought encouragement and friendship – from author and reformer Thomas Wentworth Higginson among others. But more and more she withdrew. Alone with her thoughts and her pen, she crafted poetry in experimental form that anticipated modern style. She knew what she had achieved: "I have a horror of death; the dead are so soon forgotten. But when I die, they'll have to remember me."

Nearly 1800 poems were discovered by her family after her death.

Dorothea Dix
1802–1887

An unhappy childhood helped Dorothea Dix to identify with society's outcasts. Like many young women of her day, she became a school teacher.

Surrounded by the ferment of reform in pre-Civil War Boston but untouched by it, she was drifting towards a life of spinsterly aimlessness until one cold day in March 1841. She had volunteered to teach a Sunday school class at the jail in East Cambridge. Among the convicts, shivering in an unheated room, she found some women who were mentally ill. Why was there no stove to warm them, she demanded? Lunatics, she was told, could not feel the cold, and they would only burn themselves or set the building afire.

Dorothea Dix determined to act; she had found her cause. She spent over a year touring every jail, almshouse, and house of correction in Massachusetts. She then presented a report, or "memorial" to the Legislature asking for funds for an institution specially designed to treat the mentally ill. She did the same in state after state, traveling thousands of miles alone and publicizing the terrible conditions she found.

Always observing the rules of feminine propriety, she rarely spoke publicly, but she was a persuasive lobbyist behind the scenes. When the Civil War broke out she was appointed superintendent of nurses for the Union Army. Unfortunately, this was a role for which she was ill-suited, and controversy swirled around her.

After the war she toured hospitals in the South and in Europe, slowing up but never abandoning her role as crusader for humane treatment of the insane.

Elizabeth Hanford Dole

1936–

Throughout her life, Elizabeth Hanford Dole has been a trailblazer and precedent-setting leader of great accomplishment, basing her life's work in public service.

Dole graduated with distinction from Duke University and earned her law degree from Harvard in 1965. She held two Cabinet positions – Secretary of Transportation under President Reagan (the first woman ever to hold that position) and Secretary of Labor for President George H.W. Bush. In 2002, she won 54% of the vote to become U.S. Senator from North Carolina.

Dole served as President of the American Red Cross – the first woman to hold that position since the organization's founder, Clara Barton, held it in 1881. As Secretary of Transportation, Dole increased automobile safety requirements and spearheaded the campaign to raise the drinking age to 21. She imposed tougher aviation security measures at airports, and worked to increase the use of passive restraints in vehicles.

As Secretary of Labor, Dole initiated the "Glass Ceiling Study" to identify barriers to senior management opportunities for women and minorities and make recommendations for effective change. 62% of her senior staff at Labor were women or minorities. Of this work Dole said, "My objective as Secretary of Labor is to look through the 'glass ceiling' to see who is on the other side, and to serve as a catalyst for change."

Dole also advocated increased support to disadvantaged and unskilled young people to help find employment for at-risk youth. As president of the American Red Cross, Dole directed the work of nearly 30,000 staff members and more than a million volunteers. She overhauled the disaster relief program, turning a $30 million deficit to an on-hand fund of $100 million. She implemented a multi-million dollar program to retool the blood collection, processing and distribution system, which is responsible for one-half of the nation's blood supply.

Elizabeth Dole has received numerous awards in recognition of her outstanding service, from honorary doctoral degrees to Churchwoman of the Year honors and the Raoul Wallenberg Award for Humanitarian Service. In 2012, she established the Elizabeth Dole Foundation, whose purpose is to assist caregivers of "wounded warriors."

arjory Stoneman Douglas
1890–1998

Marjory Stoneman Douglas's 1947 best seller, *The Everglades: River of Grass*, raised America's consciousness and transformed the Florida Everglades from an area that was looked upon as a useless swamp – to be drained and developed commercially – to a national park that is seen as a valuable environmental resource to be protected and preserved. After this successful campaign to preserve the Everglades as a national park, Douglas continued her work by founding the Friends of the Everglades, a conservation organization still active today.

Always ahead of her time, Douglas graduated from Wellesley College as an English major in 1912. A few years later, Douglas went to Miami to be a reporter for her father's newspaper, which later became *The Miami Herald*. During World War I, she served with the American Red Cross in Europe. After the war, she launched her career as a newspaper editor at her father's paper. Many of her editorials focused on what she perceived to be Florida's increasing problem of rapid commercial development. In the 1920s, she left the newspaper to launch a second career as an author. Over the years she published many books and short stories, both fiction and non-fiction – most for adults but several for children – especially focusing on women, the history and life in southern Florida and environmental issues. She also engaged in a number of other campaigns and charity work to improve society: campaigns against slum-lords and for improved housing conditions, for free milk for babies whose parents needed aid, and for the ratification of the Women's Suffrage Amendment.

Most important, she dedicated her life to preserving and restoring the Everglades. She lived long enough to witness great successes. In 1996, for example, Florida voters passed a constitutional amendment that held polluters primarily responsible for cleaning up the Everglades. And the Florida and federal governments have authorized multimillion-dollar projects to restore and expand the Everglades. In recognition of her tireless and successful struggle, the state of Florida named the headquarters of its Department of Natural Resources after her.

Awarding Mrs. Douglas the Presidential Medal of Freedom in 1993, President Clinton recognized her achievements. Upon her death in 1998 at the age of 108, President Clinton said: "Long before there was an Earth Day, Mrs. Douglas was a passionate steward of our nation's natural resources, and particularly her Florida Everglades."

St. Katharine Drexel
1858–1955

A missionary who dedicated her life and fortune to aid Native Americans and African Americans, Saint Katharine Drexel is only the second recognized American-born saint.

Saint Drexel was born into a prominent family in Philadelphia, PA in 1858. Her mother died shortly after her birth, and her father remarried two years later, providing Drexel with a new mother. Drexel and her sisters were raised in a loving family atmosphere permeated by deep faith, and were taught that wealth was meant to be shared with those in need.

When Drexel was growing up, her family would open their home to serve the needs of the poor three days a week, and when Drexel was old enough, she learned to assist her mother. Later, when the family purchased a summer home in Torresdale, Pennsylvania, Drexel began teaching Sunday school classes. It was there that she met Reverend James O'Connor, later the Bishop of Omaha, who became her spiritual director.

When Drexel was in her twenties, her mother was diagnosed with cancer and passed away. Shortly thereafter in 1885, her father died suddenly, and Drexel and her sisters inherited the income from his estate. Throughout 1887 and 1888, Drexel was introduced to the plight of Native Americans and visited several remote reservations with Monsignor Joseph Stephan and Bishop O'Connor. After witnessing the poverty endured by Native Americans, Drexel began building schools and providing food, clothing and financial support to the reservations.

In 1889, Bishop O'Connor urged Drexel to found a congregation to work with Native Americans and African Americans. Although she initially hesitated, through prayer, Drexel eventually accepted this as her vocation and pronounced her vows as the first Sister of the Blessed Sacrament (1891). During her lifetime, Drexel and her order founded more than sixty missions and schools, including Xavier University of Louisiana. Today, the Sisters of the Blessed Sacrament remains a religious order devoted to the education and care of Native Americans and African Americans.

Saint Drexel was beatified in 1988, and canonized by Pope John Paul II on October 1, 2000.

Anne Dallas Dudley
1876–1955

In the final years of the struggle to pass the 19th Amendment to the Constitution giving women the right to vote, Anne Dudley was central to both the national campaign (serving as National Director) and the critical struggle in her home state of Tennessee, which was to become the 36th and final state to support women's suffrage, thus making the Amendment the law of the land.

Dudley, a woman of elegance and high social standing, ignored the natural constraints of her position to speak out with great force and persuasion on behalf of suffrage. She viewed women's voting as "a matter of simple justice," and became the founder and first president of the Nashville Equal Suffrage League, and president of the Tennessee Equal Suffrage Association.

In 1917 she was chosen Vice President of the National American Women's Suffrage Association, working closely with President Carrie Chapman Catt in planning the master strategies of the campaign that finally succeeded in 1920. Dudley became a vigorous and outspoken campaigner throughout the South, matching her speeches with articles for publication and work introducing legislation.

Dudley became the first woman in Tennessee to make an open-air speech, given after she led a march of 2,000 women from downtown Nashville to Centennial Park – the first suffrage parade in the South, in May 1914. She was also the first female associate of the Tennessee Democratic Committee, and the first female delegate-at-large of the National Democratic Convention in 1920.

Throughout her life and political career, Dudley lived and modeled her conviction regarding women and the rights they were due: "This is a government of, by and for the people, and only the law denies that women are people!"

Mary Barret Dyer
1611–1660

Mary Barrett Dyer, a martyred Quaker, originally was a faithful Puritan. As such, she and her husband settled in Massachusetts Bay Colony in 1635. However, as a follower of the dissenter Anne Hutchinson, she and her family were banished by Puritan rulers after Hutchinson was convicted and banished for preaching heretical ideas.

Dyer eventually returned to England where she became a protégé of George Fox, the founder of Quakerism. Returning to Boston as a Quaker, she was expelled for preaching Quakerism. Refusing to accept her exile, she returned again and again.

Finally, the rulers of the Massachusetts Bay Colony tried and convicted her of preaching heresy and condemned her to death. Reprieved and expelled, she returned again. Again, she was tried and convicted of violating the statute against preaching Quakerism. This time her sentence was carried out – she was hanged June 1,1660.

When offered her life if she would leave Massachusetts and return no more she said: "Nay, I cannot; for in obedience to the will of the Lord God I came, and in His will I abide faithful to death."

Gradually, many came to consider her death the death of a martyr. Some claim that she was ahead of her time, searching for a religion that held women to be equal to men. Her hanging hastened the easing of anti-Quaker statutes and began a process that contributed to the move for more religious tolerance in the colonies and would, ultimately, result in freedom of religion and the separation of church and state in the United States of America.

Amelia Earhart
1897–1937

She was a vigorous tomboy in her Kansas girlhood. Yet unlike generation after generation of American women, Amelia Earhart did not have to give up action and daring in adulthood. She worked as a volunteer in a Red Cross Hospital during World War I, studied briefly as a premed student, and taught English to immigrant factory workers. But her first love was the airplane, then captivating the public imagination.

Surrounded by the excitement of stunt fliers and air shows, she made her first solo flight in 1921 and scraped together the money to buy her own plane. In 1928, when Amelia Earhart was working in a settlement house in Boston, she was approached by the organizers of a transatlantic flight. The woman originally scheduled to be part of the team could not go, so would Amelia take her place? "How could I refuse such a shining adventure!"

As the first woman to fly the Atlantic, she won the public's affection. The press dubbed her "Lady Lindy," a female Charles Lindbergh.

She became aviation editor of *Cosmopolitan*, was active in Zonta International, and helped establish an organization of women pilots.

In 1931 she married George Palmer Putnam, of the publishing family, and his promotional skills kept her name in the press. After achieving a number of flight "firsts," she determined to do "just one more long flight," In 1937 she took off from Miami heading east on an around-the-world course. Her Lockheed Electra was specially equipped, and she was accompanied by a navigator, Fred Noonan. On July 2 they took off for the most difficult leg of the trip, from New Guinea to tiny Howland Island in the mid-Pacific. They never arrived, and an extensive air and sea search failed to turn up any trace of them.

Sylvia Earle, Ph.D.
1935–

Sylvia Earle, oceanographer, conservationist, and entrepreneur, has overcome the resistance of both the scientific and general communities to women traveling with men on long scientific expeditions, to become internationally recognized as one of our nation's leading marine biologists and one of the world's leading advocates for safeguarding the seas – the earth's largest and most vital natural resource.

Dr. Earle's adventures and her sense of wonder and excitement about the living underwater world has opened our eyes and inspired us to protect the ocean and respect its role in our lives. Earle has led over 100 expeditions worldwide, involving in excess of 7,000 hours underwater in connection with her research. In 1970, after being rejected from participating in Tektite I because she was a woman, she led the first team of women aquanauts, known as the Tektite II Project, on a two-week exploration of the ocean floor. In 1979, she walked un-tethered on the sea floor at a depth lower than any other person before or since (1,250 feet).

Determined to inform the world of her discoveries and the importance of ocean conservation, Earle has authored more than 190 publications on marine science and technology and participated in numerous television productions and lectures in more than eighty countries. Her 1995 book, *Sea Change: A Message of the Oceans*, has been described as a Rachel Carson-like plea for the preservation of the oceans.

Sometimes referred to as "Her Deepness," Dr. Earle served for two years as the first female chief scientist of the National Oceanographic and Atmospheric Administration. In 1992, she founded Deep Ocean Exploration and Research, now DOER Marine, an ocean engineering firm which designs, operates, supports, and consults on manned and robotic sub-sea systems. In addition to serving as Chairperson of her company, she led the Sustainable Seas Expeditions, from 1998-2002, served as adjunct scientist at the Monterey Bay Aquarium Research Institute, and a member of various boards, foundations, and committees dealing with marine research, policy, and conservation. Her more than 100 national and international honors include honorary degrees as well as the prestigious United Nations Environment Award, the Explorers Club Lowell Thomas Award, and the Director's Award of the National Resources Council.

Dr. Earle continues to plead for understanding and preservation of the oceans, reminding us that if we do not care for our water, we will simply cease to exist.

Catherine East
1916–1996

The woman Betty Friedan described as "the midwife to the contemporary women's movement" spent many years working for the federal government, and it was from this position that much of East's invaluable data and strategic thinking came to the fore to help women progress in society.

A staff member on the Kennedy Commission on the Status of Women, East saw the range and degree of discrimination women faced nationwide, and she became a feminist, working to help end gender discrimination. She encouraged the creation of state-level commissions on women, in order to collect information and generate activism at that level.

While continuing to serve various government bodies working on women's issues, East also saw the need for the creation of a powerful national women's organization to spearhead the drive to end gender discrimination and helped found the National Organization for Women.

NOW was central to the signing of the federal anti-discrimination legislation. Catherine East was also the architect of the strategy to bring the Equal Rights Amendment out of committee and to passage in House of Representatives.

Crystal Eastman, J.D.
1881–1928

Crystal Eastman, co-founder of the American Civil Liberties Union, struggled throughout her life for equal rights and civil liberties for all. Acquiring her law degree from New York University in 1907, Eastman was one of only a few hundred women lawyers in the early twentieth century. Her first job as an attorney was to investigate labor conditions for the Russell Sage Foundation. Her pioneering report, *Work Accidents and the Law* (1910), led New York Governor Charles Evans Hughes to appoint her the first woman on New York State's Commission on Employers' Liability and Causes of Industrial Accidents, Unemployment and Lack of Farm Labor. As a member of that commission, Eastman drafted the country's first workers' compensation law. That legislation became the model for workers' compensation throughout the nation. Then, during Woodrow Wilson's administration, Eastman became investigating attorney for the United States Commission on Industrial Relations.

Meanwhile, Eastman also struggled to further women's rights – first suffrage and later equal rights – as co-author of the first Equal Rights Amendment. During World War I, she was a leader of the peace movement, working with Carrie Chapman Catt to organize the Carnegie Hall meeting that led to the founding of the Woman's Peace Party of New York – later renamed the Women's International League of Peace and Freedom – the oldest women's peace organization. Eastman became Executive Secretary of the Women's Peace Party. A leading advocate for civil liberties and the rights of conscientious objectors during World War I, she joined Norman Thomas and Roger Baldwin in founding the American Civil Liberties Union as the "watch dog" organization protecting Americans' rights under the Bill of Rights and providing legal assistance to those whose rights may have been violated, regardless of partisan persuasion.

A brilliant orator and effective writer, Eastman campaigned throughout her life for peace, equal rights, and civil liberties. In a eulogy written for *The Nation*, Freda Kirchney remembered Eastman's sincerity and enthusiasm. "When she spoke to people – whether it was to a small committee or a swarming crowd – hearts beat faster…She was for thousands a symbol of what the free woman might be."

Mary Baker Eddy
1821–1910

Mary Baker Eddy overcame years of ill health and great personal struggle to make an indelible mark on society, religion and journalism.

Her life has been described as a continual struggle for health amid tumultuous relationships. Ill health in childhood spent in New Hampshire meant a limited home education, and the death of her first husband left her penniless and pregnant.

With family help and a deep religious faith, she recovered over a period of years, but her son was raised throughout his life by others. She remarried ten years after her widowhood, an unsuccessful union that further aggravated her fragile health.

She then met Dr. Phineas Quimby, a healer, who helped her regain her full strength. It was with Quimby's tutelage that Eddy began to believe that the cause and cure of disease was mental. Later, after Quimby's death, she fell on the ice, causing great injury. After several days, Eddy pronounced herself healed, after reading from the Bible. This led to years of reflection, study and false starts, but in 1875 she opened a "Christian Scientists' Home" in Lynn, Massachusetts, and soon began holding public services.

She then helped found the Christian Science Publishing Society and published the first edition of *Science and Health*, a 456-page book of her beliefs.

In 1877 she married for the third time, and in 1879, the First Church of Christ, Scientist was formally chartered. In 1881 she also obtained a charter for the Massachusetts Metaphysical College as a degree-granting institution – and all of this moved to Boston in 1881.

Eddy proved effective at teaching hundreds of students, most of them women, to go out across the nation as Christian Science practitioners, organizing societies and recruiting still more practitioners as they went. In 1883 Eddy founded the monthly *Christian Science Journal* and later the *Christian Science Sentinel*. Her seminal work, *Science and Health*, continued to grow and be reprinted.

In 1908, just two years before her death at 89, Eddy started a newspaper dedicated to public service, *The Christian Science Monitor*, because she felt that the "yellow journalism" of the American press was unfairly prejudicial against her faith. In her work *No and Yes*, printed in 1909, Eddy wrote, "True prayer is not asking God for love; it is learning to love, and to include all mankind in one affection."

arian Wright Edelman, J.D.

1939–

Marian Wright Edelman, civil rights activist and founder of the Children's Defense Fund, has dedicated her life to those who cannot always lift themselves up. Edelman obtained a law degree at Yale and worked in Mississippi, becoming the first African-American woman to be admitted to that state's bar.

As a leader with the NAACP Legal Defense and Education Fund, Edelman helped coordinate the Poor People's Campaign after Martin Luther King, Jr.'s assassination. She founded the Children's Defense Fund in the 1970s, to apply pressure on the federal government to help poor children, and to coordinate nationwide activities to help children.

Considered the nation's most powerful children's lobby, CDF secured the 1990 Act for Better Child Care, bringing more than $3 billion into daycare facilities and other programs. Many consider this law the first federal government acknowledgment that children matter.

With millions of American children living in poverty, Edelman continues her advocacy, focusing on expanding Head Start, health care and support for homeless children. In 1993 Edelman published her book, *The Measure of Our Success: A Letter to My Children and Yours*. She is the recipient of many awards including the Presidential Medal of Freedom.

Gertrude "Trudy" Ederle
1906–2003

Gertrude "Trudy" Ederle, learned to swim as a young child. She began to compete as a teenager and eventually achieved a lifetime record of twenty-nine U.S. and world swimming records. Ederle won a gold medal in the 400 meter freestyle relay and bronze medals in the 100 meter and 400 meter freestyle races in the 1924 Paris Olympics.

The next year she conceived of the idea of swimming the English Channel and made her first try. The sea was rough and she didn't succeed in her 1925 attempt. In 1926, she succeeded, becoming the first woman to swim the English Channel. Her time of 14 hours, 31 minutes for the 35-mile (56K) distance broke the previous record held by a man, bettering it by almost two hours, and it stood for 35 years as the woman's record. "People said women couldn't swim the Channel but I proved they could!"

Ederle not only showed athletic strength, endurance and skill at levels unexpected and unforeseen in her time, she bested the previous male swimming record for the Channel swim by close to two hours. The English Channel waters were high, gray and icy on August 6, 1926. Ederle suffered back injuries and hearing impairment as a result of her Channel swim.

She went on, after her competitive swimming days were over, to a successful career in fashion design and to create breakthrough techniques for teaching people with hearing impairments to swim. Ederle's extraordinary accomplishment and the broad public recognition that she received at the time set a milestone in the achievement of expanded opportunity for women in athletics.

𝒢ertrude Belle Elion
1918–1999

One of the nation's most distinguished research scientists, Gertrude Elion's Nobel Prize in 1988 capped a career devoted to research to combat some of the world's most dangerous diseases.

Elion, working predominantly with George Hitchings, created drugs to combat leukemia, gout, malaria, herpes and autoimmune disorders. She and Hitchings devised a system for designing drugs that led to the development of the AIDS drug AZT.

In the 1950s she pioneered the development of two drugs that interfered with the reproductive process of cancer cells to cause remissions in childhood leukemia. In 1957 she created the first immuno-suppressive agent, leading to successful organ transplants. In 1977, her work led to the development of the first drug used against viral herpes.

Gertrude Elion, who lost her grandfather and mother to cancer, never lost sight of the human beings whose lives her research affects. She said, "When you meet someone who has lived for 25 years with a kidney graft, there's your reward."

Dorothy Harrison Eustis
1886–1946

A philanthropist, Dorothy Harrison Eustis combined her love of animals and her passion for helping others to co-found the nation's first dog guide school, The Seeing Eye.

Born in Philadelphia, Pennsylvania in 1886, Eustis was educated at the Agnes Irwin School and later at the Rathgowrie School in England. In 1906, she married Walter Abbott Wood and moved to New York. Together, with the state department of agriculture, they operated an experimental dairy farm. There, they demonstrated that selective breeding could increase the milk production and commercial value of dairy cattle. That work continued until 1917, two years after Wood's death.

In 1921, Eustis relocated to Switzerland, where she began an experimental breeding kennel for dogs. She married George Morris Eustis in 1923, and at their estate, Fortunate Fields, they worked to breed and train German shepherds for civic duty. In 1927, Eustis discovered a school in Potsdam that taught dogs to serve as guides for blind war veterans. Impressed by the school's work, Eustis wrote an article entitled *The Seeing Eye*, which ran in the November 5, 1927 edition of the *Saturday Evening Post*.

When a young, blind American man named Morris Frank read the article, he was inspired to write to Eustis and request a guide dog. Eustis agreed to help, bringing Frank to Switzerland and providing him with a dog. When Frank returned to the United States with his dog, they earned much publicity and received many inquiries from other blind people. Shortly after, Eustis moved back to the United States. In 1929, she and Frank established the nation's first guide dog school, The Seeing Eye, to help make the world accessible to those who are blind or visually impaired.

Throughout her lifetime, Eustis devoted much of her fortune to The Seeing Eye; she served as the organization's President until 1940 and Honorary President thereafter.

lice Evans
1881–1975

Alice Evans identified the organism causing undulant fever. This discovery, one of the most medically important in the early 20th century, led to laws mandating milk pasteurization, saving countless lives in America and throughout the world.

Evans, one of the first woman scientists to hold a permanent appointment in the USDA Bureau of Animal Husbandry (she later worked at the National Institute of Health), initiated her studies of bacterial contamination of milk in 1910 and revealed her findings in 1917. Fierce opposition to her results developed but in the 1930s, milk pasteurization laws were enacted.

Although she was herself infected with undulant fever in 1922, she worked throughout her life as a widely-respected scientist, serving as the first woman president of the American Society of Bacteriologists.

After retirement in 1945, Evans lectured frequently on female career development, emphasizing scientific careers.

Geraldine Ferraro, J.D.
1935–2011

Geraldine Ferraro was the first woman nominated by a major political party as its candidate for Vice President of the United States.

A teacher and then attorney, Ferraro worked in the Queens, New York District Attorney's office, where she started the Special Victims Bureau. Ferraro ran successfully for Congress from New York City's 9th District in 1978. There, she was a women's and human rights advocate, working for passage of the Equal Rights Amendment, sponsoring the Women's Economic Equity Act ending pension discrimination against women, and seeking greater job training and opportunities for displaced homemakers.

In 1984, Ferraro was picked to run as Vice President of the United States on the Democratic Party ticket with former Vice President Walter Mondale as the candidate for President. In her acceptance speech, she spoke of the realization of the American dream: "Tonight, the daughter of an immigrant from Italy has been chosen to run for vice president in the new land my father came to love…" The ticket lost, but Ferraro's candidacy forever reshaped the American political and social landscape.

Ella Fitzgerald
1917–1996

The woman who was perhaps the nation's greatest jazz and pop artist began singing by accident, as legend has it.

When Ella was fifteen years old, she appeared as a contestant in a talent competition intending to dance. Her knees shook too much, and so she sang instead – and was heard by a musician in the famed Chick Webb Band. Webb brought the young girl along to sing for a one-night stand tryout, and the rest is history.

By 1937, only three years after beginning her career, Fitzgerald won her first *Down Beat Magazine* award for most popular girl vocalist, and in 1938 she had her first major hit, *A-Tisket, A-Tasket*. Dizzy Gillespie introduced her to the world of bop, and she began her lifelong improvising with *Lady Be Good*.

Of the magic her voice produced, the *New York Times* drama critic Brooks Atkinson wrote, "She manages things that the human voice can't do." Fitzgerald, with *Jazz at the Philharmonic* producer Norman Granz, began touring worldwide in 1948 – and Granz and Fitzgerald demanded equal pay for her with white artists, forcing an important issue that affected many musicians and artists thereafter.

Throughout her long career, Fitzgerald recorded the music of the Gershwins, Irving Berlin, Johnny Mercer, Ellington, Armstrong, Harold Arlen, Cole Porter and more, singing with the world's finest musicians, including Benny Goodman, Teddy Wilson and Duke Ellington, to list a few.

Fitzgerald was also an inspiration for her lifetime of good works, receiving the Whitney M. Young, Jr., Award of the Los Angeles Urban League, the first woman to receive it, for those who build bridges among races and generations. She received the National Medal of Arts, and was the first woman and first pop singer to receive the Lincoln Centre Medallion, previously awarded only to internationally-famed classical musicians. Her honorary doctorates and Grammies and other awards are almost numberless – and yet when we think of Ella, what we will always hear is that pure, passionate, endlessly creating voice, and the soul behind it, telling us what she knows about life and love and hope and courage.

Induction Year: 2013

Betty Ford
1918-2011

A groundbreaking First Lady, Betty Ford is often remembered for her candor in addressing the controversial issues of her time.

Elizabeth Anne "Betty" Bloomer was born in Chicago and raised in Grand Rapids, Michigan. After graduating from Central High School, she went on to study modern dance at Bennington School of the Dance. While a student at Bennington, she met renowned choreographer Martha Graham and became a member of her Auxiliary Performance Troupe in New York City.

Bloomer returned to Michigan in 1941 and became a fashion coordinator for a department store. During this time, she continued to pursue her love of dance by starting her own performance group and teaching dance to handicapped children.

Shortly after her marriage to Gerald Ford, the Fords moved to Washington, DC, where Mr. Ford served as a member of the House of Representatives and Mrs. Ford assumed the duties of a congressional spouse.

In 1973, Mr. Ford was appointed Vice President of the United States. One year later, in a dramatic turn of political events, upon the resignation of President Nixon,

Gerald Ford became the 38th President of the United States and Mrs. Ford became the First Lady. A few months later, Mrs. Ford was diagnosed with breast cancer and underwent a radical mastectomy. Rather than suppressing the diagnosis, she courageously shared her story and inspired countless women across the nation to get breast examinations. During her tenure as First Lady, Mrs. Ford continued to be an outspoken advocate of women's rights, addressing public issues like the Equal Rights Amendment and increasing the number of women appointed to senior government posts.

The Fords left politics in 1976 and moved to Rancho Mirage, California. In 1978, following a family intervention, Mrs. Ford underwent successful treatment for addiction to alcohol and prescription drugs. She again used her personal story to raise public awareness of addiction, and in 1982, she co-founded the Betty Ford Center to treat victims of alcohol and chemical dependency.

Mrs. Ford was awarded the Presidential Medal of Freedom in 1991 and the Congressional Gold Medal, with President Gerald R. Ford, in 1999.

$\mathscr{D}$r. Loretta C. Ford, Ed.D.

1920–

An internationally renowned nursing leader, Dr. Loretta C. Ford has transformed the profession of nursing and made health care more accessible to the general public.

In the early 1960s, Dr. Ford discovered that, because of a shortage of primary care physicians in the community, health care for children and families was severely lacking. In 1965, she partnered with Henry K. Silver, a pediatrician at the University of Colorado Medical Center, to create and implement the first pediatric nurse practitioner model and training program. The program combined clinical care and research to teach nurses to factor in the social, psychological, environmental and economic situations of patients when developing care plans.

When the program became a national success in 1972, Dr. Ford was recruited to serve as the Founding Dean of the University of Rochester School of Nursing. At the university, Dr. Ford developed and implemented the unification model of nursing. Through the model, clinical practice, education and research were combined to provide nurses with a more holistic education.

Dr. Ford is the author of more than 100 publications and has served as a consultant and lecturer to multiple organizations and universities. She holds many honorary doctorate degrees and is the recipient of numerous awards, including the Living Legend Award from the American Academy of Nursing and the Gustav O. Lienhard Award from the Institute of Medicine of the National Academies.

Abby Kelley Foster
1811–1887

During her lifetime, Abby Kelley Foster followed the motto, "Go where least wanted, for there you are most needed." A major figure in the national anti-slavery and women's rights movements, she spent more than twenty years traveling the country as a tireless crusader for social justice and equality for all.

Foster was born into a Quaker family in Pelham, Massachusetts in 1811, and raised in Worcester, Massachusetts at a time when society demanded that women be silent, submissive and obedient. After attending boarding school, she held teaching positions in Worcester, Millbury and Lynn, MA.

In Lynn, she joined the Female Anti-Slavery Society, where she became corresponding secretary and later, a national delegate to the first Anti-Slavery Convention of American Women in 1837. The following year, Foster made her first public speech against slavery, and was so well received that she abandoned her teaching career and returned to Millbury. There, she founded the Millbury Anti-Slavery Society and began lecturing for the American Anti-Slavery Society.

During the next two decades, Foster served as a lecturer, fundraiser, recruiter and organizer in the fight for abolition and suffrage. In 1850, she helped develop plans for the National Women's Rights Convention in Massachusetts. There, she gave one of her most well-known speeches, in which she challenged women to demand the responsibilities as well as the privileges of equality, noting "Bloody feet, sisters, have worn smooth the path by which you come hither."

In 1854, Foster became the chief fundraiser for the American Anti-Slavery Society, and by 1857, she was its general agent. Through the American Anti-Slavery Society, Foster continued to work for the ratification of the fourteenth and fifteenth amendments.

In her later years, once slavery was abolished and the rights of freedmen were guaranteed, Foster focused her activism primarily on women's rights. She held meetings, arranged lectures, and called for 'severe language' in any resolutions that were adopted. In 1868, she was among the organizers of the founding convention of the New England Woman Suffrage Association, the first regional association advocating woman suffrage. Foster's efforts were among those that helped lay the groundwork for the nineteenth amendment to the U.S. Constitution.

Photo: American Antiquarian Society

Helen Murray Free
1923–

A pioneering chemist, Helen Murray Free conducted scientific research that revolutionized diagnostic testing in the laboratory and at home.

Free attended college intending to major in English and Latin. However, due to the events of Pearl Harbor and subsequent enlistment and drafting of men into the army, women were strongly encouraged to pursue careers in science. Helen then changed her major to chemistry, receiving her B.S. from the College of Wooster in 1945.

Upon her graduation, Free immediately began work as a quality control chemist at Miles Laboratories, later acquired by Bayer Diagnostics. While at Miles, Free served as a researcher, director, and manager. She also met Alfred Free, a noted biochemist. They married in 1947.

Together, the Frees became life-long scientific partners and changed the face of medical diagnostics. Some of their early work centered around the improvement of the Clinitest, a tablet that measured glucose levels in the urine of diabetic patients. They went on to develop the Acetest, another tablet test for diabetes. Their research culminated in the development of Clinistix, the first dip-and-read diagnostic test strips for monitoring glucose in urine.

In 1975, the Frees co-authored their second book, *Urinalysis in Laboratory Practice*, which is still a standard work in the field. They also developed additional strips for testing levels of key indicators for other diseases.

Although she retired in 1982, Free continues to be a strong advocate of science education, paying special attention to female and underprivileged students through programs like Kids & Chemistry and Expanding Your Horizons.

Free holds seven patents and is the recipient of numerous awards including the American Chemical Society's Garvan Medal (1980), the National Medal of Technology and Innovation (2010), and the American Chemical Society's 66th National Historic Chemical Landmark designation (2010).

Today, the availability and low cost of dip-and-read strips make testing for diabetes, pregnancy, and other conditions available in underdeveloped regions of the United States and in foreign countries, saving or extending countless lives.

Photo: American Chemical Society

Betty Friedan
1921–2006

Betty Friedan has been central to the reshaping of American attitudes toward women's lives and rights. Through decades of social activism, strategic thinking and powerful writing, Friedan was one of contemporary society's most effective leaders.

Friedan's 1963 book, *The Feminine Mystique*, detailed the frustrating lives of countless American women who were expected to find fulfillment primarily through the achievements of husbands and children. The book made an enormous impact, triggering a period of change that continues today.

Friedan was central to this evolution for women, through lectures and writing (*It Changed My Life: Writings on the Women's Movement* in 1976 and *The Second Stage* in 1981). She was a founder of the National Organization for Women, a convener of the National Women's Political Caucus, and a key leader in the struggle for passage of the Equal Rights Amendment.

Friedan published *The Fountain of Aging in Fall*, 1993 and was co-chair of Women, Men and Media, a gender-based research organization that conducts research on gender and the media. She remained active in politics and advocacy for the rest of her life.

Margaret Fuller
1810–1850

In her short life, Margaret Fuller, whose thoughts and writings inspired leaders of the women's movement, was a literary critic, free thinker, Transcendentalist leader, editor, teacher and women's rights author.

Fuller, well-educated and driven by boundless intellectual curiosity, was captivated by the Transcendentalist movement in New England, and became a colleague of Emerson, Bronson Alcott and other movement leaders while she taught. She became the editor of *The Dial*, the Transcendental journal, and advocated the philosophy of liberation and fulfillment of the highest potential of all human beings – including women.

From 1839 to 1844 she held her series of "Conversations" for women in Boston, encouraging women to think and talk together about ideas. These dialogues led Fuller to write her most important work, *Women in the Nineteenth Century* (1845), considered a classic work of American feminist thought that had a profound influence on the Seneca Falls Women's Rights gathering in 1848. The book's message was that women must fulfill themselves as individuals, not subordinates to men. She wrote, "We would have every arbitrary barrier thrown down. We would have every path laid open to woman as freely as to man…then and then only will mankind be ripe for this, when inward and outward freedom for woman as much as for man shall be acknowledged as a right, not yielded as a concession."

Fuller was recruited by publisher Horace Greeley in 1844 to become the literary critic for his *New York Tribune*, and in 1846-47 she traveled as a foreign correspondent in Europe, where she became friends with Thomas Carlyle, Giuseppe Mazzini, George Sand and many other intellectual and political leaders.

She fell in love with an Italian revolutionary and was caught up in that nation's political situation, not sailing for home with her husband and son until 1850. She and her family drowned off Fire Island in the wreck of the ship returning her to America.

Throughout her relatively short life, Margaret Fuller pursued both knowledge and experience with boundless energy and a brilliant mind, having a strong influence on generations of women to come and fulfilling her own statement that "Very early, I knew that the only object in life was to grow."

Matilda Joslyn Gage
1826–1898

Best known in history as the co-author (with Elizabeth Cady Stanton and Susan B. Anthony) of the first three volumes of *The History of Woman Suffrage*, Matilda Joslyn Gage holds a significant position in history as a radical feminist thinker and historian whose writings shaped her times.

An excellent speaker and writer, Gage held a variety of offices in the National Woman Suffrage Association and helped form suffrage groups in New York and Virginia. She edited the NWSA suffrage paper, *The National Citizen and Ballot Box* for four years, and wrote much material for suffrage publications. Gage tried to cast a ballot in the 1872 presidential elections and failed, but she actively supported Anthony during the court case which arose from Anthony's successful casting of a ballot. She co-authored the Declaration of Rights for Women (1876) with Stanton, which was presented at the Independence Day ceremonies that summer in Philadelphia.

After becoming discouraged with the slow pace of suffrage efforts in the 1880s, Gage turned her attention to the teaching of the churches, which she perceived as teaching men to devalue women. In 1890 she formed her own organization, the Women's National Liberal Union, to fight moves to unite church and state, and her book *Women, Church and State* (1893) articulated her views.

Gage remained a suffrage supporter throughout her life, but spent her elder years concentrating on religious issues. Her lifelong motto appears on her gravestone: "There is a word sweeter than Mother, Home or Heaven; that word is Liberty."

Ina May Gaskin
1940–

A certified professional midwife who has attended more than 1,200 births, Ina May Gaskin is known as the "mother of authentic midwifery."

Gaskin joined the Peace Corps after college and taught English in Malaysia for two years before returning to the United States to obtain her master's degree.

During the birth of her first child in the 1960's, Gaskin experienced the terrible practice of having her child pulled into the world with forceps. The incident fueled her determination to find a saner way to give birth. A few years later, during a five-month long speaking tour with her husband, Stephen Gaskin, and more than two hundred young idealists, she witnessed her first birth, one of many that would occur during the trip. Because many of the women were without health insurance or money to pay for a doctor, Gaskin often assisted in births by default, eventually aided by the instruction and support of a sympathetic obstetrician.

In 1971, the group purchased a large tract of land in rural Tennessee and established a cooperative community. Gaskin located a doctor willing to serve as a mentor and medical liaison, and the Farm Midwifery Center was born.

During a stay in Guatemala in 1976, Gaskin learned a technique for preventing and resolving shoulder dystocia, a condition that occurs during birth when the baby's head is born, but the shoulders are stuck in the birth canal. After using the method with great success, she began to teach and publish articles about the method. Now referred to as the Gaskin maneuver, it is the first obstetrical procedure to be named after a midwife.

Gaskin has lectured in numerous countries and is the author of several books, including *Spiritual Midwifery* (1975), the first text written by a midwife published in the United States. In 2011, Gaskin received the Right Livelihood Award, an honor bestowed each year by the Swedish Parliament; the award is often referred to as the "Alternative Nobel Prize."

Photo: Susanna Frohman

Althea Gibson
1927–2003

Widely regarded as one of the most talented athletes in the United States, Althea Gibson overcame extreme racism to break barriers in tennis and pave the way for talented athletes of all races to compete equally.

Born in South Carolina, she moved to Harlem at the age of three. After being given a tennis racquet at the age of 13, Gibson displayed such talent that she was invited to become an honorary member of the elite Cosmopolitan Tennis Club.

In 1942, at the age of 15, Althea began playing in the American Tennis Association (ATA) and won the first tournament she ever entered. The ATA was a counterpart to the United States Lawn Tennis Association (now the USTA), which did not allow African-American players to enter tournaments at the time.

In 1957, Gibson became the first African-American to win the All-England Championships at Wimbledon and the U.S. National Tennis Championships at Forest Hills, forever changing the face of tennis. She repeated these feats in 1958.

After retiring from tennis, Gibson went on to play professional golf, again smashing barriers by becoming the first African American to earn her LPGA card.

Althea Gibson's tremendous feats continue to inspire generations of athletes from all races and walks of life.

$\mathscr{L}$illian Moller Gilbreth
1878–1972

Lillian Gilbreth, industrial engineer and expert in motion studies, was a pioneer in recognizing the interrelationship between engineering and human relations. She understood – and convinced industrial managers and equipment developers – that the behavior and efficiency of individual workers was often the product of the quality and effectiveness of the work environment.

Her ideas helped encourage the development of industrial engineering curricula in engineering schools, and her ideas about the qualities that produce good supervisors and what kind of workers were best suited to particular kinds of work was equally innovative, and contributed to the growing field of career assessment.

Gilbreth developed many of her ideas and co-authored numerous books and scientific studies with her husband, Frank – and while doing so, she had 12 children in 17 years. When she was widowed, she carried on managing the company she and her husband had formed and managed to put all of her children through college.

Gilbreth continued to apply the principles of modern business methods to the home, and published two books about the topic, *The Home-Maker* and *Her Job and Management in the Home*, as well as many articles in popular periodicals about the topic.

Gilbreth also had a special concern for the needs of those with physical handicaps, and used the techniques of motion analysis to design special equipment to make housework easier for these individuals. She was also a consultant to the Institute of Rehabilitation Medicine. She was active in volunteer organizations, notably the Girl Scouts and served as a member of the President's Emergency Committee for Unemployment Relief in 1930 and as an educational adviser to the Office of War Information during World War II.

She was named an honorary member of the Society of Industrial Engineers (which did not then admit women to membership) and in 1966 was the first woman to receive the Hoover Medal for distinguished public service by an engineer. She encouraged women to become engineers, and was honored for that commitment by the Society of Women Engineers. Her family is recalled by humorous reminiscences by her children Frank Jr. and Ernestine in the books *Cheaper By the Dozen* and *Belles on Their Toes*.

Photo: Ernestine Gilbreth Carey Collection

Charlotte Perkins Gilman
1860–1935

Called by Carrie Chapman Catt "the most original and challenging mind which the (women's) movement produced," Charlotte Perkins Gilman was a philosopher, theoretician, writer, educator and activist. She demanded equal treatment for women as the best means to advance society's progress.

Gilman's landmark work, *Women and Economics*, was written in 1898. In the book she makes clear that until women learn to be economically independent, true autonomy and equality could not be found. A bestseller, the book was translated into seven languages. Gilman's denunciation of the romanticization of domesticity as a goal for women was revolutionary.

Gilman was a much-sought after lecturer, and she continued to write, producing six nonfiction works, eight novels, nearly 200 short stories, hundreds of poems, plays and literally thousands of essays.

Gilman was not often directly involved in the social movements of her time. From 1909 to 1916, she wrote much of and published *The Forerunner*, a monthly feminist magazine. At the end of her life, she wrote *The Living of Charlotte Perkins Gilman: An Autobiography*.

The Honorable
Ruth Bader Ginsburg, J.D.
1933–

"Justice, justice, thou shalt pursue," the Old Testament words Justice Ruth Bader Ginsburg keeps on the wall of her chambers, epitomize the outlook and achievement of this distinguished jurist. Ginsburg has worked her entire career to eliminate gender-based stereotyping in legislation and regulations. Appointed Associate Justice of the United States Supreme Court by President William Clinton in 1993, she is the second woman to sit on the bench of the United States Supreme Court in its 212 year history.

After graduating from Cornell University in 1954 with highest honors in government, Justice Bader Ginsburg attended Harvard Law School and Columbia Law School, making *Law Review* in both and graduating at the top of the class at Columbia. Despite these excellent academic credentials, Bader Ginsburg had difficulty finding a job in the male-dominated law profession. She began her career by serving a clerkship in the United States District Court of Appeals in New York, continued by teaching at Rutgers University School of Law, and then at Columbia Law School, where she became the school's first tenured female professor.

Her teaching and litigation on behalf of the American Civil Liberties Union, where she headed the Women's Rights Project, drew national attention. In 1971, she helped write the ACLU brief in *Reed v. Reed,* a case argued before the Supreme Court that involved discrimination against women in awarding the administration of a child's estate. The Court struck down the state law that favored men over women as estate administrators.

In 1980, President Jimmy Carter appointed her to the United States Court of Appeals for the District of Columbia, where she served until her 1993 appointment to the Supreme Court. Justice Ginsburg has become known for her scholarly, balanced opinions and forthright personal courage. A cancer survivor herself, she has assisted thousands by her example of frank discussion of the state of her health and early diagnosis.

Maria Goeppert-Mayer, Ph.D.

1906–1972

Maria Goeppert-Mayer silently fought the injustices of the male-dominated field of science while at the same time tackled the mysteries of physics. The first American woman and the second woman ever to win the Nobel Prize in Physics, Goeppert-Mayer made extensive contributions to several different technical fields in physics.

By 1930, the same year she was married to Joseph Mayer, she completed her thesis. In it, she calculated the probability that an electron orbiting an atom's nucleus would emit not one, but two, photons or quantum units of light as it jumps to an orbit closer to the nucleus, a concept still cited today. That same year they moved to the United States from Germany when Joseph received an assistant professorship at Johns Hopkins University. Because the University had strict nepotism rules which forbade the hiring of Goeppert-Mayer, she continued to work without pay or formal academic status.

Within nine years, she produced ten papers applying quantum mechanics to chemistry, one of which became a milestone. Also, with her husband, she wrote *Statistical Mechanics*, a textbook that sold for 44 years.

Avoiding controversy and with little recognition, she quietly laid the groundwork for the later development of nuclear physics. As her husband changed positions, she continued her work unofficially at Columbia University and later at the University of Chicago. In Chicago, she worked part time as a senior physicist at the Argonne National Laboratory supported by a federal grant. Here she began her Nobel Prize winning project developing the shell model of the nucleus of the atom, the basic model for the description of nuclear properties.

In 1956, Goeppert-Mayer was elected to the National Academy of Sciences. In 1959, at age 53, after a thirty year career, she was appointed a full time professor, with pay, at the University of California at San Diego. In 1963, she was awarded the Nobel Prize in Physics.

Katharine Graham
1917–2001

Katharine Graham, who had worked in the editorial and circulation departments of the *Washington Post*, became the owner of the newspaper upon the death of her husband Phlip Graham in 1963. She served as publisher from 1969 until 1979, and from 1973 until 1991 as Board Chair and CEO. In 1965, she hired Benjamin Bradlee as editor of the *Washington Post* and together they developed a staff of reporters and editors that moved the paper into the top ranks of American newspapers. Mrs. Graham remained Chair of the Board until her death in 2001.

"To love what you do and feel that it matters – how could anything be more fun?" said Katharine Graham, when she led the *Washington Post*. Considered to have been one of the most influential women in the United States, Graham's courageous decisions to publish the Pentagon Papers, a top-secret government study of U.S. military involvement in Vietnam – after the *New York Times* had been court ordered not to do so, and to proceed with the Watergate investigation earned her a reputation as a courageous, fair and thorough journalist. She was committed to giving readers full access to important information.

As a businesswoman, Mrs. Graham led the Washington Post Company into a conglomerate of newspaper, broadcast, cable, and magazine properties. She believed that editorial excellence and profitability were interrelated. She served on numerous philanthropic boards and received countless awards in recognition of her accomplishments as a journalist, publisher, woman, and entrepreneur.

In 1998, Katharine Graham won the Pulitzer Prize for biography with her reminiscence, *Personal History*. Her story and actions stand as an example for all women that anything is possible. Describing herself as originally a shy, insecure woman, unprepared for the responsibilities she inherited, she became successful and one of the most powerful women of the century.

Martha Graham
1894–1991

Recognized as one of the greatest artists of the 20th century, Martha Graham created a movement language based upon the expressive capacity of the human body. Her creativity crossed artistic boundaries and embraced every artistic genre. She collaborated with and commissioned work from the leading visual artists, musicians, and designers of her day, including sculptor Isamu Noguchi; fashion designers Halston, Donna Karan, and Calvin Klein; and composers Aaron Copland, Samuel Barber and Gian Carlo Menotti.

Influencing generations of dancers and choreographers including Merce Cunningham, Paul Taylor, and Twyla Tharp, Ms. Graham forever altered the scope of dance. Artists of all genres were eager to study and work with her, including classical ballet dancers Margot Fonteyn, Rudolf Nureyev, and Mikhail Baryshnikov. She also taught many actors how to utilize their bodies as expressive instruments including Bette Davis, Kirk Douglas, Madonna, Liza Minelli, Gregory Peck, Tony Randall, and Joanne Woodward.

She founded The Martha Graham Studio in 1926 after teaching a group of dancers who had been drawn to her work. She remained at the helm for 66 years. During her illustrious career, she created 181 masterpiece dance compositions that continue to challenge and inspire generations of performers and audiences. Through her compositions she personified a commitment to addressing challenging contemporary issues that distinguish her as a conscientious and politically powerful artist, capturing throughout the ages the soul of the American people.

Her many honors included receiving the Presidential Medal of Freedom from President Gerald Ford, the National Medal of the Arts, named as "Dancer of the Century" by Time magazine, and featured on a U.S. postage stamp. In 1986, her theater colleagues presented her with the Local One Centennial Award – an honor given only once every 100 years. The first dancer to perform at the White House and to act as a cultural ambassador abroad, she captured the spirit of a nation and expanded the boundaries of contemporary dance.

*E*lla Grasso
1919–1981

Young Ella Grasso wrote, "It is not enough to profess faith in the democratic process; we must do something about it." Her life and career embody her words.

Ella Grasso spent her life in her home state of Connecticut, and won her first election – to the General Assembly of the state – in 1952; she never lost an election thereafter. She became Secretary of State of Connecticut, and then served two terms in the U.S. Congress. She was elected governor in 1974 – the nation's first woman elected state governor in her own right. She served as governor until illness forced resignation in 1980.

Ella Grasso, who overcame religious prejudice and sexism to succeed, was a champion for those who needed help, including minorities, women, young people, working people and the elderly. She inspired affection and trust as she improved the state's economy and created a more effective government.

Marcia Greenberger
1946–

Marcia Greenberger is the founder and co-president of the National Women's Law Center. The creation of the Center over 40 years ago established her as the first full-time women's rights legal advocate in Washington, D.C. She is a recognized expert on women and the law, particularly in the areas of education and employment, health and reproductive rights and family economic security.

A recognized expert on sex discrimination and the law, Ms. Greenberger has participated in the development of key legislative initiatives and litigation protecting women's rights, has been a leader in developing strategies to secure the successful passage of legislation protecting women and counsel for landmark litigation establishing new legal precedents for women. Some of the notable legislative successes in which she had a key role are the Civil Rights Restoration Act of 1987, the Pregnancy Discrimination Act (1978), the Civil Rights Act of 1991, and the Lilly Ledbetter Fair Pay Act, each of which provided critical protections against sexual harassment on the job. Her work has resulted in Supreme Court victories strengthening protections for students and teachers against sex discrimination in schools.

Ms. Greenberger served as the first female lawyer at the Washington, D.C., firm of Caplin and Drysdale. In 1972 she became Director of the Women's Rights Project of the Center for Law and Social Policy, which became the National Women's Law Center in 1981. Over the years of the Center's existence, Ms. Greenberger has trained a cadre of women's rights advocates who now teach in law schools, serve as judges, and hold high government positions.

Her leadership and contributions are reflected in the many articles she has published, the numerous professional honors she has received and the multiple boards on which she serves.

Martha Wright Griffiths
1912–2003

Throughout her career – as state legislator, judge, Congresswoman, practicing attorney and Michigan's first woman lieutenant governor – Martha Griffiths fought and won important victories for equal rights for women and minorities.

Griffiths' first try for public office in 1946 resulted in defeat, but she was elected to the Michigan House of Representatives in 1948 and served two terms.

After serving as Recorder's Court Judge in Detroit (the first woman to do so) she ran successfully for the U.S. Congress in 1955, where she served with great distinction until retiring in 1975.

In Congress, Griffiths was best known for successfully adding sex discrimination as a prohibited act in the landmark 1964 Civil Rights Act, opening the door for gender equity. She shepherded the Equal Rights Amendment through the U.S. House (it had always been defeated in the past) and worked for positive changes in Social Security and pension fund benefits to help widows, as well as on behalf of education, and people with disabilities. After Congress Griffiths practiced law until running successfully for lieutenant governor of her state in 1982, serving two terms.

She said: "I don't know really that I have so much perseverance as I do a sense of indignity at the fact that women are not justly treated. I have the same sort of feelings for Blacks, Latinos, and Asiatics. If we are America, then we ought to be what we say we are. We ought to be the land of the free and the brave. What people sought in this land was justice."

$\mathcal{S}$arah Grimké
1792–1873

Sarah and Angelina Grimke eloquently fought the injustices of slavery, racism and sexism during the mid-19th century. As daughters of a prominent South Carolina judge and plantation owner, the Grimke sisters witnessed the suffering of slaves. Determined to speak out, they were eventually forced to move to the North, where they continued to appeal to northerners and southerners to work toward abolition. They also urged white northerners to end racial discrimination.

The Grimke sisters were pioneering women. Among the first female abolitionists, they were the first women to speak publicly against slavery, an important political topic. Faced with criticism from clergy and others that they were threatening "the female character," they continued their crusade.

In 1838, Angelina became the first woman to address a legislative body when she spoke to the Massachusetts State Legislature on women's rights and abolition.

Active in the women's movement, they helped set the agenda later followed by Elizabeth Cady Stanton, Susan B. Anthony, Lucretia Mott and others, calling for equal educational opportunities and the vote.

One historian said of Sarah's writings: "[They were] a milestone on the road to the Woman's Rights Convention at Seneca Falls" and "central to the feminist writings in the decades that followed." Sarah was one of the first to compare the restrictions on women and slaves, writing that "woman has no political existence…She is only counted like the slaves of the south, to swell the number of lawmakers."

After the Civil War, they continued to champion the causes of equality and women's rights. Through their examples and their words, the Grimke sisters proved that women could affect the course of political events and have a far-reaching influence on society.

Colonel Mary A. Hallaren, WAC
1907–2005

In war and peace, Colonel Mary Hallaren proved herself a true leader of women. Described as "one of the giants among military women," Hallaren enlisted in 1942 in the newly organized Women's Auxiliary Army Corps (WAACS, later to become the Women's Army Corps, WAACS). One year later, she commanded the first battalion of WAACS to serve in Europe, the largest contingent of women serving overseas throughout World War II.

By war's end, Hallaren stood in the highest ranks of WAC leadership, serving as Director from 1947-1953. Many of her military colleagues, male and female, favored the peacetime demobilization of women. Army Chief of Staff Dwight D. Eisenhower believed women were necessary to meet post-war personnel needs. Hallaren, refusing to "write 'finis' to women's contribution," became the primary exponent and dynamic force advocating permanent status for military women.

In 1948, despite strong opposition, Hallaren was instrumental in seeing that the Women's Armed Services Integration Act was adopted, enabling women to serve as permanent regulator members of all of the armed forces, not just in the military in times of war.

In 1965, Hallaren assumed direction of new organizations, Women in Community Service, sponsored by a coalition of diverse women's organizations. Through its program, at-risk women were able to secure job training and economic opportunity. Because of Hallaren's vision and inspiration, women who might have failed economically and socially, succeeded.

Hallaren was also instrumental in the creation of the "Women in Military Service Memorial," erected at the entrance of Arlington National Cemetery in the nation's capital to honor the contributions and achievements of all military women.

Fannie Lou Hamer
1917–1977

Fannie Lou Hamer, a Mississippi sharecropper, changed a nation's perspective on democracy.

Hamer became involved in the civil rights movement when she volunteered to attempt to register to vote in 1962. By then 45 years old and a mother, Hamer lost her job and continually risked her life because of her civil rights activism. Despite this and a brutal beating, Hamer spoke frequently to raise money for the movement, and helped organize the Mississippi Freedom Democratic Party, to challenge white domination of the Democratic Party.

In 1964, the MFDP challenged the all-white Mississippi delegation to the Democratic Convention, and in 1968, the Convention seated an integrated challenge delegation from Mississippi.

Deeply committed to improving life for poor minorities in her state, Hamer, working with the National Council of Negro Women and others, helped organize food cooperatives and other services. She continued political activities as well, helping to convene the National Women's Political Caucus in the 1970s.

She is buried in her home town of Ruleville, Mississippi, where her tombstone reads, "I am sick and tired of being sick and tired."

Alice Hamilton, M.D.
1869–1970

Alice Hamilton chose medicine because "as a doctor I could go anywhere I pleased – to far-off lands or to city slums – and be quite sure I could be of use anywhere."

She quickly discovered she felt more at home in the laboratory than at the bedside. Her first job, teaching pathology at Northwestern University, gave her the chance to realize her dream to live at Hull House. There she came to know Jane Addams and other reformers who encouraged her to find a way to apply her scientific knowledge to social problems.

Alice Hamilton began to investigate industrial diseases. She saw cases of lead palsy and carbon monoxide gassing among workers in the area. Because they were Poles, Italians, or Blacks, their fate had passed unnoticed. Industries denied responsibility, and states had no workmen's compensation laws.

Dr. Hamilton conducted pioneering surveys of industrial disease, and found that European countries not only outdistanced the U.S. in research but also legislated sickness insurance programs.

She studied the poisons affecting workers in the lead, munitions, and copper industries, traveling the country and touring mines and factories, smelters and forges. Her reports were always meticulously fair and impartial.

In 1918 Alice Hamilton was appointed assistant professor of industrial medicine at the Harvard University School. She was the first and, for many years, the only woman on the Harvard faculty. Though she was treated shabbily, excluded from the faculty club and the commencement procession, her research continued to help promote safety in the American workplace.

Martha Matilda Harper
1857–1950

Groundbreaking entrepreneur, Martha Matilda Harper became a servant at seven years of age and spent twenty-two years in domestic service in Canada. She immigrated to Rochester, New York at age thirty-five and continued in service for three more years.

Encouraged by Susan B. Anthony and her activist circle, Harper struck out on her own, opening the area's first public hair care salon. Harper was a marketing innovator. Using her own floor length hair as a demonstration tool, she focused on customer comfort and individualized consultation. She employed only former servant women, produced her own natural hair care products and developed her own hair and skin care methods. She used only naturally occurring substances and refused the new chemical dyes and synthetic permanents.

Harper launched a new business model, which is today known as retail franchising. In thirty years, there were over 500 franchised Harper shops worldwide. Harper customers included royalty, prime ministers, social reformers, men and women.

The franchised Harper shops were a powerful economic innovation that changed the realities of poor women's lives. Hundreds of women became owners, purchasing a Harper shop through her flexible financing. Thousands of women trained and worked in the Harper network.

Harper was customer focused. She invented the reclining shampoo chair that is today found in salons worldwide. Harper offered scalp massages and other relaxation services and provided childcare and evening hours. Flextime, profit sharing and paid personal time off were employment practices Harper introduced. Harper employees were trained to assure consistency and high quality service.

She was recognized in her time as a successful businesswoman and became the first woman member of the Rochester Chamber of Commerce. Harper is now acknowledged as a model for such beauty industry women entrepreneurs as: Madam C.J. Walker, Elizabeth Arden, Helena Rubinstein, Estee Lauder, and Anita Roddick. She created a franchising system and built a model that included centralized management, quality control, independent operators, and wider opportunities for women.

The Honorable Patricia Roberts Harris, J.D.
1924–1985

Patricia Roberts Harris was dedicated to public service, civil rights and the promotion of social justice. A woman of many firsts, she was the first African-American woman to serve the nation as Ambassador, the first African-American woman to become dean of a law school, and the first African-American woman to serve in a Presidential cabinet.

Patricia Roberts excelled academically and won a scholarship to Howard University, graduating in 1945. She married in 1955, and at her husband's urging entered law school. She earned her law degree from George Washington University and was admitted to the District of Columbia Bar and to practice before the United States Supreme Court.

Harris was appointed co-chair of the National Women's Committee for Civil Rights by President John F. Kennedy. She returned to Howard University as an associate Dean of Students and lecturer in the law school and became a full professor in 1963. In 1965, Harris accepted an appointment as Ambassador to Luxemburg. She then served briefly as Dean of Howard Law School in 1969.

In 1977, Harris was appointed as Secretary of Housing and Urban Development. At her confirmation hearing, she was queried as to her ability to represent the interests of the poor. Her response was: "I am one of them. You do not seem to understand who I am. I am a Black woman, daughter of a dining-car worker. I am a Black woman who could not buy a house eight years ago in parts of the District of Columbia. I didn't start out as a member of a prestigious law firm, but as a woman who needed a scholarship to go to school. If you think that I have forgotten that, you are wrong." In 1980, Harris was appointed Secretary of the Department of Health, Education and Welfare.

Helen Hayes
1900–1993

Helen Hayes was known as America's premier actress and dubbed, "First Lady of the Theatre." She has described herself as an ordinary woman who led an extraordinary life. But, how many others entered the theatre at age five and at age nine experienced her first hit on Broadway.

In 1911 she returned to Washington D.C. to resume acting with the Columbia Players and to finish school at the Sacred Heart Convent. Following a long run of Pollyanna from 1916-1918, she began a long and distinguished career.

The first actress to earn the coveted Tony Award, she performed in more than eighty plays and was the first woman to have two successive Broadway theatres bear her name.

Entering the world of motion pictures, Helen Hayes then became the first actress from the stage to win an Academy Award, and the first person to win an *Oscar* in two categories, Best Actress (*The Sin of Madelon Claudet*, 1931) and Best Supporting Actress (*Airport*, 1970).

Her 88 years as an actress spanned theatre, film, radio and television. Considered "a trouper" with grace and good humor, Hayes possessed none of the airs of a temperamental star and became a perennial favorite with audiences. She is one of the few people to have won an Emmy, a Grammy, an Oscar and a Tony Award.

$\mathcal{D}$orothy Height
1912–2010

It is said of Dorothy Height that her lifetime of achievement measured the liberation of Black America, the advance of women's rights and a determined effort to lift the poor and the powerless.

Height began her career as a staff member of the YWCA in New York City, becoming director of the Center for Racial Justice. She became a volunteer with the National Council of Negro Women when she worked with NCNW founder Mary McLeod Bethune. When Bethune died, Height became president, a position she held for forty years.

NCNW, an organization of national organizations and community sections with outreach to four million women, developed model national and international community-based programs, sent scores of women to help in the Freedom Schools of the civil rights movement, and spearheaded voter registration drives. Height's collaborative leadership style brought together people of different cultures for mutual benefit. Her belief in the importance of strong families became the primary energy behind the Black Family Reunion Celebration.

She received many honors including the Presidential Medal of Freedom, the Congressional Gold Medal, the Presidential Citizens Medal, and the Jefferson Award for Public Service.

Beatrice A. Hicks
1919–1979

Beatrice A. Hicks broke new ground for women as an engineer, inventor and engineering executive, expanding the advancement and recognition of women engineers in an era when less than 1% of the engineers employed in the United States were women. She strove to open the doors of engineering education closed to women prior to 1970.

At age 13, inspired by the Empire State Building and the George Washington Bridge, she told her engineer father that she, too, would become an engineer. She earned degrees in chemical engineering, electrical engineering and physics, was the first woman engineer employed by Western Electric Company, pioneered in the theoretical study, analysis, development and manufacture of sensing devices, patented a molecular density scanner, and developed an industry model for quality control procedures. In 1955, she became president of the firm founded by her father, Newark Controls, Inc., which designed and manufactured environmental sensing equipment, much of which was used in the space program.

In 1950, she was chosen as the first president of the newly organized Society of Women Engineers, which then consisted of 60 members. Hicks received several honorary degrees and in 2013 was recognized by the New Jersey Inventors Hall of Fame with the Advancement of Invention Award.

Induction Year: 1996

Colonel Oveta Culp Hobby
1905–1995

Throughout her professional career, Oveta Culp Hobby held leadership positions, shaped major institutions and influenced large numbers of people.

At 21, Hobby became an expert in the intricacies of parliamentary law, serving as parliamentarian for the Texas House of Representatives and composing a widely-read textbook on parliamentary law, *Mr. Chairman*, in 1937. She also rose through the ranks to become manager of the *Houston Post*, one of the nation's major newspapers.

In 1941, Hobby accepted a $1-a-year position as Director of the Women's Interest Section of the War Department. Army Chief of Staff George C. Marshall instructed her to organize a military unit for women. In 1942 Congress authorized the Women's Auxiliary Army Corp (WAACS, later become the Women's Army Corps, WACS).

Hobby became America's first woman Colonel. Her leadership and organizational skills were challenged by recruiting, organizing and training women in a military environment as often hostile as helpful. She and the WAACS met every test. As she often said, "a debt to democracy and a date with destiny."

When she retired in 1945, she had commanded 100,00 women at more that 200 posts and in every theater of wartime operations. After the war, Hobby returned to the *Post*, serving as co-editor.

From 1952-1955 she played another pioneering role in government as the first Secretary of the Department of Health, Education, and Welfare. She was the only woman to serve in the Cabinet of President Dwight D. Eisenhower.

Barbara Holdridge
1929–

Barbara Holdridge co-founded Caedmon Records in 1952 with Marianne Mantell. Their woman-owned business pioneered the concept and most significant treasury of spoken word literary recordings featuring great writers and outstanding actors of the 20th century. The success of Caedmon Records launched the spoken word industry, created a broad audience for diverse, high quality literature, and helped lay the foundation for today's audio books industry.

The Caedmon catalog is extraordinary for the dramatic gender equality and cultural inclusiveness it achieved. It expanded the audience for American women's writing and women's writing in general. Ms. Holdridge bridged many different cultures and voices, establishing a legacy of recordings that are a vast resource of American cultural history, at a time when publishing was not open to women's writing or cultural diversity.

She also discovered and documented with her husband, Lawrence Holdridge, the American Portrait painter Ammi Phillips. Phillips was responsible for 700 portraits, many attributed to other artists or to "anonymous." After the successful sale of Caedmon, Ms. Holdridge founded Stemmer House Publishers, devoted to fine illustrated books and a small list of spoken word recordings.

Billie Holiday
1915–1959

Considered by many to be one of the greatest jazz vocalists of all time, Billie Holiday triumphed over adversity to forever change the genres of jazz and pop music with her unique styling and interpretation.

Holiday left employment as a maid to pursue work as a dancer in Harlem nightclubs. At one of those clubs, she was asked to sing. She quickly began singing in many of the Harlem nightclubs and soon established a following of admirers, despite having had no formal musical training.

Holiday's career began to grow, thanks in part to the interest of John Hammond of Columbia Records, who organized her first recording with Benny Goodman in 1933. She debuted at the Apollo Theater in 1935, and began recording under her own name in 1936.

Holiday toured extensively in 1937 and 1938 with the Count Basie and Artie Shaw bands. While on tour, Holiday was often subjected to discrimination.

Perhaps Holiday's most notable collaborations were with legendary saxophonist Lester Young, who gave Holiday her moniker "Lady Day." Together, they created some of the most important jazz music of all time. Of her groundbreaking vocal style and delivery, Holiday once said, "I hate straight singing. I have to change a tune to my own way of doing it. That's all I know."

As both a vocalist and a songwriter, Holiday penned God Bless the Child and Lady Sings the Blues, among others. Her interpretation of the anti-lynching poem Strange Fruit was included in the list of Songs of the Century by the Recording Industry of America and the National Endowment for the Arts.

Holiday's autobiography, Lady Sings the Blues, was written in 1956. She won five Grammy Awards and was inducted into the Rock and Roll Hall of Fame in 2000 and the Nesuhi Ertugan Jazz Hall of Fame in 2004.

Holiday, known for her deeply moving and personal vocals, remains a popular musical legend more than fifty years after her death. In spite of personal obstacles, Holiday inspired many with her vocal gifts and continues to be recognized as a seminal influence on music.

Photo: Carl Van Vechten

Wilhelmina Cole Holladay
1922–

A personal interest quickly developed into a social and educational cause for Wilhelmina Holladay. During a tour of Vienna with her husband, Holladay became interested in the work of the artist, Clara Peeters, a contemporary of Rembrant.

Holladay was amazed and dismayed to learn that the talented woman artist was not listed in major art references, nor were many other deserving women artists. She also found that the major American art museums had devoted few shows to the work of women artists.

In an effort to correct the inequity, Holladay established The National Museum of Women in the Arts (NMWA). Opened in 1987, it promotes a greater awareness of women in the arts and their contributions to aesthetics throughout the ages.

Six years after the museum opened its doors in Washington, D.C., it boasted an organization of national and international chapters and a membership of more than 125,000, which makes its the third largest museum in the world in terms of membership. To fulfill its mission, the museum cares for and displays a permanent collection, presents special exhibitions and conducts educational programs. A state-of-the-art, 200 seat auditorium serves as a center for the performing arts and other creative disciplines in which women excel.

NMWA also maintains a Library and Research Center containing substantial specialized holdings for research. Numerous publications have been developed by the Center, including a quarterly newsletter, exhibition catalogues, books, brochures and curriculum materials. Said Holladay, "When substantial accomplishments and excellence are known, the right to be taken seriously surely will follow. Women should know their heritage which has been so long ignored."

Major General Jeanne Holm, USAF
1921–2010

Major General Jeanne Holm, USAF (Ret.) was a driving force in achieving parity for military women.

After enlisting during World War II as a truck driver in the Women's Army Auxiliary Corps, Holm graduated from Officer Candidate School and, after the war, received a regular commission in the newly formed United States Air Force. There she held a variety of positions in the United States and overseas, including landmark ork with NATO. From 1965 to 1973, as Director of Women in the Air Force, she worked tenaciously to enhance the status and expand the roles and opportunities for women in the armed services. She led efforts to remove outdated laws and policies that discriminated against women in the military. She advocated opening ROTC to women and admitting women to flying programs.

In 1971, Holm became the first Air Force woman to be promoted to Brigadier General. Two years later, she became the first woman in all the armed forces to achieve the rank of Major General. Among her military awards are the Legion of Merit and two Distinguished Service Medals. She is also the author of two books detailing the history of women in the armed forces during World War II and throughout history, the most noted being *Women In The Military: An Unfinished Revolution*.

Upon her retirement from the military, Holm served President Gerald Ford as a Special Assistant focusing on women's issues. She initiated a Justice Department review of all laws and policies discriminating against women. As a member of the Defense Advisory Committee on Women in the Services, she advocated the need for the removal of artificial barriers to military women's careers. She continued these efforts during the Carter Administration as a consultant on military women to the Under Secretary of the Air Force. During the Reagan Administration, she became the first chairperson of the Veterans Administration's Committee on Women Veterans, successfully advocating parity for women veterans, their benefits, and needs.

General Holm is recognized as the driving force behind the successful movement for women achieving equal opportunities and equal rights in the military. Her challenge to the military leadership to utilize the talents of military women was the foundation for sweeping increases in the numbers of, and opportunities for, women in the military.

Bertha Holt
1904–2000

Bertha Holt was a pioneer in international adoption who became known to thousands of internationally adopted children as "Grandma Holt". She and her husband Harry, already the parents of six children, adopted eight Korean children in 1955, after seeing a documentary film about the wretched conditions of orphaned Amerasian children in Korea.

An Act of Congress was required to allow the Holts to adopt these eight children, ranging in age from eight months to two years. The national attention that followed prompted numerous requests to the Holts for help in adopting children from Korea.

In 1956, the Holt Adoption Program, later called Holt International Children's Services, was established to help hundreds of people interested in intercountry adoptions. Hundreds of thousands of orphaned children worldwide now have families through the efforts of this agency.

Her work helped change the world's attitudes about adoption. She challenged the then established policy of matching children and adoptive parents by appearances and demonstrated that differences in race or national origin are not barriers to forming strong families.

Bertha Holt also became an advocate for children with special needs. She planned and designed the Ilsan Center in Korea to accommodate children with disabilities. Mrs. Holt developed principles for the temporary care of children that are still used today as models.

Numerous awards and honors were bestowed on Bertha Holt including America's Mother of the Year, two National Civil Merit Awards from Korea, the Decade of the Child Medallion from the Philippines, and several honorary doctoral degrees.

The Holt International Children's Services, headquartered in Eugene, Oregon, is regularly asked by the United States Congress and by other countries for advice in determining adoption and child welfare policies. Guided always by their motto, "Every child deserves a home of his own," the Holt agency continues the legacy of its founders.

dmiral Grace Murray Hopper, USN, Ph.D.
1906–1992

A mathematics genius and computer pioneer, Grace Hopper created computer programming technology that forever changed the flow of information and paved the way for modern data processing.

Born in New York City, Hopper earned her B.A. in mathematics and physics from Vassar College and her M.A. and Ph.D. from Yale University,. Hopper began her professional career teaching mathematics at Vassar College, and remained there until the early 1940s.

In 1943, wanting to aid her country during World War II, Hopper joined the United States Navy. She was soon assigned to the Bureau of Ordnance Computation Project at Harvard University, where she began her legacy of groundbreaking computer programming with the Mark I, a precursor to electronic computers. Hopper became a faculty member at Harvard's computation laboratory in 1946 and continued her programming work with the Mark II and Mark III computers.

Believing that a much wider audience could operate a computer if it was more user-friendly and more programmer-friendly, Hopper joined the Eckert-Mauchly Computer Corporation (later the Sperry Corporation) in 1949. There, she worked on the UNIVAC I, the first commercial electronic computer. In 1952, Hopper was credited with creating the first complier for modern computers, a program that translates instructions written by a programmer into codes that can be read by a computer. Hopper went on to develop the FLOW-MATIC computer programming language (1957) and shortly after, pioneered the Common Business Oriented Language (COBOL).

Hopper retired from the Navy in 1986 as a Rear Admiral, the first woman to hold the rank. She continued her career as a consultant to Digital Equipment Corporation, where she worked until her death in 1992.

Throughout her lifetime, Hopper received many awards and commendations. In 1969, the Data Processing Management Association awarded her the first computer sciences Man of the Year Award, and in 1973, she became the first person from the U.S. and first woman from any country to be recognized as a Distinguished Fellow of the British Computer Society. Hopper was awarded the National Medal of Technology in 1991 for her "pioneering accomplishments in the development of computer programming languages that simplified computer technology and opened the door to a significantly larger universe of users."

$\mathcal{J}$ulia Ward Howe
1819–1910

Julia Ward Howe, author of *The Battle Hymn of the Republic*, was a pioneer in literature and women's rights.

As a writer, poet, reformer, and lecturer, Howe worked throughout her life for justice. In 1861, she authored *The Battle Hymn of the Republic*, as an inspiration to Union soldiers fighting against slavery.

More importantly, she helped found the New England Women's Club, which later became the American Woman Suffrage Association. Throughout the later 19th and early 20th centuries, Howe lectured and wrote on women's rights. She fought for the right to vote and to liberate women from the confinement of the traditional "woman's place" in stifling marriages like her own, where none of her ideas were ever valued. She also worked for world peace, founding the American Friends of Russian Freedom in 1891 and serving as a president of the United Friends of Armenia in 1894.

In 1907, Howe became the first woman elected to the American Academy of Arts and Letters. As stated in her citation for an honorary Smith College degree, she was a "Poet and patriot, lover of letters and learning… sincere friend of all that makes for the elevation and enrichment of women."

$\mathscr{D}$olores Huerta
1930–

Dolores Huerta is one the century's most powerful and respected labor movement leaders.

Huerta left teaching and co-founded the United Farm Workers with Cesar Chavez in 1962: "I quit because I couldn't stand seeing kids come to class hungry and needing shoes. I thought I could do more by organizing farm workers than by trying to teach their hungry children." Huerta raised her own eleven children while organizing for the labor movement.

The 1965 Delano Grape Strike launched UFW into a period of fast-paced organizing, with Huerta negotiating contracts with growers, lobbying, organizing strikes and boycotts and well as spearheading farmworker political activities. Always politically active, she co-chaired the 1972 California delegation to the Democratic Convention. She led the fight to permit thousands of migrant/immigrant children to receive services. She also led the struggle to achieve unemployment insurance, collective bargaining rights, and immigration rights for farmworkers under the 1985 Rodino amnesty legalization program. The recipient of the Presidential Medal of Freedom, Huerta continues as an outstanding labor and political activist.

Helen LaKelly Hunt
1949–

Helen LaKelly Hunt saw a major unmet need – the absence of funding programs and opportunities to help women – and chose to use her personal resources and energy to create positive change.

Hunt has made her primary work the establishment of women's rights as human rights as a principal of grantmaking. In 1981 she became president of the Hunt Alternatives Fund and in 1984 co-founded the National Network of Women's Funds, an organization created to unify the women's giving and funding communities.

In 1985 she founded the New York Women's Foundation and in 1987 she helped found the Dallas Women's Foundation. In 1992, Hunt became president of The Sister Fund, dedicated to the social, political, economic and spiritual empowerment of women and girls.

Hunt's belief that women know best how to launch programs and meet needs in their own communities has been ratified by the success of many programs. She is a powerful example to a woman pioneering new ways to lead and transform society for women's growth and success.

The Honorable Swanee Hunt, Ph.D.
1950–

Philanthropist, ambassador, and social activist, Swanee Hunt, has made her presence known the world over. Hunt began her philanthropic work in Denver where in 1981 she, with her sister, Helen, founded the Hunt Alternatives Fund.

For 16 years the Fund gave millions to neighborhood and minority groups, not funded by larger foundations, in the Denver area. Most of these more than 600 grassroots organizations were focused on families in poverty, particularly women and children, and included mental health care, homeless services and battered women shelters, areas of special concern to Hunt.

In 1987, she co-founded The Women's Foundation of Colorado, which makes grants to empower women of all ages.

In 1993, President Clinton appointed Hunt United States Ambassador to the Republic of Austria, where she served for four years. During that time she worked extensively as a political and social activist. She brought together business executives, politicians, government leaders, as well as cultural leaders, in order to further U.S. and Austrian interests.

Hunt played a key role in the creation of the Bosnian Women's Initiative in 1996 and within that context, she was the keynote speaker for a women's conference in Sarajevo with more than 500 participants from all over Europe. She personally funded the Vienna Women's Initiative, which provided an opportunity for women leaders across all fields to come together to join forces.

In January 1998, she became the Director of Harvard's Women and Public Policy Program (WAPPP) at the Kennedy School of Government. Hunt continued in her role as an educator and supporter of women leaders worldwide. The WAPPP focuses on public policies that significantly impact women and on the women who shape these policies.

In 2005, Hunt's book *This Was Not Our War: Bosnian Women Reclaiming the Peace* won the Pen/New England Award for non-fiction. In addition to her writing, she is a talented photographer, composer, and speaker. Her mission is to achieve gender parity, especially as a means to end war and rebuild societies as well as to alleviate poverty and other human suffering.

Zora Neale Hurston
1891–1960

Novelist, anthropologist, folklorist – Zora Neale Hurston's work in a range of fields contributed greatly to the preservation of African-American folk traditions, as well as to American literature.

Born in Eatonville, Florida, the first incorporated all-Black city, Hurston studied anthropology at Barnard College in New York with famed scholar Franz Boas (she was the first African-American woman to graduate from the college), and did graduate work at Columbia University.

She conducted field work in African-American folklore all over the South. She began publishing novels; *Their Eyes Were Watching God* is often considered her finest novel. She taught for some years at what is now North Carolina Central University, and won a Guggenheim fellowship to pursue her writing. Her 1942 autobiography, *Dust Tracks on a Road*, was one of her last major works; in it, she wrote, "I want a busy life, a just mind, and a timely death." Hurston's work encouraged the study of folklore and anthropology nationwide. Her intense focus on the lives of African-American women has been of equal or greater impact.

Anne Hutchinson
1591–1643

"She was a woman of haughty and fierce carriage, a nimble wit and active spirit, a very voluble tongue, more bold than a man," said Governor John Winthrop of religious pioneer Anne Hutchinson, whom he expelled from the Massachusetts Bay Colony in 1638 for her insistence on practicing religion as she chose, and on preaching herself.

An émigré from England who settled in the New World in 1634, Anne Hutchinson came under fire from the colony elders when she began expounding her theology at meetings in her home. She believed in a "covenant of grace," in which faith alone was enough to achieve salvation. Others disagreed, and when Winthrop became governor, Hutchinson was banished and excommunicated. She moved with her family to the area of the country that became Rhode Island, and after her husband's death, she moved to Long Island, where in 1643 she and five of her six children were killed in an Indian attack. This advocate of freedom of religion, the right to free assembly and women's rights was honored in the naming of the Hutchinson River and the Hutchinson River Parkway.

*B*arbara Iglewski, Ph.D.
1938–

Dr. Barbara Iglewski's landmark discovery that pathogenic bacteria communicate with each other via a system known as "quorum sensing" showed how this system is a global regulator of virulence in humans. Her work served as the foundation for an entire field of study into how this system works across the various types of bacteria. Several drugs that interrupt the bacterial communication process, thereby preventing infections, have been developed based on her work.

Dr. Iglewski pursued her scientific career as a result of accompanying her country physician father on house calls, answering the phone at his office, and playing with his microscopes. She became the first woman to lead a department at the University of Rochester School of Medicine and Dentistry, chairing the Department of Microbiology and Immunology at the University from 1986 to 2009.

Her work on the bacteria *pseudomonas aeruginosa*, its production, modes of ction and regulation and, specifically, how it damages the lungs of patients with cystic fibrosis, has had an enormous positive impact nationally and globally. She is considered the leader in this field of research, particularly as it relates to implications for, and applications to, many different genera and species. In addition, she has studied biofilms made by pathogenic bacteria that cause intractable problems both in the body (lungs, oral cavity, and bladder) and in clinical pipes (catheters and intravenous lines) and industrial pipes (any pipe carrying water or fluids in factories).

She holds seven patents, has published more than 180 papers and book chapters and has received many awards and honors, including from the National Institutes of Health and the American Society for Microbiology. Known as a mentor and role model, she has received numerous awards for her encouragement and development of young women in science. Dr. Iglewski has been instrumental in helping women achieve placement in editorial positions at various scientific journals as part of her goal to increase the number of women on scientific editorial boards.

The Honorable Shirley Ann Jackson, Ph.D.
1946–

Shirley Ann Jackson, noted physicist and former head of the United States Nuclear Regulatory Commission (NRC), was one of the first two African-American women to receive a doctorate in physics in the U.S. and the first to receive a doctorate from the Massachusetts Institute of Technology.

Jackson was elected a fellow of the American Physical Society for her work in the interaction of electrons on liquid helium films with surface excitations as a polaron problem. As the first African-American woman to serve on the NRC and the first woman and African American to lead the NRC, Jackson reaffirmed that agency's commitment to public health and safety.

She enhanced its regulatory effectiveness, and initiated a bottom-up strategic assessment of all NRC activities. Committed to promoting social justice, she organized MIT's Black Student Union and worked to increase the number of blacks entering MIT. After only one year, the number entering rose from 2 to 57. On numerous educational and corporate boards, she works to advance science and the role of women in science. She has led a transformation of Rennselaer Polytechnic Institute in her role as President.

Jackson's numerous awards demonstrate the capability of women and minorities to join the leadership ranks in science and technology, education and public policy. *Time* magazine has called her "perhaps the ultimate role model for women in science."

Mary Putnam Jacobi, M.D.
1842–1906

Mary Putnam Jacobi empowered and inspired nineteenth century women to become physicians by raising the level of medical education for women and overcoming public doubt about women's capabilities to study and practice medicine.

Dr. Jacobi was dissatisfied with the quality of medical education available to women and so, after studying abroad, she established a large private practice in New York City and taught at the New York Infirmary for Women & Children and other hospitals.

Dr. Jacobi, a brilliant physician whose skills and training surpassed that of most male physicians, founded the Association for the Advancement of Medical Education of Women in 1872, serving as its president for several years. She was also an activist in the consumer and woman suffrage movement, inspiring female colleagues to excel in medicine and as citizens.

Frances Wisebart Jacobs
1843–1892

An outstanding example of the difference one dedicated person can make, Frances Wisebart Jacobs, known as Colorado's "Mother of Charities," was the driving force behind the concept of today's United Way, the founder of a major medical institution, an educator and an important philanthropist.

Jacobs, an Ohio native, relocated with her husband to Denver in 1874. President of the Hebrew Benevolent Ladies Society, known today as Jewish Family Service of Colorado, and an officer of the nonsectarian Ladies' Relief Society, in 1887 she spearheaded the creation of the Charity Organization Society, which became a federation of charities that coordinated fundraising and other efforts and shared the proceeds. This was the model that led to the creation of today's United Way, which recognizes Jacobs as its founder.

Jacobs also founded Denver's first free kindergarten to help poor children. After her death, a new hospital she had helped found was named the Frances Jacobs Hospital – and today it stands as the internationally-known National Jewish Health, the leading respiratory hospital in the nation.

Jacobs is the only woman among the 16 pioneers honored with stained glass portraits in the Colorado Capitol Rotunda.

$\mathcal{M}$ae Jemison, M.D.
1956–

Medical doctor, engineer, astronaut – Mae Jemison's skills and expertise reflect a determined individual whose contributions to the nation and the world make a difference.

Jemison, determined from childhood to explore space, became the first African-American woman in space when she traveled on the *Endeavor* on September 12, 1992. Earlier, Jemison spent several years as a Peace Corps physician in West Africa and opened a private practice in Los Angeles.

After her space flight, Jemison took leave from NASA to lecture and teach at Dartmouth College, focusing on space-age technology and developing nations. She says that space "is the birthright of everyone who is on this planet. We need to get every group of people in the world involved because it is something that eventually we in the world community are going to have to share."

Jemison heads her own firm in Houston, and travels throughout the world. Jemison encourages women and minorities to enter scientific fields: "I want to make sure we use all our talent, not just 25 percent." In 1999 Jemison accepted appointment as the President's Council of Cornell Women Andrew D. White Professor-at-Large at Cornell University.

Mary "Mother" Harris Jones
1837–1930

Mary Harris Jones was over fifty years old before she began her career as a labor organizer. She was born in Ireland, but her family was forced to emigrate because they rebelled against British rule.

While living in the northeast, she completed school, became a teacher, and married an iron moulder. From her husband, George E. Jones, she learned how workers were struggling against abuses by unscrupulous employers.

Two tragic events changed her from a bystander to a fighter for the rights of labor. In 1867 Mary Jones lost her husband and four children in a yellow fever epidemic. And as she was rebuilding her life in Chicago four years later, her successful dressmaking business was destroyed in the famous Chicago fire.

Destitute and alone, Mary Jones strongly identified with working people who had no protection against low wages, long hours, and dangerous working conditions. Owners often used blacklists and violence to intimidate workers and prevent unionism.

"Mother" Jones, as she came to be called, was neither frightened nor discouraged. She fearlessly began to organize both men and women to fight for their rights. A fiery and electrifying speaker, "Mother" Jones specialized in creating a public outcry over the inhuman treatment of workers. She once put together a caravan of children on a march to dramatize the evils of child labor. Her most famous efforts were attempts to organize the miners of West Virginia and Colorado.

Scorning jail, deportation to other states, and threats on her life, "Mother" Jones became an enemy of the wealthy business owners. Well into her eighties, she continued to agitate and actively assist in the struggle to unionize streetcar, garment, and steel workers.

Unique as a woman in the predominately male labor movement, "Mother" Mary Harris Jones became a symbol of labor's insistence on its right to decent treatment and wages.

$\mathcal{B}$arbara Jordan
1936–1996

Elected to the U.S. House of Representatives from Texas in 1972, Barbara Jordan became the first African-American congresswoman to be elected, and re-elected, from the deep South.

Before her election to Congress, she was a Texas State Senator, the first African-American woman to serve there. Jordan captured the attention of the nation during the 1974 Nixon impeachment hearings. As a member of the House Judiciary Hearings, she served on the committee charged with hearing and evaluating the evidence bearing on the possible impeachment of then-President Nixon. It was on this committee that her incisive questioning and her impassioned defense of the Constitution made her a respected national figure.

In 1976, Barbara Jordan became the first woman and first African American to give the keynote speech at the Democratic National Convention.

In 1978 she announced that she would not seek re-election and returned to Texas as a full professor at the Lyndon B. Johnson School of Public Affairs at the University of Texas. She remained there, and became a counselor to Texas Governor Ann Richards. Her many honors included the Presidential Medal of Freedom.

Helen Keller
1880–1968

When she was nineteen months old, an illness left Helen deaf, blind, and mute.

Though a wild, destructive child, she showed such signs of intelligence that her mother sent for a special teacher. The teacher, young Anne Sullivan, herself formerly blind, managed to break through to communicate with Helen. The child loved to learn, and her remarkable achievements in reading, writing and even speaking soon made her internationally famous.

Helen earned a bachelor's degree from Radcliffe College, where Anne Sullivan accompanied her to every class and spelled the lectures into her hand. Keller wrote poetry, toured on the Chautauqua lecture circuit, and published an autobiography, *The Story of My Life*. Helen became a member of the Socialist Party. She also supported controversial groups like the Industrial Workers of the World, the American Civil Liberties Union, the National Association for the Advancement of Colored People, and Margaret Sanger's birth control crusade.

In the 1920s, the newly established American Foundation for the Blind asked Helen Keller to help them raise funds. She was living testimony to the capabilities of a group once assumed to be retarded and helpless, and she spent most of the rest of her life as the most prominent advocate for the needs and rights of the handicapped. She lobbied for measures to aid the blind, including reading services and Social Security acceptance.

*ℬ*ishop Leontine T. Kelly
1920–2012

Bishop Leontine Kelly, pioneer religious leader, came from a family of Methodist ministers. Her life as high school social studies teacher, mother of four and wife of a Methodist minister was like that of many other women until her husband's death in 1969. Kelly then received her own "call" to ordained ministry. After studying at Wesley Theological Seminary and Union Theological Seminary, she received her degree in divinity and became an ordained minister. She was pastor of two churches, held several important positions in the United Methodist Church, and gained a reputation as an excellent administrator and dynamic preacher.

In 1983, Kelly became Assistant General Secretary in the area of Evangelism for the United Methodist General Board of Discipleship in Nashville, Tennessee. In 1984, the Western Jurisdictional Conference of the United Methodist Church elected her to the episcopacy, the first African-American woman to be elected bishop in her denomination. She served as bishop of the California-Nevada Annual Conference and as president of the Western Jurisdiction College of Bishops. She was the chief administrative officer and spiritual leader of more than 100,000 United Methodists in California and Nevada.

After retiring in 1988, Kelly served as visiting and adjunct professor of religion at several universities and she continued to speak and teach throughout the United States and the world. She also played a significant role in the development of Africa University, a United Methodist-related institution in Zimbabwe. As a role model for women and men all over the world, she mentored and counseled women – both young women and older women – in the ministry. In addition, she was a social activist, advocating many progressive and controversial issues, including the end to nuclear arms, opening up the church to gays and lesbians, and ministry to AIDS victims. Her work for social justice was recognized with numerous honors and awards, including ten honorary doctorate degrees, the Martin Luther King, Jr. "Drum Major for Justice" and "Grass Roots Leadership" awards from the Southern Christian Leadership Conference, and the California-Nevada Annual Conference's Leontine Kelly Social Justice Award.

As a spiritual and moral leader, Bishop Kelly advanced the cause of justice in the United States and throughout the world.

Susan Kelly-Dreiss
1942–

For over thirty years, Susan Kelly-Dreiss has worked to enact legal protections, implement innovative services and heighten public awareness on behalf of battered women and their children.

Having grown up in a violent home, Kelly-Dreiss began her career in victim advocacy by helping to start a shelter for battered women in Harrisburg, Pennsylvania. In 1976, she joined with a handful of other women to successfully lobby for passage of Pennsylvania's first domestic violence law, the Pennsylvania Protection from Abuse Act.

She co-founded the nation's first domestic violence coalition, the Pennsylvania Coalition Against Domestic Violence (PCADV). This group grew from an idea to an official coalition at Kelly-Dreiss's kitchen table, where women met to raise consciousness and plan their legislative strategy. As the founding Executive Director of PCADV, Kelly-Dreiss oversaw the growth of the network from nine to sixty-one community-based programs now operating throughout the state.

In 1993, she was instrumental in securing federal funding to establish the National Resource Center on Domestic Violence at PCADV, providing information and technical assistance on domestic violence and related issues.

Kelly-Dreiss was a founding member of the National Network to End Domestic Violence. She played a key role in drafting federal legislation including the Federal Violence Prevention and Services Act and the Violence Against Women Act. She has served in leadership positions on family violence task forces under two Pennsylvania attorneys general, and was appointed by Governor Tom Ridge and re-appointed by Governor Ed Rendell to the Pennsylvania Commission on Crime and Delinquency. Kelly-Dreiss was the recipient of a National Crime Victim Service Award.

Kelly-Dreiss has mentored and motivated generations of women to carry out the work of the Battered Women's Movement. Perhaps most importantly, Kelly-Dreiss has demonstrated an unwavering commitment to battered women and their children. PCADV and its member organizations have provided life-saving services to millions of domestic violence victims and their children.

Frances Kathleen Oldham Kelsey, Ph.D., M.D.
1914–2015

Frances Kathleen Oldham Kelsey, Ph.D., M.D., physician and pharmacologist, was a leading compliance officer with the Federal Food and Drug Administration. She became nationally known in the 1960s when she withstood great pressure by a leading drug company to quickly approve the drug thalidomide, which was then widely used in Europe primarily to allay morning sickness suffered during pregnancy. Demanding more testing before she would consider approval, Dr. Kelsey saved countless women in the United States from giving birth to terribly deformed children. President Kennedy awarded Kelsey the President's Medal for Distinguished Service for her exceptional judgment in evaluating this new drug. Kelsey was only the second woman to receive this award – the highest award the government gives to civilians.

Dr. Kelsey's brought to the FDA the rigorous standards that typified high quality research in major academic institutions. Her alertness and careful review of the thalidomide application and the subsequent evidence of the danger of that drug resulted in significant strengthening of drug legislation in the United States. Today drug companies must prove not only that drugs are safe, but also that they are effective. Perhaps even more important, drug companies now have to submit enough research to the FDA to prove a drug's safety before it can be tested on humans.

Dr. Kelsey helped open the door to women in medical and scientific research by proving that women can compete at top academic institutions. She received her Ph.D. in pharmacology in 1938 from the University of Chicago and became an instructor and then assistant professor of pharmacology there. In 1950, after many years of course work, she earned her M.D. degree, also from Chicago. This was at a time when less than ten percent of graduate students and medical students in her field were women. Dr. Kelsey authored numerous articles in well recognized scientific journals and was the recipient of several prestigious awards and honorary degrees.

A woman of courage and a woman of reason, Dr. Kelsey demanded of herself and others in her profession high standards of science and integrity.

*N*annerl O. Keohane, Ph.D.
1940–

As the first contemporary woman to head both a major women's college (Wellesley) and a great research university (Duke), Nan Keohane is a major force in changing the perception about women's capabilities to lead major institutions of higher learning.

Educated at Wellesley (B.A., 1961, Durant Scholar), Oxford University (St. Anne's College, 1963, Philosophy, Politics and Economics – First Class Honours) and Yale University (Ph.D., Political Science, 1967 – Sterling Fellow), Keohane served on the faculties of the University of Pennsylvania, Swarthmore College and Stanford University, and is the author of scholarly books as well as numerous articles.

She became president and professor of political science at Wellesley in 1981, and led the largest fundraising drive in the history of American private colleges, overturning conventional wisdom that women would not become heavily involved in a major philanthropic effort and were not supportive of higher education.

Also during Keohane's tenure at Wellesley, she implemented an improved affirmative action program and increased both minority student enrollment and faculty hiring.

She became President and Professor of Political Science at Duke University in 1993, where she champions increased faculty diversity and promoted the hiring and advancement of women faculty. Later, she joined the faculty at Princeton University.

Keohane has been active in her field of political science, holding various position in the American Political Science Association and serving as an editor of its journal. She served on the Trilateral Commission, the Council of Foreign Relations, and on the boards of directors of IBM, the Colonial Williamsburg Foundation, Massachusetts Institute of Technology and the Director's Advisory Committee of the National Institutes of Health.

She is a powerful contemporary role model for women, a trailblazer who has performed with excellence and who has shattered centuries of prejudice about women's capabilities in academe.

Jean Kilbourne
1943–

Through her pioneering work studying images of women in advertising, Jean Kilbourne has transformed the way in which organizations and educational institutions around the world address the prevention of many public health problems including smoking, high-risk drinking, eating disorders, obesity, sexualization of children, and violence against women. In the late 1960s, she began her exploration of the connection between advertising and its impact on several public health issues, most notably violence against women and eating disorders. Ms. Kilbourne launched a movement to promote media literacy as a way to prevent these problems – a radical and original idea at the time that is today mainstream and an integral part of most prevention programs.

Internationally recognized for her groundbreaking work, Ms. Kilbourne's speaking, writing, films and videos have impacted the way in which we publicly communicate with each other about ideal beauty, the connection between the objectification of women and violence, the themes of liberation and weight control, the targeting of alcoholics by the alcohol industry, and the image of addiction as a love affair. Her first film *Killing Us Softly: Advertising's Image of Women* (and the remakes *Still Killing Us Softly* and *Killing Us Softly 3*) are among the most popular and widely used educational films of all time.

In addition to the many awards and honors she has received, Ms. Kilbourne has served as an authority on addictions, gender issues and the media, and as an advisor to former United States Surgeons General, Dr. C. Everett Koop and Dr. Antonio Novello. She has also provided testimony for the United States Congress. She lectures at a wide range of conferences including those focusing on addictions and public health, violence, women and the media and has appeared on hundreds of television and radio programs to encourage an open dialogue that moves and empowers people to take action in their own and in society's interest.

*B*illie Jean King
1943–

As one of the most celebrated tennis players in history, and one of the 20th century's most respected women, Billie Jean King has dedicated her life to breaking barriers both on and off the tennis court.

Billie Jean Moffit began playing tennis at the age of 11. After one of her first tennis lessons, she told her mother, "I'm going to be No. 1 in the world", a title she would come to hold five times between 1966 and 1972.

For more than 20 years, King dominated the world of tennis. As a player, she won 39 Grand Slam singles, doubles and mixed doubles tennis titles, including a record 20 titles at Wimbledon. In 1973, King defeated Bobby Riggs in the most talked-about tennis match in history. The "Battle of the Sexes" was a turning point for women in athletics, proving that skill is not dependent upon gender.

King's efforts turned women's tennis into a major professional sport. Outraged at the disparity between men's and women's prizes at major tournaments, King spearheaded the drive for equal prize money and equal treatment of women. She helped establish the Virginia Slims Tour, founded the Women's Tennis Association and the Women's Sports Foundation, and co-founded World TeamTennis.

As a female athlete, King achieved a number of "firsts". In 1971, she became the first female athlete in any sport to earn more than $100,000 in a single season, and in 1974, she became the first woman to coach a co-ed team in professional sports, the Philadelphia Freedoms. In 1984, King became the first woman commissioner in professional sports history.

In honor of her contributions to tennis, sports and society, the National Tennis Center was renamed the USTA Billie Jean King National Tennis Center in 2006. In the same year, the Sports Museum of America and the Women's Sports Foundation announced the Billie Jean King International Women's Sports Center.

King is the author of numerous books, including, *Pressure is a Privilege: Lessons I've Learned from Life and the Battle of the Sexes*. In 2009, she was awarded the Presidential Medal of Freedom, the nation's highest civilian honor.

King's groundbreaking achievements spearheaded the women's movement in tennis, affording today's female athletes equal opportunity in the world of sports.

Photo: Carol L. Newsom

Coretta Scott King
1927–2006

One of the most celebrated champions of human and civil rights, Coretta Scott King, in partnership with her husband, Reverend Dr. Martin Luther King, Jr., ignited democracy movements worldwide.

King received her B.A. in music from Antioch College in Ohio and went on to study concert singing at Boston's New England Conservatory of Music, where she earned a degree in voice and violin. It was also while in Boston that Coretta met her husband, Martin Luther King, Jr.

Together, the Kings devoted their lives to social change. As a leading participant in the American Civil Rights Movement, King recognized the importance of women to that movement. She implored, "Women, if the soul of the nation is to be saved, I believe that you must become its soul."

After her husband's assassination in 1968, King devoted time and energy to developing social programs and building the Martin Luther King, Jr. Center for Nonviolent Social Change as a living memorial to her husband's life and dream. In 1969, she became the Founding President, Chair and Chief Executive Officer of The King Center.

In 1974, she formed and co-chaired the National Committee for Full Employment. She also formed the Coalition of Conscience (1983), and co-convened the Soviet-American Women's Summit (1990).

For over forty years, King traveled throughout the world speaking out on behalf of racial and economic justice, women's and children's rights, gay and lesbian dignity, religious freedom, the needs of the poor and homeless, full employment, and nuclear disarmament.

King lent her support to emerging democracies worldwide and consulted with leaders around the world, including Corazon Aquino and Nelson Mandela. In 1985, King and three of her children were arrested at the South African Embassy in Washington, DC for protesting against apartheid.

King received over 60 honorary doctorates and served on and helped found dozens of organizations including the Black Leadership Forum and the Black Leadership Roundtable.

King's legacy of peace, justice and social action resonates still today.

Photo: CSK Legacy, LLC on behalf of the Estate of Coretta S. King

Julie Krone
1963–

With more than 3,700 career wins, Julie Krone is the leading female Thoroughbred horse racing jockey of all time.

Raised on a horse farm in Eau Claire, Michigan, Krone began riding horses at an early age and won her first horse show when she was five years old. At the age of 14, after watching 18 year-old Steve Cauthen win a Triple Crown race, she set her sights on becoming a jockey.

Two short years later, Krone made her debut riding Tiny Star at Tampa Bay Downs; less than a month later, she won her first race aboard Lord Farkle at the same track (1981). She soon became the first female leading rider at Monmouth Park, The Meadowlands, Belmont Park, Gulfstream Park and Atlantic City Race Course. Among her myriad achievements, Krone won six races in one day at both The Meadowlands (twice) and Monmouth Park, and won five races in one day at Saratoga Race Course and Santa Anita Park.

In 1993, Krone rode Colonial Affair to victory at the Belmont Stakes and made history as the first woman to win a Triple Crown event. She set records again in 2003 as the first woman to win a Breeders' Cup event at the Juvenile Fillies and the first woman to win a million dollar event at the Pacific Classic.

Krone is the recipient of many awards, including ESPN's Professional Female Athlete of the Year (1993) and the Women's Sports Foundation's Wilma Rudolph Courage Award (2004). In 2000, she became the first woman inducted into the National Museum of Racing's Hall of Fame.

Initially retired from horse racing in 1999, Krone became a commentator and analyst for the TVG racing network and the Hollywood Park simulcast network. She returned to the sport in 2002, retiring for the final time in 2004. Today, she maintains a close relationship with the Thoroughbred racing business and shares her love of horses through motivational speeches, clinics and private tutoring.

*E*lisabeth Kübler-Ross, M.D.
1926–2004

In her journal, Elisabeth Kübler-Ross wrote, "There is within each of us a potential for goodness beyond our imagining, for giving which seeks no reward; for listening without judgment; for loving unconditionally." It was this spirit that directed much of her psychiatric work with terminally ill patients, AIDS patients, and maximum-security prisoners.

She was born in Zurich, Switzerland, a tiny two-pound baby, the first of triplets. In spite of her father's objections, Elisabeth was determined at an early age to study medicine and in 1957 received her medical degree from the University of Zurich. She married Dr. Emanuel Ross, an American, who also studied at the university and they moved to the United States to fulfill their medical residency requirements.

During her first residency at Manhattan State Hospital, Dr. Kübler-Ross was horrified by the routine neglect and poor treatment of mental patients. It was here that she began her life-long approach to medical practice as she developed a program of individual care and attention for each patient. This protocol resulted in significant improvement in the mental health of 94% of her patients.

She continued in the field of psychiatry at the University of Colorado School of Medicine. There she became a teaching fellow and began a lecture series for medical and theological students on death and dying, with terminally ill patients as part of her presentations.

As an assistant professor of psychiatry at the University of Chicago in 1965, Dr. Kübler-Ross continued these seminars, which were incorporated into her first book, *On Death and Dying*, a 1969 worldwide bestseller. This book and her lectures are credited with helping people put aside a long-held Western reluctance to openly talk about death and dying. This, in turn, helped to strengthen the hospice movement in the United States and to make the study of the psychological, social, and physical issues associated with dying an important and accepted part of medical training. Based on her many patient interviews, she identified the five now widely accepted stages that patients encounter as they confront death; denial, anger, bargaining, depression, and acceptance. Today, these stages are associated with any major loss or life-changing experience.

During her career, Dr. Kübler-Ross was associated with 16 different hospitals and universities, wrote more than 20 books, many of which were translated into other languages, and received more than 47 awards and honors including *Time* Magazine, 1999, 100 Most Important Thinkers of the Century and many honorary degrees.

Maggie Kuhn
1905–1995

At age 65, when many people prepare for quiet years, Maggie Kuhn embarked on the greatest adventure and most important work of her life.

In 1970, forced to retire from her career with the Presbyterian Church at age 65, Kuhn and a group of her friends in similar circumstances organized and founded an organization which became the Gray Panthers. The organization was created to work on issues of concern to the elderly, such as pension rights and age discrimination, but also to concern itself with larger public issues, such as the Vietnam War and other social concerns. At the core of the Gray Panthers' message was that older people needed to seize control of their lives and be in the active world working for issues in which they believed.

Kuhn's candor, charisma and lively approach to the needs and problems of the old drew major media attention, and the group was successfully launched, coming to represent in the public mind that power and energy that the elderly can represent. Kuhn fought off efforts by everyone from politicians to the managers of nursing homes to treat the elderly like amusing children, instead insisting on a place at the table and voice in decision-making that affected the lives of the old.

Kuhn's advice to activists interested in creating social change shows the strength of her convictions: "Leave safety behind. Put your body on the line. Stand before the people you fear and speak your mind – even if your voice shakes. When you least expect it, someone may actually listen to what you have to say. Well-aimed slingshots can topple giants. And do your homework."

Kuhn, who continued to play a role in the Gray Panthers until her death at age 89, is considered by many to have started nothing less than a contemporary cultural revolution, both in terms of redefining the meaning of age and through her insistence on "young and old together." She and the Panthers have been directly instrumental in enacting significant national reforms, including nursing home reform, ending forced retirement provisions, and combatting fraud against the elderly in health care. She authored several books and an autobiography.

Photo: Julie Jensen Photography, Philadelphia

Stephanie L. Kwolek
1923–2014

Stephanie L. Kwolek spearheaded the discovery, development and processing of high performance aramid fibers. These fibers, most notably Kevlar offer opportunities across the globe to save lives and assist humanity.

As a child, Kwolek was encouraged by her father to learn about nature and enjoyed math and science. Initially, she planned upon a career in medicine, graduated from Margaret Morrison Carnegie College, now a part of Carnegie Mellon University, and earned her BS degree in chemistry.

Searching for employment to save money for medical school, Kwolek was hired by the Dupont Company for a research position at the textile fibers laboratory. Working with great determination, she earned a transfer to Dupont's pioneering research laboratory in Delaware. She specialized in low-temperature processes for the creation of long molecule chains that resulted in petroleum-based synthetic fibers of tremendous rigidity and strength.

In 1965, she discovered a new fiber, an aramid fiber and a new branch of synthetics, liquid crystal-line polymers. Thoughts of medical school faded. Kwolek engaged in four decades of cutting edge chemical research. It was ten years before the first Kevlar bulletproof vests came on the market (1975). Kevlar today has hundreds of uses and has saved thousands of lives.

Kwolek was the recipient or co-recipient of 17 U. S. patents, including one for the spinning method that made commercial aramid fibers feasible, and five for the prototype from which Kevlar was created. An Inductee into the National Inventors Hall of Fame and the Engineering and Science Hall of Fame, Kwolek received many other awards and honors including the 1999 Lemelson-MIT Lifetime Achieve-ment Award, the 1996 National Medal of Technology, the Perkin Medal from the American Chemical Society, and the American Innovator Award (1994). She was known for mentoring women scientists and for her contributions to science education of young children.

*S*usette La Flesche
1854–1903

Susette La Flesche, an Omaha, campaigned tirelessly for Native American rights, becoming the first Native American lecturer and the first published Native American artist and writer.

Daughter of Chief Joseph La Flesche, Chief of the Omahas, La Flesche was a teacher on her reservation after completing her education at the Elizabeth Institute in New Jersey. She generated national attention in 1879 when she accompanied newspaperman Thomas Tibbles of the *Omaha Herald* on a lecture tour to publicize wrongs against the Ponca Indians. The tribe had been brutally displaced and relocated to unfamiliar grounds, and more than a third had died.

La Flesche, going by the English translation of her Native American name Inshta Theumba ("Bright Eyes"), was able to reach influential Easterners and brought about passage of the Dawes Act in 1887, at the time considered a progressive law of benefit to the tribes.

La Flesche married Tibbles in 1881 and continued to tour and lecture in America and England. She also became a writer, contributing regularly to a variety of magazines and newspapers. She anonymously edited *Ploughed Under, The Story of an Indian Chief*.

Photo: Nebraska State Historical Society

Winona LaDuke
1959–

Native American land rights activist, environmentalist, economist, politician, and author Winona LaDuke has spent her career working on a national level to advocate, raise public support and create funding for environmental groups. A graduate of Harvard and Antioch Universities, LaDuke has become known as a voice for Native American economic and environmental concerns around the globe.

LaDuke is an Anishinaabekwe (Ojibwe) enrolled member of the Mississippi Band Anishinaabeg. While attending Harvard University, LaDuke met Jimmy Durham, a well-known Native American activist, and her own interest in issues related to Native tribes began. At the age of 18, LaDuke spoke to the United Nations regarding Native American concerns.

After graduation, LaDuke moved to the White Earth Ojibwe reservation in Minnesota, where she became principal of the reservation high school. There, she quickly became involved in a lawsuit to recover lands promised to the Anishinaabeg people by an 1867 federal treaty. After four years of litigation the case was dismissed, prompting LaDuke to found the White Earth Land Recovery Project. The project's mission centers on land recovery, preservation and restoration of traditional practices and the strengthening of spiritual and cultural heritage. In 1985, she established the Indigenous Women's Network, a group devoted to increasing the visibility of Native Women and empowering them to participate in political, social, and cultural processes.

LaDuke is program director of the Honor the Earth Fund, a national advocacy group that seeks to educate and create public support and funding for native environmental groups. In 1998, her work was recognized by *Ms.* Magazine, which named her Woman of the Year. Four years earlier she was nominated by *Time* Magazine as one of the country's fifty most promising leaders under the age of 40.

In 1996 and again in 2000 she was a vice-presidential candidate, joining Ralph Nader on the Green Party ticket. A mother of three, LaDuke has written extensively on Native American and environmental issues.

Dorothea Lange
1895–1965

Pioneering documentary photographer Dorothea Lange was challenged in her childhood by contracting polio and by the abandonment by her father, She decided at a young age to become a photographer. After graduation, she obtained work in leading photographers' studios.

She became an empathic observer of people in the context of their lives by walking through many parts of New York City. In 1918, Lange and a friend planned to work their way around the world, but were stranded in San Francisco after losing their savings in a robbery. Lange settled in San Francisco, married artist Maynard Dixon and raised their family of two sons.

She created commercially successful studio photographs but her most influential work became focused on the visual depiction of people's changing lives and the interrelationships of people, environment, and major historical events.

Lange became one of the outstanding photo-documentarians of farmers and migrant workers when she worked for the Farm Security Administration during the Great Depression. Her famed photograph *Migrant Mother* (Nipomo, 1936) has been acclaimed as the summation of the rapidly changing realities of the time.

In 1940, Lange became the first woman awarded a Guggenheim Fellowship in photography. In 1942, Lange and Ansel Adams photographed Richmond, California's rapidly changing wartime communities.

Lange sensitized America and the world to the injustices of the Japanese American internment of World War II, through her War Relocation Authority photographs.

After the war, Lange traveled the world with her second husband Paul Taylor, creating photo-essays for leading magazines such as *Life* and *Fortune*. She chronicled the new industrial expansion of San Francisco, the societal change from rural small town communities to mass urban culture in America, and photographed scenes across the globe. Her dedication, breadth, compassion, empathy, graphic power, and superb technique set standards that stand today.

Carlotta Walls LaNier
1942–

Carlotta Walls LaNier, at age 14, was the youngest of the nine courageous African-American students known as the Little Rock Nine who integrated Little Rock Central High School in 1957. The integration of the Arkansas high school was a catalyzing event in the American Civil Rights Movement testing the landmark decision by the U.S. Supreme Court declaring segregation in public schools unconstitutional (*Brown v. Board of Education of Topeka, 1954*).

Ms. LaNier and her fellow students initially were escorted to Central High School by the 101st Airborne Division of the U.S. Army and later the Arkansas National Guard. Daily, they endured verbal taunts and physical harassment while at school. Ms. LaNier was one of three Little Rock Nine students to return to Central High School after the closing of all Little Rock high schools in 1958-1959, and became the first African-American woman to walk across the Central High School stage to receive her diploma.

After graduating from Central High in 1960, she studied at Michigan State University for two years before moving to Colorado. She enrolled at the University of Northern Colorado and earned her bachelor's degree in 1968.

She, along with the other members of the Little Rock Nine, is the recipient of the nation's highest civilian honor, the Congressional Gold Medal, awarded by President Bill Clinton in 1999, the prestigious Spingarn Medal from the NAACP, and the Lincoln Leadership Prize awarded by the Abraham Lincoln Presidential Library Foundation. Ms. LaNier is a recipient of four honorary doctorate degrees and is an inductee into the Colorado Women's Hall of Fame.

Ms. La Nier has documented her journey with Lisa Frazier Paige in *A Mighty Long Way…My Journey to Justice at Little Rock Central High*. She remains active in numerous community organizations in Colorado and serves as the President of the Little Rock Nine Foundation, a financial aid and mentoring organization dedicated to ensuring equal access to education for children of color.

$\mathscr{A}$llie B. Latimer, J.D.
1929–

An attorney, civil rights activist and humanitarian, Allie B. Latimer has been active in legal, civic and religious activities throughout her lifetime.

After graduating from Hampton Institute (now Hampton University). she volunteered for two years with the American Friends Service Committee, performing work in prisons and mental institutions. She participated in the effort to desegregate the New Jersey State Hospital at Vineland and an effort to integrate a suburban community outside Philadelphia.

Latimer later enrolled in Howard University School of Law and earned her Juris Doctor in 1953. In 1958, she went on to earn a Master of Legal Letters degree from The Catholic University of America Columbus School of Law, and earned both a Master of Divinity degree and a Doctor of Ministry degree from Howard University School of Divinity.

Latimer was instrumental in organizing Federally Employed Women (FEW) in 1968, and served as the organization's founding president until 1969. The organization began as a grassroots effort with the major objective of equality of opportunity for all. Today, FEW is an itnernational organization. FEW's many accomplishments and activities have impacted the federal work-place and contributed to improved working conditions for all.

In 1969, Latimer became an Ordained Elder at Northeastern Presbyterian Church in Washington, DC. She has traveled to more than fifty countries to participate in various church related conferences.

In 1977, as a federal attorney, Latimer was the first African American and first woman to serve as General Counsel of a major federal agency as well as the first African American and first woman to attain the GS-18 salary level at the General Services Administration. Veteran Feminists of America (VFA) recognized Latimer as part of the 'second wave of feminist pioneers' She was also the recipient of the Ollie May Cooper Award, presented by the Washington Bar Association for a lifetime of legal humanitarianism and outstanding contributions to the legal profession.

Photo Courtesy of FEW National Office

*E*mma Lazarus
1849–1887

"Give me your tired, your poor, your huddled masses yearning to breathe free." These famous words from *The New Colossus* were written by Emma Lazarus, one of the first successful Jewish-American authors. Although best known for penning this sonnet, Lazarus was also a novelist, playwright, teacher and translator.

Lazarus was an enthusiastic student who immersed herself in many subjects, including the study of literature, languages and the arts. As a teenage author, Lazarus enjoyed the emotional and financial support of her father, a successful sugar merchant.

Lazarus's growing position as part of New York's literary elite afforded her the opportunities to interact with and gain inspiration from notable authors like George Eliot and Ralph Waldo Emerson. In fact, Lazarus viewed Emerson as a mentor throughout much of her early career.

Lazarus often used her writings to advocate against anti-Semitism and for the creation of a Jewish homeland. In the 1880s, considered as perhaps her most productive period, Lazarus published *Songs of a Semite: The Dance to Death and Other Poems*. It was celebrated by many as her best work and consisted of Jewish-themed poems and a lyric drama.

Through her 1882-1883 essays in the *Century*, Lazarus put forth the notion of a Jewish homeland in Palestine. She was an important forerunner of the Zionist movement, having argued for the creation of a Jewish homeland thirteen years before the term Zionist was even coined.

In 1883, Lazarus wrote *The New Colossus* for an auction to raise money for the Statue of Liberty's pedestal. It was later inscribed in bronze beneath the statue and has come to symbolize a universal message of hope and freedom for immigrants coming to America. In 1924, the Statue of Liberty was declared a national monument.

Photo: American Jewish Historical Society, NY, NY and Newton Centre, MA

Lilly Ledbetter
1938–

For more than a decade, Lilly Ledbetter fought to achieve pay equity.

It was in Alabama, where Ledbetter was born and raised, that she began a crusade that would eventually lead her all the way to the nation's capital.

In 1979, Ledbetter took a job at the Goodyear Tire & Rubber Company in Gadsen, Alabama. Although she was the only woman in her position as an overnight supervisor, Ledbetter began her career earning the same salary as her male colleagues. By the end of her career, however, Lilly was earning less than any of the men in the same position.

Although she signed a contract with her employer that she would not discuss pay rates, just before Ledbetter's retirement an anonymous individual slipped a note into her mailbox listing the salaries of the men performing the same job. In spite of the fact that Ledbetter had received a Top Performance Award from the company, she discovered that she had been paid considerably less than her male counterparts.

Ledbetter filed a formal complaint with the Equal Employment Opportunity Commission and later initiated a lawsuit alleging pay discrimination. After filing her complaint with the EEOC, Ledbetter, then in her 60s, was reassigned to such duties as lifting heavy tires. The formal lawsuit claimed pay discrimination under Title VII of the Civil Rights Act of 1964 and the Equal Pay Act of 1963.

Although a jury initially awarded her compensation, Goodyear appealed the decision to the U. S. Supreme Court. In 2007 the Supreme Court ruled on the *Ledbetter v. Goodyear Tire & Rubber Co.* case. In a 5-4 decision, the court determined that employers cannot be sued under Title VII of the Civil Rights Act if the claims are based on decisions made by the employer 180 days ago or more. Due to the fact that Ledbetter's claim regarding her discriminatory pay was filed outside of that time frame, she was not entitled to receive any monetary award.

Since that decision, Ledbetter has lobbied tirelessly for equal pay for men and women. Her efforts finally proved successful when President Barack Obama signed the Lilly Ledbetter Fair Pay Act into law on January 29, 2009.

Ledbetter said of her continuous and persistent efforts, "I told my pastor when I die, I want him to be able to say at my funeral that I made a difference."

$\mathscr{M}$ildred Robbins Leet
1922–2011

Mildred Robbins Leet made philanthropy the cornerstone of her life's work.

Today, she is recognized worldwide as a distinguished public advocate and proponent of human rights. Her activism spanned multiple arenas: health, education, international development, peace, women's issues, and the alleviation of family poverty through entrepreneurship.

In 1948, Leet was one of the founders of United Cerebral Palsy and became the first president of the women's division. From 1957 to 1964, she was the representative of the National Council of Women of the U.S.A. to the United Nations. From 1964 to 1968, she served as President of the National Council of Women, and participated in the development of the International Peace Academy.

In 1977, she was the Chair for International Relations for New York State to the First United States Conference on Women at Houston. In 1984, she helped found the U.S. Committee for the United Nations Development Fund for Women (UNIFEM), and became vice president of the that organization. She was the recipient of countless awards and honors.

Leet is best known for creating TrickleUp, Inc., with her late husband Glen Leet. TrickleUp, launched in 1979, with $1,000 of the couple's own money, is now a leading international nonprofit organization that has assisted more than 500,000 of the world's poorest people build their own businesses, educate themselves and their children, and become contributors to their communities.

One of the originators of micro-enterprise capitalization, the TrickleUp program has helped start over 100,000 businesses, aided the original entrepreneurs and their families through small start-up grants, training and technical assistance. The professionalism, integrity, organization, and unsurpassed vision of TrickleUp have made its pioneering program one of the leaders of the micro-enterprise movement. Her work has been described as outstanding and transformative.

*M*aya Y. Lin
1959–

Maya Lin, architectural designer and sculptor, blazed across the consciousness of America when, as a 21-year old architecture student at Yale University, she won the design competition for the Vietnam Veterans War Memorial.

Her visionary design, selected from a field of 1,420 entries, inspired interaction between viewers and the memorial. It made no political statement but commemorated the sacrifice and heroism of every service person through engraving the names of all the fallen in chronological order of loss on two highly polished, black granite, intersecting walls. Its silent, massive, shining presence, two V-shaped wings, one pointing to the Lincoln Memorial and the other to the Washington Monument, opened officially to the public November 11, 1982. It has become the most visited monument in Washington, DC and one of the most well-known memorials in the world.

In 1981, her selection stirred reflection, debate, opposition, and intense controversy. By 1989, when her design for the Southern Poverty Law Center's Civil Rights Memorial in Montgomery, Alabama was completed, Maya Lin was established as a pre-eminent architectural designer.

Over the last few decades, she has executed numerous other architectural projects such as private homes, landscape sculptures and other memorials. Her co-design of the Museum of African Art, Pennsylvania Station, sculptural works such as *Topographic Landscape*, the *Wave Field* located at the Francois-Xavier Bagnoud building for aerospace engineering at the University of Michigan, *Ten-Degrees North* at the Rockefeller Foundation in New York City, *Avalanche, Groundswell* at the Wexner Center for the Arts at Ohio State University, Columbus, OH, and the traveling *Topologies* show treat the themes of love of nature, landscape and the environment, while utilizing technological elements.

She draws inspiration from widely diverse sources; her Chinese-American immigrant heritage, Japanese gardens, European multi-use parks such as Denmark's Norbrow, Hopewell Indian earthen mounds, and American earthworks artists of the 1960s and 1970s. Weaving an American fabric from differing threads, Maya Lin broke opened new avenues and expanded public understanding. Focusing on "how humanity deals with mortality in the built form," she connects the viewer, through immediate sensory experience, with major historic events. Inspiring thoughtful examination, emotional bonding and the reconciliation of oppositions, Maya Lin's work has promoted human rights and changed the way people view the world and the events of their times.

Anne Morrow Lindbergh
1906–2001

Anne Morrow Lindbergh first won literary acclaim when she was very young. At her graduation from Smith College, she won the Mary Augusta Jordan Prize for the most original literary piece and the Elizabeth Montagu Prize for the best essay on women of the 18th Century. The novels, essays and diaries she later composed have been described as "small works of art."

In 1929, her life dramatically changed with her marriage to America's "last hero," aviator Charles A. Lindbergh. Throughout their marriage the legendary pair flew together constantly on goodwill tours and on business trips to explore transcontinental routes for commercial aviation.

In the early 1930s, she became the first woman in the United States to obtain a glider pilot license. In 1931, she received her private pilot's license. Later, they covered 30,000 miles over five continents. For her part in the expedition, Lindbergh received the United States Flag Association Cross of Honor.

In 1934, she became the first woman to receive the National Geographic Society Hubbard Gold Medal, one of several awards won for her piloting and navigational skills.

Throughout her aviation career, Lindbergh continued to write. Her first book, *North to the Orient*, chronicled the couple's flight in a single engine airplane over uncharted routes through Canada and Alaska to Japan and China. *Listen! The Wind* documents their 30,000-mile survey of north and south Atlantic air routes. In all, Lindbergh published 11 major works. Her 1955 essay, *Gift from the Sea*, led the non-fiction bestseller list for many weeks, and a special anniversary edition was reissued 25 years later.

Photo: The Missouri Historical Society

Patricia A. Locke
1928–2001

Patricia Locke, *Tawacin WasteWin*, she of good consciousness – compassionate woman, was born in Idaho, a Standing Rock Sioux-Hunkpapa Lakota, and Mississippi Band of White Earth Chippewa. She received her college education at the University of California at Los Angeles and became a world-renowned educator, making her home at the Standing Rock Lakota Reservation in South Dakota.

During her more than 40 years as an educator, Native American languages and culture were suppressed by official schools that served indigenous peoples. She worked tirelessly to change that situation, becoming a preserver of the languages, cultures and spiritual traditions of Native Americans and other indigenous peoples. Serving as an instructor, curriculum designer and executive of the International Native Languages Institute, she influenced changes in Federal law, helped organize 17 tribally run Lakota colleges and was recognized for her creative and indefatigable efforts by being awarded a MacArthur Foundation Fellowship in 1991. She served as President of the National Indian Education Association, as Chair of the American Indian Advisory Committee of the Martin Luther King, Jr. Holiday Commission, wrote a regular column for the *Lakota Times*, "Unlocking Education," wrote or contributed to more than two dozen published articles, and served as a member of many advisory boards of organizations dedicated to social justice, human rights and environmental issues.

Patricia Locke developed policies, procedures and education codes for Indian communities in several regions of the country. She co-chaired the United States Department of Interior Task Force on Indian Education Policy and helped develop a Bureau of Indian Affairs Mission Statement and policies that were written into statute.

She was an active advocate for the American Indian Religious Freedom Act of 1978, which guaranteed Native Americans the right to freely practice their spiritual traditions, and was a strong voice for tribal independence in deciding how and what Native American children should study.

She became instrumental in starting Native American run colleges and developing educational curricula on reservations across the country.

She taught and lectured at UCLA, San Francisco State University, Alaska Methodist University, the University of Colorado, and the University of Southern Maine. She was active internationally at the World Assembly of First Nations in Canada (1982), Chair of the Indigenous Women's Caucus at Beijing (1995), and among the speakers at the Parliament of World Religions, Cape Town, South Africa (1999). Late in her life, Patricia Locke accepted the Baha'i faith and became the first Native American woman to be elected to an office of the National Spiritual Assembly (1993).

Belva Lockwood, J.D.
1830–1917

Belva Lockwood began to teach school at fifteen and married at nineteen. When her husband died soon after, she was left with an infant daughter to support. She returned to teaching and determined to continue her education.

In 1857 she graduated with honors from Genesee College (later Syracuse University). After a move to Washington, D.C., she married Ezekiel Lockwood. She was nearly forty when she decided to study the law. She finally found a law school that would admit her, but even there her diploma was held up until she demanded action.

Lockwood was admitted to the bar of the District of Columbia, but was refused admission to practice before the Supreme Court. She spent five years energetically lobbying a bill through Congress, and in 1879 Belva Lockwood became the first woman to practice law before the US Supreme Court.

In 1884 she accepted the nomination of the National Equal Rights Party and ran for president. Although suffrage leaders opposed her candidacy, Lockwood saw it as an entering wedge for women. She polled over 4,000 votes and ran again in 1888.

Using her knowledge of the law, she worked to secure woman suffrage, property law reforms, equal pay for equal work, and world peace. Thriving on publicity and partisanship, and encouraging other women to pursue legal careers, Lockwood helped to open the legal profession to women.

Juliette Gordon Low
1860–1927

An educator and humanitarian, Juliette Gordon Low made history as the founder of the Girl Scouts of the USA, the largest organization for girls in the world.

Low earned the nickname "Daisy" at an early age and quickly became known for her stubborn but charismatic spirit. In her youth, Low developed a passion for the arts and often painted, performed plays, sketched and wrote poetry.

Following her education, Low traveled throughout the United States and Europe. She met and married a wealthy Englishman, William Mackay Low (1886); however, the couple's marriage quickly fell apart and the Lows were separated at the time of William's death in 1905.

In 1911, while in England, Low began a close friendship with Sir Robert Baden-Powell, founder of the Boy Scouts and Girl Guides. Low quickly became interested in the Girl Guides program, believing that girls should be given the opportunity to develop physically, mentally and spiritually outside of isolated home environments. She returned to Savannah, Georgia and on March 12, 1912, held a meeting to register eighteen girls as members of the American Girl Guides. In 1913, the name of the organization was changed to the Girl Scouts, and in 1915, the Girl Scouts of the USA was incorporated. Low served as the organization's first president and gave freely of her own money in the early years.

Having suffered from the improper treatment of an ear infection in her youth and from a punctured eardrum in her twenties, as an adult, Low was completely deaf in one ear and nearly deaf in the other. She was known to exaggerate her deafness when she pretended not to hear friends who tried to beg off commitments to work for the Girl Scouts. When attending a fashionable luncheon, she would trim her hat with carrots and parsley, exclaiming to guests, "Oh is my trimming sad? I can't afford to have this hat done over – I have to save all my money for my Girl Scouts. You know about the Scouts, don't you?"

Today, Girl Scouts is the preeminent leadership development organization for girls.

$\mathcal{S}$hannon W. Lucid, Ph.D.

1943–

Shannon W. Lucid grew up during the 1940s and 1950s when women rarely thought of careers in the sciences and aviation, but ignored conventional restrictions to pursue a dream. Confronted by discriminatory attitudes, she persisted, earning a Ph.D. in biochemistry from the University of Oklahoma in 1973.

Dr. Lucid broke ground in 1979, when she became a member of the first astronaut class to admit women. She went on to become the first woman to hold an international record for the most flight hours in orbit by any non-Russian, and, until June 2007, she also held the record for the most flight hours in orbit by any woman in the world – 5,354 hours or 223 days in space. Moreover, the science experiments she performed during her five highly visible space flights broke new ground in spacecraft deployment, earth science studies, space materials processing, biomedical experimentation and atmospheric ozone research.

During her six-month flight aboard the Russian Space Station *Mir*, Dr. Lucid performed space experiments with poise and professionalism while enduring orbital problems and delays. She was a pioneer role model and diplomat par excellence, becoming highly respected and genuinely liked by the Russian crew members as well as by the Russian people.

Dr. Lucid became the ninth person and the first woman to receive the Congressional Space Medal of Honor (1996). She retired from NASA in January 2012.

Mary Lyon
1797–1849

Mary Lyon founded the Mount Holyoke Female Seminary (now College) in 1837 at South Hadley, Massachusetts, the model for institutions of higher education for women in the United States.

A teacher herself, Lyon struggled to finance her education – and determined to create a new form for women's education based on principles of sound financial endowment, the inclusion of all economic groups, an advanced curriculum equivalent to that available to men, and the preparation of women for more than homemaking and teaching.

Defying conventional behavior, Lyon traveled and fundraised in the public eye to win support for her ideas. In 1837 Mt. Holyoke Female Seminary opened with 80 students. It was an immediate success, besieged by more students than could be accommodated. Lyon headed the organization for twelve years.

For more than 150 years, Mt. Holyoke has empowered women for serious intellectual pursuits, public leadership and service to humanity, as its founder envisioned through her words "Go where no one else will go, do what no one else will do."

Mary Mahoney
1845–1926

Mary Mahoney was the first African-American woman to study and work as professionally trained nurse. She was a hospital worker before entering training and receiving a diploma in 1879 from the nursing school of the New England Hospital for Women and Children.

Trained nurses were a relatively new institution then, but standards were rigorous, and only four of 18 women who started the course with Mahoney graduated. Her high level of performance thwarted racial bias and paved the way for other African-American women to enter the profession.

Mahoney developed a successful career as a private duty nurse and as one of the few early African-American members of the American Nurses Association. She was an active member of the National Association of Colored Graduate Nurses.

A longtime advocate of woman suffrage, Mahoney is believed to be one of the first women to register and vote in Boston following passage of the 19th Amendment. The Mary Mahoney Award of the American Nurses Association honors significant contributions to race relations.

*W*ilma Mankiller
1945–2010

The powerful, visionary first woman Principal Chief of the Cherokee Nation, Wilma Mankiller spent her formative years in San Francisco, where she learned about the women's movement and organizing. When she returned to her native Oklahoma, Mankiller used her skills to help the Cherokee Nation, starting community self-help programs and teaching people ways out of poverty. In 1983 she ran for deputy chief of the Nation, and in 1985 Mankiller became Principal Chief. Mankiller brought about important strides for the Cherokees, including improved health care, education, utilities management and tribal government. She was instrumental in attracting higher-paying industry to the area, improving adult literacy, supporting women returning to school and more. Mankiller also lived in the larger world, active in civil rights matters, lobbying the federal government and supporting women's activities and issues. She said: "We've had daunting problems in many critical areas, but I believe in the old Cherokee injunction to 'be of a good mind.' Today it's called positive thinking."

Mankiller was instrumental in establishing the Nation to Nation relationship between the Cherokee Nation and the Federal Government. Her many honors included the Presidential Medal of Freedom in 1998, the Elizabeth Blackwell Award, and Ms.Magazine's Woman of the Year.

*P*hilippa Marrack
1945–

Immunologist Dr. Philippa "Pippa" Marrack is one of the world's leading research scientists investigating T-cells, the family of cells that help the body fight off disease. Her pioneering work isolating the T-cell receptor has led to a greater understanding of the molecular basis of the immune system, and has contributed to medicine's current understanding of vaccines, HIV, and other immune disorders.

Dr. Marrack works in conjunction with her husband, Dr. John Kappler, studying the basic biology of lymphocytes and the application of the knowledge about lymphocytes to human disease. Much of their work concentrates on T-cells as they relate to protection against infection, their role in driving autoimmune and allergic diseases, and their possible role in rejection of cancers. In 1990, they discovered superantigens, extremely virulent toxins that cause an overwhelming and disastrous immune response, such as occurs in toxic shock syndrome. In a continuing drive to understand why some auto-immune diseases occur more frequently in women than men, she and Dr. Kappler have recently described a population of B cells that may account for some of this observation.

Recognized as one of the most influential immunologists in the world, Dr. Marrack's work in unraveling the immune system has led to numerous important discoveries that have impacted the health of millions. Dr. Marrack is an inductee in the Colorado Women's Hall of Fame, a member of the National Academy of Sciences, the United States Institute of Medicine, and The Royal Society. Her many awards include the prestigious 2015 Wolf Prize and the Louisa Gross Horwitz Prize, often considered a predictor of the Nobel Prize.

$\mathscr{B}$arbara McClintock, Ph.D.
1902–1992

America's most distinguished cytogeneticist, Barbara McClintock entered Cornell University in 1919 where she concentrated in plant breeding and botany in the College of Agriculture. Since the Plant Breeding department discouraged women from doing graduate work due to a lack of job prospects, she instead studied plant cytology, genetics and zoology in the Department of Botany and received her Ph.D. in 1927.

She worked at Cornell and the University of Missouri until 1942, when she secured a research position with The Carnegie Institution of Washington's Department of Genetics at Cold Spring Harbor, New York. For the next 43 years, Dr. McClintock studied genetic mutations by examining changes in color and texture of the pigment in kernels and leaves of growing plants.

In 1950, Dr. McClintock first reported in a scientific journal that genetic information could transpose from one chromosome to another. Many scientists assumed that this unorthodox view of genes was peculiar to the corn plant and was not universally applicable to all organisms. They believed that genes usually were held in place in the chromosome like a necklace of beads.

Twenty years later, after many discoveries in molecular biology, scientists finally acknowledged Barbara McClintock's view of genes as universal, and in 1983 she received the Nobel Prize in Physiology or Medicine for her pioneering discovery of mobile genetic elements. Her work has assisted in the understanding of human disease. "Jumping genes" help explain how bacteria are able to develop resistance to an antibiotic and there is some indication that jumping genes are involved in the transformation of normal cells to cancerous cells.

Katharine Dexter McCormick
1875–1967

Katharine Dexter McCormick made a significant impact on women's equality in the areas of suffrage, contraception, and scientific education.

First, as an officer of the National Woman's Suffrage Association, McCormick helped achieve the ratification of the 19th Amendment giving women the right to vote. In 1919, she helped Carrie Chapman Catt found the League of Women Voters. As its first vice president, she educated women in the political process and worked to promote their political power.

Second, McCormick funded the essential research that led to the discovery and development of "the pill" (1956). Thereafter, she helped finance research on the pill's long-term effects.

Finally, as a rare 1904 female graduate of the Massachusetts Institute of Technology (MIT), she realized that one of the key barriers to women entering MIT was the lack of campus housing for them. In 1959 she fully funded MIT's first on-campus residence for women, helping increase the number of women at MIT from 3% to 40% of the undergraduates.

As a philanthropist and activist, McCormick significantly improved women's social, political, economic and intellectual position in America.

Photo: MIT Museum

Louise McManus, Ph.D.
1896–1993

The first nurse to earn a Ph.D., Louise McManus worked to establish schools of nursing in colleges and universities, which provided the fundamental basis for a nursing science to evolve.

McManus created the Institute for Nursing Research at Teachers College, Columbia University, and worked tirelessly with the state boards of nursing, state legislators and national nursing organizations to develop a standardized national approach to nursing licensure. This standardization continues today, protecting patients nationwide and ensuring the quality of care received.

McManus was always a patient advocate, and developed a "Patient Bill of Rights" adopted by the Joint Commission in Accreditation of Hospitals. She has been widely recognized in the nursing science profession as the major figure in furthering the professionalization of nursing, and received many awards for her work, including the Columbia University Bicentennial Award, the Florence Nightingale International Red Cross Society Citation and Medal and the Mary Adelaide Nutting Award for Leadership.

Margaret Mead
1901–1978

Although her father taught economics at the Wharton School, Margaret Mead had to struggle to persuade him to send her to college.

At Barnard she studied with Franz Boas and his brilliant student Ruth Benedict. They convinced her to join them in a new science, anthropology, devoted to the study of varieties of human culture. Over Boas's opposition, Mead went by herself to Samoa to do field work. The result was a tremendously popular and influential book, *Coming of Age in Samoa*. Adolescence, she argued, is not inevitably a time of stress and conflict. While portraying the free and easy Samoan life, she was critical of American society for shrouding sexuality in secrecy.

Mead went on to a career of brilliant field work. While other anthropologists spent a lifetime studying one primitive tribe, she studied half a dozen.

In the 1920s and 30s the Pacific Islands and New Guinea still offered conditions that tested a scholar's mettle. "The natives are superficially agreeable," she once wrote home, "but they go in for cannibalism, headhunting, infanticide, incest, avoidance and joking relationships, and biting lice in half with their teeth." She pushed back the boundaries of her science, and her clear style of writing and public speaking brought advanced ideas to the general public.

$\mathscr{S}$enator Barbara A. Mikulski
1936–

The first female Democratic United States Senator elected in her own right, Barbara Mikulski has been a political trailblazer for more than thirty years.

Mikulski learned the values of hard work at a young age, as she often watched her father open the family grocery store early so that local steelworkers could buy lunch before their morning shift. Mikulski graduated with a B.A. from Mount Saint Agnes College (now part of Loyola College in Maryland), and an M.S.W. from the University of Maryland School of Social Work in 1965.

Determined to make a difference in her community, Mikulski first became a social worker in Baltimore. Her work later evolved into community activism when Mikulski successfully organized communities against a plan to build a sixteen lane highway through Baltimore's Fells Point neighborhood.

Her first election effort was a successful run for Baltimore City Council in 1971, where she served for five years. In 1976, she ran for Congress and won, representing Maryland's 3rd district for 10 years. In 1986, she ran for Senate and won, becoming the first Democratic woman Senator elected in her own right. She was re-elected with large majorities in 1992, 1998 and 2004 and 2010.

During her tenure as a United States Senator, Mikulski has developed and supported legislation promoting equal healthcare for American women, Medicare reform, better care for veterans, greater student access to quality education, increased funding for scientific research, and more. Mikulski is the Dean of the Women in the U.S. Senate – mentoring other female Senators when they first take office and building coalitions. She is also a senior member of the Health, Education, Labor and Pensions Committee; a senior member of the Appropriations Committee; and a member of the Senate Select Committee on Intelligence.

Her commitment to women is evidenced in her actions and her words. "I don't want women and their families to be left out and left behind. We can fight for them. We will fight for them. They deserve better and I want to give them better."

In 2011, Senator Mikulski officially became the longest serving female Senator in United States history.

$\mathscr{K}$ate Millett, Ph.D.
1934–

A feminist activist, writer, visual artist, filmmaker, teacher and human rights advocate, Kate Millett has been described as one of the most influential Americans of the twentieth century.

Dr. Millett began her academic career as an English instructor at the University of North Carolina, Greensboro, and has held several additional teaching positions over the years. Some of the institutions she has worked for include, Tokyo's Waseda University, Barnard College, Bryn Mawr College, Sacramento State University, and University of California at Berkeley.

As a political activist, Dr. Millett has long fought for the rights of women, gay liberation, mental patients and the elderly. Her first significant contribution came in 1966, when she was named as the first Chair of the Education Committee of the newly formed National Organization for Women (NOW). In 1968, she authored a pioneering report published by NOW, *Token Learning: A Study of Women's Higher Education in America*, in which she challenged women's colleges to provide educational opportunities for women equal to those being provided to men.

A few years after joining NOW, Dr. Millett authored *Sexual Politics* (1970), a landmark work in feminist theory that fueled the second-wave of the women's movement in the U.S. Since then, she has authored numerous articles and essays and ten additional books.

In 1971, Dr. Millett formed Women's Liberation Cinema and produced the feminist classic, *Three Lives*. Between 1963 and 2009, she had several international solo art exhibitions and installations in sculpture, drawing, serigraphs and photography.

She currently serves as the Director of the Millett Center for the Arts, a creative work space that provides artist-in-residence accommodation and studio facilities to women artists from around the world. Dr. Millett founded the Center in 1978, on her own ten acre farm in LaGrange, New York.

She is the recipient of many awards, including The Yoko Ono Lennon Courage Award for the Arts and The New York Foundation for Contemporary Arts Award.

Photo: Cynthia MacAdams

Patsy Takemoto Mink, J.D.
1927–2002

Patsy Takemoto Mink was a distinguished, dedicated and innovative legislator who served as a member of the territorial House of Representative of Hawaii, State Senator of Hawaii, and for over two decades as the representative of Hawaii's 2nd Congressional District.

Compassionate, articulate, and focused, Patsy Mink riveted audiences and moved governmental bodies in ways that changed history. Mink was a legislative trailblazer who overcame gender and racial discrimination to become one of the most influential public servants of her generation.

A 1948 graduate of the University of Hawaii trained in chemistry and zoology, she was denied admission by all the medical schools to which she applied. She successfully gained admission to the University of Chicago Law School and graduated in 1951. She and her husband, John Mink, returned to Hawaii, where she started her own law practice, becoming the first woman of Japanese-American ancestry to practice law in Hawaii.

Mink began her political career in 1956, when she was elected to Hawaii's House of Representatives. In 1964, she made history when she was elected to the United States House of Representatives, becoming the first woman of color elected to the national legislature and the first Asian-American congresswoman.

For over four decades, Mink championed the rights of immigrants, minorities, women, and children, and worked to eradicate the kind of discrimination she had faced in her life. Known for her integrity, determination, tenacity, and honesty, she is recognized as the major mover of Title IX, the legislation that brought academic and athletic equity to American educational institutions. She was a strong environmental advocate and worked tirelessly on energy policy issues of regional, national and global impact. She was the recipient of numerous awards and honorary degrees.

Maria Mitchell
1818–1889

In thinking about equality of the sexes, astronomer Maria Mitchell wrote, "The eye that directs a needle in the delicate meshes of embroidery, will equally well bisect a star with the spider web of the micrometer."

Taught the basics of astronomy by her father as a girl on Nantucket, in 1847 Mitchell's sharp eyes and mind determined the orbit of a new comet. She was soon famous, and received a gold medal from the king of Denmark for her accomplishment, as well as membership in the American Academy of Arts and Sciences, the first woman to achieve this honor.

She was then elected to the American Association for the Advancement of Science. American women raised the funds to give her a state-of-the-art telescope, and in 1865 she accepted an appointment to Vassar College to become director of their observatory and professor of astronomy.

She was a beloved teacher, and her private research was focused on the study of the sun, Jupiter and Saturn. She was chosen for membership in the American Philosophical Society in 1869 and helped found the Association for the Advancement of Women in 1873.

Constance Baker Motley, J.D.
1921–2005

Making history and making law are the twin components of Constance Baker Motley's extraordinary life and career. Motley's legal career began as a law clerk in the fledgling National Association for the Advancement of Colored People Legal Defense and Education Fund, where she clerked for Thurgood Marshall.

She became a key legal strategist in the civil rights movement, helping to desegregate Southern schools, busses, lunch counters – and successfully argued nine of ten cases before the U.S. Supreme Court.

In 1964, Motley became the first African-American woman elected to the New York State Senate; in 1965 she was chosen Manhattan Borough President – the first woman and first African American in that position; and in 1966, President Johnson named her a Federal Court judge – the first African-American woman so named. Known as an incisive and capable judge, Motley believed her presence made a difference: "As the first black and first woman, I am proving in everything I do that blacks and women are as capable as anyone."

$\mathcal{L}$ucretia Mott
1793–1880

The daughter of a sea captain, Lucretia Coffin spent her childhood on Nantucket Island. She was reared in the Quaker faith, unique among American religions in encouraging the equality of women.

In 1811 she married James Mott and they made their home in Philadelphia. Soon she began to speak in Quaker meetings, developing confidence and eloquence that were rare at a time when women seldom spoke in public.

In the 1830s Mott advocated the radical idea that slavery was sinful and must be abolished. She was one of several American delegates to the 1840 World's Anti-Slavery Convention in London, but the women were denied seats. There she bonded with Elizabeth Cady Stanton whose husband was a delegate. The lesson was clear for Mott and Stanton. How could women fight for the rights of others unless they enjoyed rights of their own?

In 1848, while Mott was visiting her sister in Auburn, New York, she met with Stanton and helped to plan the first woman's rights convention. Mott delivered the opening and closing addresses at the Seneca Falls Convention, and her husband James chaired the proceedings at the Wesleyan Chapel.

Motivated by her religious convictions, Mott dedicated herself to the twin causes of antislavery and women's rights. She harbored runaways slaves in her Philadelphia home and agitated for Negro suffrage and education when emancipation was finally won. As she wrote, spoke, and attended women's conventions, younger feminists recognized that Mott's early leadership had been crucial in the infancy of the women's rights movement.

Photo: Schlesinger Library

Kate Mullany
1845–1906

Kate Mullany, a leading female labor organizer in the nineteenth century, worked for justice and opportunities for women in newly emerging industries after the Civil War.

Immigrating to Troy, New York, from Ireland with her family, Mullany had to go to work in the local laundry at the age of nineteen when her father died. Kate became the primary source of her family's income. She worked 12 to 14 hours a day, six days a week, for about $3 a week. And if she damaged a shirt or a collar, the company reduced her wages to pay for the damages.

Kate was unwilling to accept the low wages and dangerous, unhealthy working conditions at the laundry. Therefore, only a few months after she went to work in 1864, she founded the Collar Laundry Union, the first bona fide female union in the country. She then led a strike of two hundred laundresses, protesting menial wages and unsafe working conditions. Her efforts led to a twenty-five percent wage increase.

Mullany's efforts were recognized not only by women workers, but also by male labor organizers. In 1868, she was appointed an assistant secretary of the National Labor Union, making her the first female to hold a national labor position. Later, she led the efforts to form a laundry cooperative as well as a cooperative to manufacture collars and cuffs in order to shift ownership and control to the workers. Due to economic conditions and great pressure from the factory owners, these efforts failed. Still, Mullany remained a prominent labor union leader. As such, she worked to improve the economic lives of countless working-class women, while, during the same era, middle-class women's suffragists were focused on political rights.

Mullany recognized the connection between the struggle for economic and political rights. With no political power, women laundresses had no ability to pressure leaders to enact needed protective legislation. While Mullany was identified primarily as a workers' advocate rather than a women's rights advocate, she worked with suffragists, such as Susan B. Anthony, to further the interests of women wage earners and all trade unionists – male and female.

As a labor leader and organizer, Mullany is one of early American labor history's most important women.

Antonia Novello, M.D.
1944–

The first woman and the first Hispanic to become the Surgeon General of the United States (1990-1993), Antonia Novello brought to her work a strong empathy for people without power in society and used her position to alleviate suffering, especially for women and children.

Trained as a pediatric nephrologist and in public health, Novello became a clinical professor of pediatrics at Georgetown University Hospital in 1986, after working in private practice and later in the U.S. Public Health Service. In 1987 she was named coordinator for AIDS research at the National Institute of Child Health and Human Development and then Deputy Director.

As Surgeon General, Dr. Novello was among the first to recognize the need to focus on women with AIDS and on neonatal transmission of HIV. She found new opportunities for Hispanic/Latino Americans to participate in health issues, convening national and regional meetings to discuss community health needs. She raised national awareness in the medical profession about the domestic violence epidemic in America, and worked to elevate public consciousness about underage drinking and alcohol abuse.

A̸nnie Oakley
1860–1926

Annie Oakley was probably the nation's finest marksman. Born in 1860, she was an outstanding Ohio woman who gave freely of her time, funds and energies to benefit other women.

Oakley's shooting skills were developed early in her life and when she was age 21 she met her future husband, shooting champion, Frank Butler by defeating him in a match. They toured as a team for some years before he retired to manage her career.

She joined Buffalo Bill's Wild West in 1885 and performed as the star of that 19th century show for more than 16 years. She astonished Americans and royalty across England and Europe with her amazing skill.

She was injured in a train accident in 1901 that ended her career with the Wild West. After she recovered she went on to shoot in charity events to help orphans, widows, and underprivileged women. She campaigned for women's rights to hold paid employment, earn equal pay, participate in sports, and defend herself in her own home and on city streets.

Induction Year: 1995

$\mathcal{T}$he Honorable
Sandra Day O'Connor, J.D.
1930–

Sandra Day O'Connor, the first woman named to the U.S. Supreme Court, has made history through her appointment, breaking the ultimate "glass ceiling" in the legal profession. Named to the Court by President Reagan in 1981, O'Connor's legal beginnings probably did not suggest to her that she would one day hold a seat on the nation's highest bench.

After a distinguished legal preparation at Stanford University (LL.B., 1952), service as a deputy county attorney in California, and work as a civilian lawyer for the Quartermaster Corps while her husband was on military duty in Europe, O'Connor was unable to find work with an Arizona law firm because of her gender. Rather than retreat, she established her own successful law practice – and in 1965 was named assistant attorney general for the State of Arizona. She was named to fill a vacancy in the Arizona State Senate in 1969, and was subsequently re-elected to two, two-year terms, serving as Senate Majority Leader in her last term.

In 1975 she was elected to the Maricopa County Superior Court, and then to the Arizona Court of Appeals in 1979. Throughout her service on the U.S. Supreme Court, O'Connor has proven to be a thoughtful jurist. She has, forever, shattered the idea that women were not qualified to serve on the nation's highest court – and by her role model, further opened the door for women at all levels of the legal profession.

Georgia O'Keeffe
1887–1986

Words do not capture the spare, intense, unforgettable art of Georgia O'Keeffe; her paintings reveal her better, as Alfred Stieglitz said, "a woman on paper."

Determined from her early years to be an artist, O'Keeffe's career received a boost from famed photographer Alfred Stieglitz, who promoted her paintings in New York City after seeing her work. They married in 1924, beginning one of history's great creative partnerships. Some of Stieglitz' best work was of O'Keeffe, his muse, and in turn he promoted and encouraged her art throughout his life.

Georgia O'Keeffe was an American original, living as she chose, painting what she wanted. It is said that her art is uniquely American, shining with a bright modernism and energy. The lyrical flowers, the New Mexico-inspired vistas of light and shape, the hard-edged, energetic urban landscapes all somehow could only have been painted by an American woman. O'Keeffe painted all her days, committed as always to what she loved: "Art is a wicked thing. It is what we are."

$\mathcal{R}$osa Parks
1913–2005

"I would like to be known as a person who is concerned about freedom and equality and justice and prosperity for all people," said Rosa Parks on the occasion of her 77th birthday. And so she was.

Parks, known as "the mother of the civil rights movement," walked into history on December 1, 1955 when she refused to give up her seat for a white man on a Montgomery, Alabama bus. Parks was arrested for her defiance, and she agreed to challenge the segregation order in court. After this tactic failed, Parks and others organized the Montgomery bus boycott: "For a little more than a year, we stayed off those busses. We did not return to using public transportation until the Supreme Court said there shouldn't be racial segregation."

Parks and others lost their jobs, and she was harassed and threatened. The boycott held, and an important corner was turned in the movement. Parks and her family eventually moved to Detroit, where she worked for many years for Congressman John Conyers. She founded the Rosa and Raymond Parks Institute for Self-Development to offer guidance to young African Americans in preparation for leadership and careers.

Parks was the recipient of the NAACP's Spingarn Medal, the Presidential Medal of Freedom, and the Congressional Gold Medal. Her statue is in the National Statuary Hall.

*R*uth Patrick, Ph.D.
1907–2013

A pioneer in limnology, the scientific study of the life and phenomena of freshwater bodies, Ruth Patrick provided methods needed to monitor water pollution and understand its effects.

Patrick grew up in Kansas, where her father helped shape her interest in natural sciences. She and her family would often venture into the woods. From an early age, Patrick admitted to collecting mushrooms, worms, and rocks. She became fascinated with science after receiving her first microscope, at the age of seven. She went on to receive her bachelor's degree in biology from Coker College in 1929, and completed her masters and doctorate degrees in botany at the University of Virginia.

Patrick's long career at the Academy of Natural Sciences spanned many years, beginning in 1933 with her position as an unpaid researcher and volunteer curator. She then became curator of the Academy's Leidy Microscopical Collection and promptly revived the institution's research in diatoms. Her pioneering work, begun in the 1940s and dubbed The Patrick Principle, became the fundamental principle on which all environmental science and management is based. Patrick proved that biological diversity holds the key to understanding the environmental problems affecting an ecosystem.

In 1947, Patrick founded the Limnology Department at the Academy of Natural Sciences. She led the department until 1973, and a decade later, it was renamed the Patrick Center of Environmental Research in her honor. She was the first female elected chair of the board of the Academy of Natural Sciences and the first female board member of DuPont. Patrick received the National Medal of Science in 1996 for "her algal research, particularly the ecology and paleoecology of diatoms, and for elucidating the importance of biodiversity of aquatic life in ascertaining the natural condition of rivers and the effects of pollution."

Called "a den mother for generations of scientists," and a "visionary ecologist," Ruth Patrick was a champion of environmental protection, as well as a mentor and inspiration to future scientists for more than seventy years. Patrick is credited, along with Rachel Carson, as being largely responsible for ushering in the current worldwide concerns with ecology.

Alice Paul, J.D.
1885–1977

While earning degrees in law and social work, Alice Paul studied in London and joined the radical British suffrage movement. She was jailed several times and returned in 1910 determined to put new life into the American woman's struggle for the ballot.

The National American Women Suffrage Association (NAWSA), the old organization of Anthony and Stanton, was still focused on state-by-state campaigns, but Alice Paul preferred to lobby Congress for an amendment to the Constitution. She worked first within the NAWSA and then in her own rival organizations.

She soon demonstrated her political savvy, stealing the limelight at Woodrow Wilson's inauguration with a gigantic suffrage parade. When Wilson proved slow to aid the suffrage cause, Alice Paul adopted the British strategy of holding the party in power responsible. Her group, then called the Congressional Union, campaigned against Democrats in the states where women already voted. Alice Paul led them in militant tactics, including picketing the White House.

After World War I broke out, tensions grew and the pickets were alternately threatened by hostile crowds and thrown in jail. Placed in solitary confinement in a psychopathic ward, Alice Paul was force-fed, but her spirit remained unbroken.

In the 1920s her group, by then the National Woman's Party, set the agenda for feminism: the vote won, the next target would be an Equal Rights Amendment.

$\mathcal{N}$ancy Pelosi
1940–

Nancy Pelosi served as the first woman Speaker of the United States House of Representatives and the first woman in American history to lead a major political party in Congress.

Pelosi was born in Baltimore, Maryland, with a strong family tradition of public service. Her late father, Thomas D'Alesandro Jr., served as Mayor of Baltimore for 12 years, after representing the city for five terms in Congress. Her brother, Thomas D'Alesandro III, also served as Mayor of Baltimore. In 1962, she graduated from Trinity College in Washington, DC. One year later, she married Paul Pelosi, a native of San Francisco, where they settled with their five children.

As Pelosi raised her children, she volunteered for the Democratic Party and served on the San Francisco Library Commission. In 1987, she won a special election to represent the city of San Francisco in the House of Representatives.

Pelosi's colleagues elected her House Democratic Whip in 2001 and House Democratic Leader in 2002, making her the first woman to hold both positions. Finally breaking the marble ceiling of the Capitol, Pelosi was elected by her colleagues to serve as the first woman Speaker of the House from 2007 to 2011.

As Speaker, Pelosi spearheaded passage of the historic Affordable Care Act in the House and led the Congress in passing strong Wall Street reforms. A powerful voice for women's rights, she was instrumental in passage of the Lilly Ledbetter Fair Pay Act to restore the ability of women and all workers to fight pay discrimination. Her legislative accomplishments also include the passage of historic investments in college aid, clean energy and innovation, and initiatives to help small businesses and veterans. Under Pelosi's leadership, the 111th Congress was heralded as "one of the most productive Congresses in history" by Congressional scholar Norman Ornstein.

Pelosi has worked tirelessly to increase the number of women in public service, and through her leadership, she has paved the way for many more women to enter politics.

Mary Engle Pennington, Ph.D.
1872–1952

Today's supermarket refrigerated and frozen food sections are the direct result of the pioneering work of Dr. Mary Engle Pennington. As the population of the United States moved to cities, and people turned to stores and foods shipped long distances instead of backyard home gardens, the 1906 Pure Food and Drug Act was passed to secure the food supply. Dr. Pennington was a trailblazer in implementation of the Act, overseeing the handling, transportation and storage of perishables. She became a leading expert in the evolution of safe and sanitary methods for processing, storing and shipping milk, poultry, eggs, and fish.

Denied a bachelor's degree in 1892 because of her sex, Mary Engle Pennington received a certificate of proficiency in chemistry and then went on to earn her PhD in chemistry at the same institution, the University of Pennsylvania, in 1895. She founded the Philadelphia Clinical Laboratory in 1898, joined the U.S. Department of Agriculture in 1905 and became the Chief of its Food Research Lab in 1908. She did bacteriological analyses for subscribing doctors and developed milk and dairy standards, including checklist procedures for dairy herds that were adopted throughout the United States. She traveled the nation investigating the efficiency of refrigerator cars and recommended standards for construction and insulation.

A recognized authority on refrigeration and its effect on food products, Dr. Mary Engle Pennington spent more than forty years educating the government and the general public in the techniques and importance of proper handling of perishable food. In her later years she oversaw the design and construction of modern refrigerated warehouses, commercial and home refrigerators.

In 1923, Pennington was recognized by the American Society of Heating, Refrigeration and Air-conditioning Engineers (ASHRAE), as the foremost American authority on home refrigeration. She was profiled by the *New Yorker* as "Ice Woman" in 1941, was the first woman elected to the Poultry Historical Society Hall of Fame (1959), and was elected fellow by the American Society of Refrigerating Engineers in 1947.

Frances Perkins
1880–1965

From a comfortable background in Worcester, Massachusetts, Frances Perkins went to Mount Holyoke. There lecturers introduced her to the cause of social reform.

While teaching in Chicago, she spent her free time at Hull House and she began to move into the new field of social work. She witnessed the Triangle Shirtwaist fire in 1911. That tragedy stiffened her resolve to fight for better conditions for working people, especially women.

After her husband had to be confined to an institution, she proceeded to support herself and raise their young daughter alone. She made conscious compromises to succeed as a career woman, adopting a grandmotherly style of dress she felt was less threatening to men.

Perkins was appointed to Governor Al Smith's administration in Albany, serving on the Industrial Commission and the Bureau of Mediation and Arbitration. She continued to serve after Franklin Roosevelt was elected Governor. When FDR swept into the White House in 1932, he appointed Frances Perkins Secretary of Labor. She was the first woman cabinet officer in American history. After serving throughout Roosevelt's four terms, she continued to lecture and write, and taught at the Cornell School of Industrial and Labor Relations.

ℛ*ebecca Talbot Perkins*
1866–1956

Rebecca Talbot Perkins was a highly successful businesswoman who found time during a career of more than fifty years to engage in many philanthropic interests.

At the age of twenty-four, following her father's death from influenza, Perkins assumed leadership of the family's real estate brokerage. This was at a time when few women were in business and even fewer were running their own enterprises.

Not long after Perkins established herself in business, she became extremely active in charitable and civic work. In 1893, she joined the Brooklyn Women's Suffrage Society, a full quarter century before women gained the right to vote. For many years, she served as chair of the Alliance of Women's Clubs of Brooklyn and served as president of the People's Political League of Kings County. She was Vice President of the Memorial Hospital for Women and Children, and a director of the Welcome Home for Girls.

In 1921, Perkins was asked to find an adoptive family for an out-of-wedlock child. She placed an advertisement in a local paper seeking adoptive parents for the child. The many responses she received encouraged her to continue in this work. In 1927, a time when very few agencies existed to promote adoption, Perkins joined with the Alliance of Women's Clubs of Brooklyn to create The Rebecca Talbot Perkins Adoption Society. Later know as Talbot Perkins Children's Services, the organization provided foster care and adoption services to countless families across the country for seventy-five years. She served as the organization's president from 1927-1949, and honorary president until her death in 1956.

Over several decades, Perkins fought for causes including better schools, improvements in the courts, increased pay for civil service workers and expanded social services for women and children.

Esther Peterson
1906–1997

Throughout her life, Esther Peterson was a powerful and effective catalyst for change – for the labor movement, the women's movement and the consumer movement.

Peterson joined the staff of the Amalgamated Clothing Workers in the late l930s and later became the effective legislative representative of the AFL-CIO's Industrial Union Department. In 1961, she had her pick of positions in the Kennedy Administration and chose to head the Women's Bureau in the Department of Labor. As Assistant Secretary of Labor, she achieved the creation of the first presidential commission on women, headed initially by Eleanor Roosevelt. This pioneering group for the first time focused federal attention on the status and condition of women in the workplace. Peterson served Presidents Johnson and Carter as adviser in consumer affairs.

She continued to work actively in international affairs. On the occasion of her honoring by Radcliffe College Peterson said, "We have a tremendous responsibility to future generations to leave an accurate record of our history, one which lays bare not only the facts, but the process of change."

Photo: Boston Globe

Judith L. Pipher, Ph.D.
1940–

Dr. Judith L. Pipher, an infrared astronomer, has a career that people at the first women's rights convention, held in Seneca Falls in 1848, could not even imagine. Her work as an astrophysicist at two acclaimed universities, Cornell University and the University of Rochester, is a significant first among women's achievements.

Dr. Pipher, a native of Toronto, Ontario, Canada, graduated from the University of Toronto where she majored in astronomy. After graduation, she moved to the Finger Lakes region of New York State, and began graduate study at Cornell University in Ithaca. Along with her part-time study, she taught science classes at the high school and college level. Her doctoral study led her to research in the new field of infrared and submillimeter astronomy. She became the first woman to pursue this brand new research into ultra sensitive light detection of celestial bodies.

She received her Ph.D. from Cornell in 1971 and then joined the faculty of the Physics and Astronomy Department at the University of Rochester, where she became the founder of a group of observational infrared astronomers. For the next 31 years she taught full time at the University of Rochester and continued her astronomy research, which included a highly successful and frequently imitated partnership between academic and industrial research groups.

As one of the first US astronomers to turn an infrared array to the skies, she and her colleagues in 1983 were able to take the first telescopic infrared pictures of the moon. After her retirement as a full-time professor in 2002, the same year she received the Susan B. Anthony Lifetime Achievement Award, her involvement in infrared technology continued.

In 2003 the NASA Spitzer Space Telescope was launched. Dr. Pipher helped design this telescope which features infrared detectors. It is being used to study clusters of forming stars and brown dwarfs, huge planet-like objects too dark to be detected by telescopes on the ground.

Dr. Pipher is a member of numerous astronomical organizations and the author of more than 150 scientific articles and papers. She has chaired or served on a number of national committees that determine astrophysics funding for NASA and the National Science Foundation.

Jeannette Rankin
1880–1973

Jeannette Rankin was the first woman elected to the U.S. Congress, serving two separate terms. She injected the first woman's voice into national political debates. A committed pacifist, Rankin was the only member of Congress to oppose entry of the United States into both World Wars.

Rankin, a lifelong Montana resident, was active in the woman suffrage movement in the West, and campaigned for election to Congress after her state gave women the right to vote. In Congress she sponsored legislation to provide federal voting rights and health services to women. Her anti-war vote in 1917 cost her her office, and she devoted much of the remainder of her life to pacifist causes.

She held leadership roles in the Women's Inter-national League for Peace and Freedom and other groups. In 1940 she ran again for Congress on an isolationist platform and in 1941 was the sole Member to oppose the declaration of war on Japan.

She later traveled extensively, studying with Ghandi, among others. She was, at age 86, a proud marcher in the Jeannette Rankin Brigade in the March on Washington to oppose the Vietnam War.

Janet Reno
1938–

Janet Reno, the first female Attorney General of the United States, has had a life filled with "firsts." Reno graduated from Cornell University in 1960 with a degree in chemistry, having worked her way through school as a waitress and dormitory supervisor. She then earned her law degree from Harvard Law School in 1963, one of sixteen women in a class of more than 500. She eventually became a partner in a law firm that had previously denied her a position because she was a woman.

Her first entry into government work was in 1971 as staff director of the Judiciary Committee of the Florida House of Representatives, where she helped revise the Florida court system. In 1978, she became the first woman to head a county prosecutor's office in Florida. As Dade County State Attorney, Reno was the first Florida prosecutor to assign lawyers to collect child-support payments from deadbeat fathers. Winning election for four terms as a Democrat in the heavily conservative, Republican Dade County, Reno helped establish the Miami Drug Court, which has served as a model for other courts, helped reform the juvenile justice system, and focused attention on needed prevention programs for children.

Appointed United States Attorney General by President Clinton in 1993,

Reno worked to reduce crime and violence; to enhance prevention and early intervention efforts to keep children away from gangs, drugs, and violence; to enforce civil rights to ensure equal opportunities for all; to prosecute violations of ecological statutes; and to build a Justice Department that strives for excellence and professionalism. She faced many controversial decisions, including the confrontation with the Branch Davidian religious cult in Waco, Texas. Despite some attacks on Reno for this action, Reno won respect from average Americans by unflinchingly taking responsibility for the operation. Similarly, Reno made the difficult decision to raid the home of Elian Gonzalez's relatives so the six-year old Cuban could be returned to his father's custody. Again, some tried to second-guess Reno's decision, but she remained firm.

Reno's childhood taught her to strive for excellence as well as stand for absolute honesty. Her father was a crusading reporter for the *Miami Herald* while her mother, also a journalist, built the family's home and was known to wrestle alligators. Significantly, her mother influenced her with this homily: "Good, better, best. Don't ever rest until good is better and better is best."

Ellen Swallow Richards
1842–1911

Ellen Swallow Richards was the first woman professional chemist in the nation, and played a major role in opening scientific education and the scientific professions to women. Applying scientific principles to domestic life, she pioneered the new study and profession of home economics, a major opportunity at the time for higher education and employment or American women.

The first woman to study at the Massachusetts Institute of Technology, Richards developed MIT's Women's Laboratory. Her innovative studies of air, water and food led to the creation of national public health standards and the new disciplines of sanitary engineering and nutrition.

The interaction between people and their environment led this visionary to predict future environmental crises and to advance the concept of ecology as an environmental science – an idea not widely accepted until almost a century passed.

Richards was central to the founding of the American Home Economics Association and served as the group's first president. She was one of the founders of what is today the American Association of University Women.

Linda Richards
1841–1930

The recipient of the first diploma awarded by the nation's first school of nursing, Linda Richards recognized the nation's need for professionally-trained nurses and dedicated her life's work toward the creation of training institutions to meet that need, in hospitals, homes and communities.

Richards' mission began when she struggled to find competent nurses' training; after her education at the New England Hospital for Women and Children, she became superintendent of the new Boston Training School and developed a curriculum for the trainees and got them admission to work in all wards of the hospital.

She learned from Florence Nightingale in England, and later traveled to Japan to establish nursing schools. During her life, Richards established and headed a large number of training schools, and became the first president of the American Society of Superintendents of Training Schools. She also established special institutions for those with mental illness.

The nation's first professional nurse had transformed her profession, bringing the work of nursing from menial chores to the great caregiving profession of today.

Sally Ride, Ph.D.
1951–2012

In 1983, twenty-two years after the first United States manned space mission, Sally K. Ride became the first American woman in space. She was a mission specialist on the *Challenger*, the seventh space shuttle flight.

Ride had applied to be an astronaut in 1977 after seeing an announcement that NASA was looking for young scientists to serve as mission specialists on its shuttle flights. Previous astronauts had been military test pilots, but NASA was looking for scientists and technicians who could monitor the complex technology of the shuttle. Eight thousand people responded to the announcement, one thousand of them women. Six women, among them Sally Ride, were selected for a group of 35 new astronauts in 1978.

Becoming an astronaut had not been a lifelong goal for Ride. A talented athlete, she had considered a professional tennis career, but decided against it because, her mother says, she could not make the ball go exactly where she wanted it. Instead, she enrolled at Stanford University, graduating in 1973 with degrees in physics and English. She continued her studies in physics, earning a Ph.D. in astrophysics shortly before joining NASA.

As a mission specialist on the six-day *Challenger* mission, her responsibilities included testing a robot arm which deployed and retrieved satellites, assisting the commander and shuttle pilot during ascent, re-entry, and landing, and acting as flight engineer. She said of that flight, "The thing that I'll remember most about the flight is that it was fun. In fact, I'm sure it was the most fun I'll ever have in my life." Ride flew into space again in 1984. In 1986, she was part of the presidential commission investigating the *Challenger* explosion.

In 1987, she left NASA to accept a fellowship at the Stanford University Center for International Security and Arms Control. In 2001, Ride founded Sally Ride Science, an innovative science content company dedicated to supporting girls' and boys' interests in science, math and technology. Ride served as the organization's President & CEO.

The Honorable Rozanne L. Ridgway
1935–

Ambassador Rozanne L. Ridgway served over three decades as an American foreign policy leader. Her expertise as an international negotiator was demonstrated in complex multilateral and bilateral agreements that she negotiated on behalf of the U. S..

In the early 1970s, Ridgway skillfully negotiated longstanding issues over fishing rights in Brazil, Peru and the Bahamas. This led to her appointment in 1976 as the Deputy Assistant Secretary of State for Oceans and Fisheries. During her tenure, she negotiated the 200-mile fishing rights treaty. Ridgway's subsequent negotiations led to the return of property of U.S. citizens from Czechoslovakia, an arrangement that will provide the basis for similar negotiations with Cuba when relations are normalized.

Her success dealing with these issues – a complicated mix of domestic politics, economics, foreign policy and international security issues – prepared her for substantial contribution at the highest level of our government. As Special Assistant to the Secretary of State for Negotiations and, subsequently, the Assistant Secretary of State for Europe and Canada, she was the lead negotiator at all five Reagan/Gorbachev summits. These brought the first substantive reductions in nuclear weapons, signaled the beginning of the end of Communism and the Cold War, and established the fundamental realignment of global power as America prepared to enter the 21st century.

Between Ridgway's positions at the Department of State, she served as America's Ambassador to Finland from 1977 to 1980 and as the Ambassador to the German Democratic Republic between 1983 and 1985. She retired as Assistant Secretary of State for European and Canadian Affairs and sits on corporate boards.

$\mathscr{E}$dith Nourse Rogers
1881–1960

Edith Nourse Rogers, political leader and outstanding legislator from the 1920s through the 1950s, was most noted for her legislative initiatives on behalf of veterans and women.

Beginning as a volunteer Red Cross worker during World War I, Rogers became the presidential representative in charge of assisting disabled veterans for Presidents Harding, Coolidge, and Hoover. This background made her an outstanding legislator, beginning in 1925 when she was elected to the 69th Congress to complete her late husband's unfinished term. Going on to win 17 more elections, she became the longest-serving woman in the history of the House of Representatives.

Among her highest achievements was drafting a major portion of the G.I. Bill of Rights. It gave returning World War II veterans opportunities to go to college, obtain job training, and get low interest mortgages.

Even more visionary was her introduction of legislation, at the start of World War II, to establish the Women's Army Auxiliary Corps (WAAC). This allowed women to serve in the armed forces. Now women are important to all branches of the military. Rogers also fought against child labor, supported the 48-hour work week for women, and backed equal pay for equal work.

Photo: The Lowell Sun

Mother Mary Joseph Rogers, MM
1882–1955

A woman of extraordinary vision and drive, Mother Mary Joseph Rogers, MM, founded the Maryknoll Sisters, the first U. S.-based Catholic congregation of religious women dedicated to a global mission.

While studying zoology at Smith College, Rogers became inspired by graduating Protestant students who were soon leaving for missionary work in China. Following her graduation, she worked as an assistant in the Biology Department for two years and then taught in Boston's public schools. Shortly thereafter, Rogers returned to Smith and started a mission club for Catholic students. While organizing the club, she met Father James A. Walsh, director of Boston's Office for the Propagation of the Faith. Father Walsh was launching a mission magazine in which Rogers took immediate interest and volunteered her time to assist with production.

Nearly a decade later, Father Walsh co-founded Maryknoll Fathers & Brothers, and Rogers was selected as one of the "secretaries" to direct the group under his guidance. Rogers took the religious name Mother Mary Joseph and oversaw the growth of the congregation and its expansion into mission. In 1920, the group became recognized as the Maryknoll Sisters, a mission society of women that ministers to the humanitarian needs of all people, especially the poor, regardless of race, creed or color. While leading the mission, Mother Mary Joseph welcomed women from all nations, stressed the need for sisters to be compassionate women, and took care to integrate prayer with apostolic ministry.

Mother Mary Joseph was awarded honorary doctorates from Smith College, Trinity University and Regis College, Boston. By the time of her death in 1955, there were 1,065 sisters working in twenty countries and several cities in the United States. The Maryknoll Sisters became a Pontifical Institute in 1954 and the name of the Congregation was changed to Maryknoll Sisters of St. Dominic.

Eleanor Roosevelt
1884–1962

As a child, Eleanor Roosevelt was made to feel that she was an "ugly duckling." After losing both her parents, she was raised by her stern and proper grandmother, and her loneliness persisted until she was befriended by the headmistress at her boarding school. She "came out" into society, but preferred volunteer work at a settlement house to the social whirl.

In 1905 she married her cousin, Franklin Roosevelt, a marriage made more complex by her domineering mother-in-law, Sara. While raising six children, Eleanor Roosevelt gradually found the determination to abandon traditional roles in favor of political and reform work. She joined the League of Women Voters, worked with trade union women, and pressed for women's causes within the Democratic Party.

After Franklin Roosevelt was paralyzed by polio in 1921, her public activities expanded. She became his political repre-sentative, especially after he was elected governor of New York State in 1928. After her husband's landslide election in 1932, she feared the White House might encase her in sterile protocol. But her broad sympathies and great energy created a whole new image of what a First Lady could be.

Eleanor Roosevelt held her own press conferences, toured the nation repeatedly, and pressed her opinions through newspaper columns and radio broadcasts. In the dark days of the Depression she made Americans feel that someone cared and would try to help. Even though Franklin Roosevelt did not always follow her advice, she pressed the cause of black people, youth, the poor, and the unemployed.

After her husband's death in 1945, President Truman named her U.S. Delegate to the United Nations. The Universal Declaration of Human Rights, adopted in 1948, was largely her work, and the delegates rose in a standing ovation for her. Eleanor Roosevelt continued to be active in politics and in work for international cooperation. At a memorial service, Adlai Stevenson said: "She would rather light candles than curse the darkness, and her glow warmed the world."

Ernestine Louise Potowski Rose
1810–1892

Ernestine Rose, often cited by Susan B. Anthony as one of the early influential leaders of the women's suffrage movement was born in a ghetto in Russian Poland, She inherited substantial property at the death of her mother. As was the custom, her father assigned Rose and her dowry in marriage to a man his age, although her refusal to consent to the marraige was quite unusual.

Instead, Rose successfully persuaded Polish officials to grant her authority over her inheritance. In 1827, she left Poland, traveled across Europe, and married William Rose. The couple emigrated to the United States in 1836. Settling in New York, she took up the cause of the married women's property bill that had been introduced in the State Legislature.

In 1840, along with Paulina Wright Davis and Elizabeth Cady Stanton, Rose circulated petitions and spoke in support of the bill before a legislative committee in Albany. Because of strong opposition, twelve years elapsed before a limited version of the bill passed both houses of the Legislature.

During the 1850's, Rose focused her efforts on women's rights. In 1850, she attended the first national women's rights convention in Worcester, Massachusetts, where she introduced a resolution calling for "political, legal and social equality with man." For the next 20 years, she attended most national and state conventions and was frequently a recognized speaker. She lectured in more than twenty states, addressing legislative bodies on the issues of antislavery, temperance and freedom of thought, as well as women's rights. Her oratorical prowess led to her title, "Queen of the Platform."

During the Civil War, Rose found herself again in the company of Stanton as they worked together in the Women's Loyal National League and later in the American Equal Rights Association. In 1869, the pair, along with Susan B. Anthony, took the lead in transforming the Equal Rights Association into the National Women's Suffrage Association, an organization critical to the success of the women's suffrage movement in 1920.

Elaine Roulet
1930–

Sister Elaine Roulet spends her energy and creativity helping some of society's most sharply disadvantaged people – the children of women in prison.

A Sister of St. Joseph, Roulet has been family liaison with the Bedford Hills Correction Center in Bedford Hills, New York since 1970. In 1980 she became founder and executive director of Providence House, Inc., affiliated with Catholic Charities, which includes multiple sites offering shelter for battered women and families, homeless women, temporary housing for women released from prison, and more. In the same year Roulet founded and became director of the Children's Center at Bedford Hills, which includes a parenting center, children's playroom, nursery and infant center. She has created support programs for mothers and their babies in prison, where this unique program permits mothers whose babies are born in prison to keep them for as long as one year.

The Bedford Hills program has become a national model for prisons, overturning conventional wisdom about prisons, women and their children. Roulet says, "Some people say that babies shouldn't be in prison. The baby doesn't know he is prison, but he does know that he's with his mother."

ilma Rudolph
1940–1994

The first American woman ever to win three gold medals in the Olympics, Wilma Rudolph overcame major obstacles to make her mark in the record books and in life.

Rudolph contracted severe polio as a child. By age 16, she was an All-State basketball player and a bronze medalist in the 1956 Olympics. She attended Tennessee State University on a track scholarship, and returned for the 1960 Olympics – and Olympic glory, winning gold medals in the 100 meter dash, 200 meter dash and the 4 x 100 meter relay. She set world records in all three events.

She was named United Press Athlete of the Year (1960), the AP Woman Athlete of the Year (1960, 1961) and received the Sullivan Award as the nation's top amateur athlete (1961).

She has been inducted into the Women's Sports Hall of Fame and named one of five sports stars selected as America's Greatest Women Athletes by the Women's Sports Foundation, she is in the Black Sports Hall of Fame and the U.S. Olympic Hall of Fame. Rudolph gave women's track a strong boost in America.

Since her competition days, she has written a best-selling autobiography, *Wilma*, and created the Wilma Rudolph Foundation to train young athletes. The "fastest woman in the world" inspired many with her life story.

Induction Year: 1995

Josephine St. Pierre Ruffin
1842–1924

An African-American leader from New England who was a suffragist, fought slavery, recruited African-American soldiers to fight for the North in the Civil War, and founded and edited a magazine, Josephine Ruffin is best known for her central role in starting and sustaining the role of clubs for African-American women.

The wife of the first African-American man to graduate from Harvard Law School and who became the first African-American municipal judge, Ruffin raised four children and was actively involved in the Civil War and African-American rights. She also served on the Board of the Massachusetts Moral Education Association and the Massachusetts School Suffrage Association, working closely with other New England women leaders, including Julia Ward Howe and Lucy Stone.

Her particular interest was the development of African-American women in New England and nationwide, and in 1894 she organized the Women's Era Club, among the very first African-American women's organizations.

In 1895, she convened in Boston a conference of representatives of other national groups, which organized the National Federation of Afro-American Women. Its mission was to demonstrate the existence of a large number of educated, cultured African-American women. At its founding meeting she said, "…we are women, American women, as intensely interested in all that pertains to us as such as all other American women; we are not alienating or withdrawing, we are only coming to the front, willing to join any others in the same work and welcoming any others to join us."

In 1896 this group merged with the Colored Women's League of Washington, forming the National Association of Colored Women; Ruffin was elected first vice-president. Continued resistance of all-white national women's clubs reinforced her commitment to the importance of the African-American clubwomen's movement, and she remained an active participant through-out her life.

Ruffin was also active in the founding of the Boston branch of the National Association for the Advancement of Colored People, and of the League of Women for Community Service.

Mary Harriman Rumsey
1881–1934

The founder of The Junior League, Mary Harriman Rumsey, was a young woman ahead of her time. The daughter of Union Pacific Railroad titan and financier, E.H. Harriman, she used her life of privilege as a platform for social reform. Mary saw an untapped resource in her debutante friends and seized the opportunity to revolutionize the experience of young women being introduced to society. Within the debutante system she saw a self-perpetuating supply of volunteers who could enrich their own lives by becoming involved in improving social conditions in their city. In 1901, 80 young women came together in New York City and formed the first Junior League as The Junior League for the Promotion of Settlement Movements.

Building on her idea, Ms. Rumsey and the League's leaders brought together experts on the Settlement Movement to provide lectures and instruction to Junior League members, thus designing the archetype of a new kind of civic leadership: volunteer-driven social services and policies grounded in education and intense training from subject-area experts. This model allowed knowledgeable volunteers to fill gaps left by government agencies, private corporations, and individual philanthropists. Her legacy can be seen in the many social service programs that exist in Junior League communities today: domestic violence shelters, children's museums, mentoring and self-esteem workshops, human trafficking awareness campaigns, support hotlines, advocacy for incarcerated juveniles, literacy programs, food pantries, nutritional and fitness counseling, community gardens, environmental clean-up efforts, education for immigrants, and enacted legislation at various levels of government.

Resulting from her League work, she was appointed by President Franklin D. Roosevelt as the Chair of the first consumer's rights group, The Consumer Advisory Board of the National Recovery Administration. She helped author the Social Security Act and was instrumental in the enactment of the 1946 National School Lunch Act, modeled in part on a similar program developed by The Junior League. An updated version of this law remains in place today.

Today, The Junior League is one of the oldest, largest, and most effective women's volunteer organizations, encompassing more than 150,000 women in 292 Leagues in the United States, Canada, Mexico and the United Kingdom.

*F*lorence Sabin, M.D.
1871–1953

She was born in the Colorado mining country, where her father was an engineer, but brought up in New England after the death of her mother. Hers was the first generation to benefit from the long struggle to open higher education to women.

She graduated in early classes at Smith College and Johns Hopkins Medical School. Unlike many women pioneering in the professions, she was fortunate to find a sympathetic mentor in her anatomy professor, Franklin Mall. He stimulated her interest in anatomy when the field was just beginning to be experimental rather than merely descriptive. Sabin proved an extremely talented researcher.

She won one of four highly prized internships at Johns Hopkins Hospital, and eventually joined the faculty at Johns Hopkins. Dr. Sabin rose to the rank of full professor in 1917, the first woman in the university to achieve that rank. She worked on embryology and did important research on the origins of the lymphatic system. She also brought back from Germany a new technique for non-toxic staining of cells.

In 1925 she became the first woman elected to the National Academy of Science. She went on to do research in tuberculosis at the Rockefeller Institute. Although Sabin retired in 1938, in her seventies she took up another highly successful career, as a reforming public health official in her native state of Colorado.

$\mathscr{S}$acagawea
C.1788–UNKNOWN

Sacagawea (Sacajawea, Sakakawea), famed Native American woman whose land survival expertise and interpretive abilities were essential to the success of the Lewis and Clark Expedition, was born in a northern Shoshone village near the Lemhi River valley, in what is today Idaho. Between her tenth and twelfth year, she was taken to live among the Hidatsas of the Knife River area, modern day North Dakota.

In April 1805, Sacagawea, her husband Toussaint Charbonneau and their infant son, Jean Baptiste (Pomp), left Fort Mandan with the Lewis and Clark Expedition to explore the western lands recently acquired in the 828,000 square mile Louisiana Purchase. Considered at first to be simply Charbonneau's wife who possessed specific native language interpretation abilities, Sacagawea became one of the most valuable members of the Corps.

Sacagawea helped supply the Corps with food foraged from the wild, roots, berries and other edibles. She was very calm and collected in crises and saved valuable records, instruments and other supplies when one of their boats almost capsized. Saving Clark's journals preserved the history of the expedition for future generations.

Lewis and Clark knew in advance that they would need the skills of a Shoshone interpreter when they would have to negotiate for horses to take them through the mountains. In August of 1805, west of the Continental Divide, when the expedition needed to secure horses, Sacagawea was joyfully reunited with her brother, Cameahwait. He provided horses and guides to the Expedition, assisting their journey across the Bitterroot Mountains and through the Salmon River country to the Clearwater and Columbia Rivers. In November 1805, the Corps reached the shores of the Pacific and Sacagawea saw the "great waters."

Though her later life is shrouded in mystery and controversy, Sacagawea's documented skill, determination, courage, and insight on the Expedition live on as an outstanding model and feat of great achievement.

Bernice Resnick Sandler, Ed.D.

1928–

For more than four decades, Dr. Bernice Resnick Sandler has been a tireless advocate of educational equality for women and girls.

From 1969-1971, Dr. Sandler served as the Chair of the Action Committee for Federal Contract Compliance of the Women's Equity Action League. In this position, she filed charges of sex discrimination against 250 educational institutions using a little-known federal Executive Order prohibiting contractors from discriminating against employees. It was this strategy that led to the first federal investigations of campus sex discrimination at a time when no laws existed to prohibit discrimination based on gender in education.

Subsequently, Sandler was instrumental in the development, passage and implementation of Title IX, the legislation that prohibits discrimination on the basis of sex in any federally funded education program or activity. Working closely with Representative Edith Green (D-OR) in 1970, Dr. Sandler organized and testified at the first congressional hearing dealing specifically with sex discrimination in education and employment.

In that same year, Dr. Sandler served as the Educational Specialist for the House of Representatives Special Subcommittee on Education, making her the first woman ever appointed to a Congressional committee staff to work specifically on women's issues. In 1971, she wrote the education section for the first federal policy report on sex discrimination in education. In 1975, Dr. Sandler was appointed by Presidents Ford and Carter as the first Chair of the National Advisory Council on Women's Educational Programs.

Today, Dr. Sandler serves as a Senior Scholar in Residence at the Women's Research and Education Institute in Washington, DC. An expert in strategies and policies to prevent and respond to sex discrimination in higher education, she has given more than 2,500 presentations. Dr. Sandler is the recipient of numerous awards, including twelve honorary degrees.

Margaret Sanger
1879–1966

Margaret Higgins learned from her nonconformist father to be a rebel and to reject prejudice.

She married William Sanger, an architect, but after three children and ten years in an affluent Westchester suburb, she yearned for more. The Sangers moved to New York City and plunged into the world of bohemian radicalism in Greenwich Village.

Perhaps the radical activist Emma Goldman first introduced her to the issue of birth control. Margaret Sanger worked as a visiting nurse on the Lower East Side. She always said that a poor woman named Sadie Sachs, dying after trying to end an unwanted pregnancy, made her determined to take up the fight.

Sanger published *The Women Rebel*, a newspaper advocating birth control, and when indicted for sending "obscene" materials through the mails, she fled to Europe and gathered information there.

In 1916 she opened a clinic in Brooklyn, was arrested, and served thirty days for distributing information about contraceptives. From then on, Sanger assumed leadership of the struggle for free access to birth control. She was persuasive, tireless, singleminded, and unafraid of a fight. Her arguments might vary – at first she saw birth control as part of a socialist reordering of society, later as a means to prevent the multiplication of the inflicted or to assure happy marriages. But always Sanger saw it as a woman's issue and she was prepared to take on the medical establishment, the churches, the legislatures, and the courts.

Katherine Siva Saubel
1920–2011

Katherine Siva Saubel dedicated her life to the preservation of the language and culture of her people. She was a nurturer, scholar, educator, museum founder, author, social activist and inspirational leader to all who knew her.

Saubel, a Cahuilla Indian, grew up in poverty on reservations in Southern California. At school, speaking her native language was punished, as was opposing how her people were portrayed in history. The first Indian girl to graduate from Palm Springs High School, Saubel's further education continued after marriage and child-rearing. Scholarships helped her learn anthropology.

In 1964, she and others founded the Malki Museum at the Morongo Reservation, the first Native American museum created and managed by Native Americans. Saubel collaborated with scholars and produced books and articles on ethnobiology, Cahuilla grammar and other topics, beginning with *Kunvachmal: A Cahuilla Tale* in 1969. Saubel's answer to pressure on Native Americans to abandon their language and beliefs to conform to society was to dedicate her life to preserving both – and with it, her people's dignity.

Betty Bone Schiess
1923–

Through persistence, leadership and wisdom, Betty Bone Schiess led the successful effort to have women ordained priests in the Episcopal Church in America, elevating the position of women in the Church, and in society.

Schiess, an ordained deacon in the Church in 1972, was one of the 11 women ordained priests in 1974. Her efforts and those of her colleagues have made it possible for girls and women to serve at all levels in the Church – impossible before "the Philadelphia Eleven" made their stand for equality.

Trained at the University of Cincinnati, Syracuse University and the Rochester Center for Theological Studies, Schiess was a chaplain at Syracuse University (1976-78) and Cornell University (1978-79) as well as rector of Grace Episcopal Church in Mexico, New York from 1984-89. She has been advisor to Women in Mission and Ministry of the Episcopal Church in the United States since 1987. She has received the Governor's Award for Women of Merit in Religion (1984), the Ralph Kharas Award of the ACLU and other awards. She is past president of the International Association of Women Ministers.

℘atricia Schroeder, J.D.
1940–

During her twelve terms in Congress, Patricia Schroeder made an indelible mark on our times through her trailblazing leadership in the House of Representatives, where she worked tirelessly to establish national family policy, including issues like parental leave, child care, family planning, and more. She was also a leader in foreign and military policy, serving on the House National Security Committee, the House Judiciary Committee and chaired the Select Committee on Children, Youth and Families.

Schroeder, who earned a law degree from Harvard University, was first elected from Colorado in 1972 and continued to serve her constituency until she announced her retirement in late 1995.

One of the few women in modern times to become a candidate for the Presidency, Schroeder has always been an outspoken advocate for what she calls "work and family issues," in recognition of the fact that issues concerning women inevitably impact all families.

She wrote and introduced the now-enacted Family and Medical Leave Act in 1985, and was a primary advocate to enact legislation and secure funding for key legislation to support women's health research. One of the nation's most respected women, Patricia Schroeder was not only a sophisticated and successful legislator; she embodies an unblinking commitment to represent the interests of women and their families at the highest levels of government, and do all in her power to see that those interests are served. She does not apologize for her feminism and her advocacy. As she expressed it to The New York Times in 1977, "I have a brain and a uterus, and I use both."

Anna Jacobson Schwartz, Ph.D.
1915–2012

Perhaps the most widely acclaimed female research economist of the twentieth century, Anna Jacobson Schwartz has been described as "one of the world's greatest monetary scholars."

Anna Jacobson became interested in economics while attending Walton High School. She graduated from Barnard College and went on to earn her Master's Degree in Economics from Columbia University. In 1936, she began her professional career with Columbia University's Social Science Research Council. Schwartz returned to Columbia University and earned a Ph.D..

Dr. Schwartz's first published paper, "British Share Prices, 1811-1850," written with Arthur Gayer and Isaiah Finklestein was published in the 1940 issue of *The Review of Economics and Statistics*. The paper was a precursor to much of her subsequent work, meticulous in the presentation, explanation and interpretation of data.

In 1941, Dr. Schwartz began a more than seventy-year tenure working for the National Bureau of Economic Research. It was during this time that she met and began working with economist Milton Friedman. Together, the two coauthored *A Monetary History of the United States, 1867 – 1960*, which was described by Federal Reserve chairman, Ben Bernanke, as "the leading and most persuasive explanation of the worst economic disaster in American history." The massive study demonstrated that changes in monetary policy have large effects on the economy and blamed a large portion of the Great Depression on the Federal Reserve; it is one of the most widely cited texts in economics today.

In 1981, Dr. Schwartz served as the Executive Director of the United States Gold Commission, a panel that was responsible for recommending the future of gold in the nation's monetary system. In 1988, she was president of the Western Economic Association.

Considered a leading financial historian and expert on monetary statistics in the United States and Britain, Dr. Schwartz authored and co-authored several publications during her lifetime. Her work demonstrated the importance of the behavior of the money supply and the importance of that behavior being stable and predictable, forever changing the entire approach to economic policy making.

Felice N. Schwartz
1925–1996

Felice N. Schwartz, a prolific writer and organizer, helped provide women with better access to the workplace and especially the top levels of corporate America.

Schwartz's several books and articles convinced major companies that it was more cost-effective to offer flexible schedules for women than fire a woman manager and train a replacement. Her work was sometimes controversial, such as her call for what was dubbed "the mommy track" by the media, but it always heightened awareness of women's career conflicts.

In 1962, Schwartz founded Catalyst, a national organization to help women re-enter the work force and help companies find women board members. In the 1960s, women represented less than 35% of the workforce. Near the end of the century, they comprised over 46%. From 1977 to 1997, the numbers of women on Fortune 500 company boards grew from 46 to over 400.

Schwartz's Catalyst efforts, her pioneering research on job-sharing, dual career couples, parental leave, and other such issues have changed corporate America. Such changes have removed barriers to women's upward mobility.

Blanche Stuart Scott
1889–1970

Blanche Stuart Scott, a pioneering aviator of indomitable spirit of adventure, became the first woman to drive across the United States and the first woman to fly in America.

When she accomplished her transcontinental auto trip, there were only 218 miles of paved roads outside of cities. The publicity led to a contract for her to learn to fly with the newly created Glenn Curtiss Exhibition Company. In August and September of 1910, she took to the air in Hammondsport, NY. On October 23, 1910, she made her first public flight and the first professional appearance of a woman aviator in the country at Fort Wayne, IN.

In those years, there was no formal training for aviators and discrimination against women was widespread. She virtually had to teach herself in dangerous and unstable aircraft, and had no career path to look forward to in the industry or the military. Yet, she launched herself into a career of firsts in fields that were completely male-dominated, new and dangerous. Most of her contemporaries felt that "if God had wanted a woman to fly, He would have given her wings." It was 1910, women couldn't vote and society still believed woman's place was in the home.

Blanche Stuart Scott's life spanned the era when airplanes were just being invented and given trials, to the moment she saw Neil Armstrong walk on the Moon. She set a long distance flying record for women of 10 miles on July 30, 1911 and then a 25-mile record in August 1911. She performed the lead role in the first movie made about flying, *The Aviator's Bride*.

In 1912, she joined aviator and designer Glenn Martin and as a Martin employee became the first woman test pilot in America. She participated in many exhibitions in the west as the headliner and became the nation's first woman stunt pilot, the "Tomboy of the Air." Accidents and fatalities were frequent in aviation's early years and Scott suffered an accident in 1913 that caused serious injury. It took her a year to recover. She made few flights after that and retired from active flying in 1916.

Her subsequent career included screenwriting and many years as a radio personality, but her passionate interest in flying never abated. In September 1948, she became the first woman passenger to ride in a jet plane. The Aeronautics Association of the United States honored her in 1953. In 1954, Scott became a consultant to the United States Air Force Museum and is credited with helping the institution acquire more than $1,000,000 worth of early aviation artifacts. On the 50th anniversary of her first flight, she was honored by the Antique Airplane Association. The U.S. Postal Service honored her with a commemorative stamp in 1980.

Florence B. Seibert, Ph.D.
1897–1991

During her long and distinguished career, Florence Seibert made important contributions to science and to the advancement of medicine. Because of her work it became possible to test accurately for tuberculosis, and intravenous drug therapy became safe.

Dr. Seibert succeeded in isolating Purified Protein Derivative, thus making possible the isolation of the active substance of pure tuberculin. This work, done in the l930s, is now the international standard for tuberculin made in the world. She perfected a new distillation process that eliminated pyrogens (fever producing chemicals) from the distilled water used in intravenous therapy, thus making that therapy safe.

Seibert worked until her retirement at the Henry Phipps Institute of the University of Pennsylvania. After retirement she volunteered for 13 more years in programs examining the etiology of cancer.

Photo: Smithsonian Institution Archives

St. Elizabeth Bayley Seton
1774–1821

The first American-born saint of the Roman Catholic Church, Elizabeth Bayley Seton's early life experiences shaped her faith. She lost her mother at the age of three. At the age of nineteen, she married William Seton and began a family of her own.

Years later, William took ill with tuberculosis and the family traveled to Italy in search of renewed health. Shortly after arrival, William passed away. Elizabeth remained in Italy with the Filicchi family who shared with her their strong Catholic beliefs. Long a pious member of the Episcopal Church, Seton converted to Catholicism in 1805, a year after her return to New York City. She was promptly disinherited, and anti-Catholic prejudice made it difficult for her to support herself and her children.

In 1809, she moved to Baltimore, Maryland and began a school for Catholic girls. The school's existence was short-lived. Later that same year, Seton took her first vows and received the title of "Mother." The vows were for a new order that would be known as the Sisters of Charity, the first American Catholic sisterhood. Mother Seton proved an inspired leader and her order quickly grew. Seton next accepted an invitation to start a school in Emmitsburg, Maryland. In 1810, she established St. Joseph's School, deriving income from boarding students to provide free schooling to needy girls of the local parish. This work led to Mother Seton being widely recognized as the foundress of the parochial school system in the United States.

In 1882, it was suggested that her cause for canonization be proposed. Investigative work began in 1907 and culminated with her beatification in 1963. At that time, Pope John XXIII named her "the flower of sanctity which the United States of America offers to the world." Mother Seton was canonized a Saint by Pope Paul VI on September 14, 1975.

$\mathscr{D}$onna E. Shalala, Ph.D.
1941–

A groundbreaking educator and politician, Dr. Donna E. Shalala has more than thirty years of experience as an accomplished scholar, teacher and administrator.

Shalala received her A.B. in history from Western College for Women in 1962. From 1962 - 1964, she served as one of the country's first Peace Corps volunteers in Iran. She earned her M.S.Sc. in 1968 and her Ph.D. in 1970 from The Maxwell School of Citizenship and Public Affairs at Syracuse University.

Dr. Shalala became an Assistant Professor at Bernard Baruch College and later at Teachers College, Columbia University. From 1980 - 1987, Dr. Shalala served as the President of Hunter College. In 1987, she became the first woman to lead a Big Ten school as the Chancellor of the University of Wisconsin-Madison, a position she held until 1993.

In 1993, President Clinton appointed Dr. Shalala U.S. Secretary of Health and Human Services. During her eight-year tenure, she directed the welfare reform process, made health insurance available to millions of children, raised child immunization rates to the highest levels in history, led major reforms of the Food and Drug Administration's approval process and food safety systems, and more. Dr. Shalala is recognized as the longest serving U.S. Secretary of Health and Human Services, and was described by *The Washington Post* as "one of the most successful government managers of modern times."

From 2001-2015, Dr. Shalala served as the President of the University of Miami. Under her leadership, the university solidified its position as one of the top research universities in the United States and continues to rise in national rankings.

Dr. Shalala serves on corporate boards and has received many honors. In 2005, she was named one of America's Best Leaders by *U.S. News and World Report* and the Center for Public Leadership at Harvard University's Kennedy School of Government. In 2007, President George W. Bush selected Dr. Shalala to co-chair, with Senator Bob Dole, the commission on Care for Returning Wounded Warriors. In 2008, she was awarded the Presidential Medal of Freedom.

The Reverend Doctor Anna Howard Shaw

1847–1919

The Reverend Doctor Anna Howard Shaw, minister, physician, ardent feminist, and masterful orator, worked to improve individual morality through her ministry, tried to improve society by moving into the temperance and suffrage movements, and finally campaigned vigorously for the League of Nations to promote world peace.

Essentially self-taught, Shaw's first career, to help support her family, was as a frontier school teacher. At the age of twelve, Shaw had to assume the burden of the survival of her semi-invalid mother and her siblings.

After the Civil War, she was able to move into the home of a married sister and attend high school. She became active in the Methodist church, preaching her first sermon when she was twenty-three and becoming a licensed to preach a year later. In 1873, she entered Albion College, paying for her two years of education there by preaching and giving lectures on temperance. In 1876, she left Albion to attend Boston Theological Seminary. Upon graduation, in 1878, as the only woman in her class, she took charge of a church in East Dennis, Massachusetts, but the General Conference of the Methodist Episcopal Church refused her application for ordination because she was a woman. It also took steps to revoke her preaching license. Finally, in 1880, Shaw convinced the Methodist Protestant Church to grant her ordination so she could administer the sacraments and continue her ministry in East Dennis. In addition to ministering at two churches, Shaw earned a medical degree from Boston University in 1886. However, she never practiced medicine. Instead, she resigned her pastorates in 1885 to take up the banners of temperance and women's suffrage. From the 1880s until her death in 1919, Shaw worked at the grass roots level throughout the country to achieve women's suffrage. For a few years she headed the Franchise Department of the Woman's Christian Temperance Union. In 1904 she became president of the National American Woman Suffrage Association. During World War I, Shaw turned her attention to foreign affairs. She became chair of the Woman's Committee of the U. S. Council of National Defense, coordinating women's contributions to the war effort. For this work, in 1919 she became the first woman to earn the Distinguished Service Medal. At the end of the war, at the request of President Wilson and former President Taft, she lectured in the United States and Europe in support of world peace and the League of Nations. It was during one of those speaking tours that she fell ill and died in July, 1919, at the age of seventy-two.

While Shaw died just before the Women's Suffrage Amendment was ratified, she fulfilled her vision of success: "Nothing bigger can come to a human being than to love a great cause more than life itself."

Catherine Filene Shouse
1896–1994

A philanthropist and patron of the arts, Catherine Filene Shouse is best remembered for her establishment of Wolf Trap National Park for the Performing Arts. It was because of her significant donations of family land in 1961 and 1966, that this one-of-kind center exists today. She later funded an amphitheater on the site named the Filene Center, in honor of her Boston retailing family.

As a result of her college efforts at Wheaton College to promote jobs for educated women, she was hired by the Women's Division of the Employment Service of the U. S. Department of Labor. She later enrolled at the Harvard Graduate School of Education and in 1923 became the recipient of the school's first degree awarded to a woman.

In 1931, she married Jouett Shouse, a former congressman from Kansas. During her residence in the nation's capital, Shouse became active in Democratic Party politics and was the first woman ever appointed to the Democratic National Committee. In 1926, President Coolidge appointed her the first chairwoman of the first federal prison for women. There, she used her educational background to establish a job-training program for prisoners.

During the next 20 years she developed a highly successful dog-breeding kennel at Wolf Trap and at the same time became very involved in the music and cultural scene in Washington. She was on the board of the National Symphony Orchestra, serving as vice-president for 17 years. In 1959, President Eisenhower appointed her to the first board of the National Cultural Center, now the John F. Kennedy Center for the Performing Arts, where she served for more than 20 years.

Her many years of philanthropic support of the arts earned Shouse many honors including Dame Commander of the British Empire from Queen Elizabeth II. The highest U.S. civilian award, the Presidential Medal of Freedom, was awarded to Shouse in 1977 by President Gerald R. Ford.

Eunice Kennedy Shriver
1921–2009

For more than thirty years, Eunice Kennedy Shriver served as a leader in the worldwide struggle to enhance the lives of people with intellectual disabilities.

After her graduation from Stanford University, she worked for the U.S. State Department in the Special War Problems Division, and later became a social worker. Relocating to Chicago, Illinois in 1951, Shriver worked with the House of the Good Shepherd and the Chicago Juvenile Court.

In 1957, Shriver took over leadership of the Joseph P. Kennedy, Jr. Foundation, named in honor of her late brother. During her tenure, the foundation aided in the creation of The President's Committee on Mental Retardation (1961) as well as the development of the National Institute for Child Health and Human Development (1962).

Throughout the late 1950s and early 1960s, Shriver visited institutions for people with intellectual disabilities. Appalled by the treatment of these individuals and motivated by the notion that given the right opportunities, they would be more capable than commonly believed, she began Camp Shriver in 1962. At the summer day camp, held at her home, Shriver led attendees through a variety of physical activities. It was here that the Camp Shriver concept – through sports people with intellectual disabilities can realize their potential for growth – was developed. The concept began to spread, and in 1968, the first International Special Olympics Games were held in Chicago. At the ceremony, Shriver announced the creation of a national program, the Special Olympics, formed to give people with intellectual disabilities "the chance to play, the chance to compete and the chance to grow."

Shrivel was the recipient of many honors, including the Presidential Medal of Freedom (1984), the nation's highest civilian award. In 2009, the U.S. National Portrait Gallery unveiled a historic painting of Shriver; this work was the gallery's first commissioned portrait of an individual who has not served as a U.S. President or First Lady.

Today, Shriver's legacy lives on through the Special Olympics.

$\mathcal{M}$uriel Siebert
1928–2013

Known as the "First Woman of Finance", Muriel Siebert forever left her mark on the business world when she became the first woman, among 1,365 men, to own a seat on the New York Stock Exchange (NYSE).

Siebert began her career as a $65 a week research trainee at Bache & Company and worked her way up through various brokerages. In 1967, she established her own firm, Muriel Siebert & Company, Inc., doing research for institutions and buying and selling financial analyses. In 1975, when members of the NYSE were first permitted to negotiate broker commissions, Siebert transformed her company into the nation's first discount brokerage.

In 1977, Siebert left her firm for five years to become the first female Superintendent of Banking for the State of New York, responsible for oversight of all banks and other financial institutions within the state. During her tenure, she often acted boldly and controversially to launch protective measures to ensure the safety of state banks. Despite the common nationwide failures of financial institutions, not one New York State bank failed during Siebert's term.

In 1990, Siebert expanded her philanthropic reach with the creation of the Siebert Entrepreneurial Philanthropic Program. Through the program, she shared half of her firm's profits from new securities underwriting with charities of the issuer's choice.

While serving as president of the New York Women's Agenda in 1999, Siebert developed a Personal Finance Program to provide youth with financial management skills. The program is currently being taught in New York City Schools and has been distributed by the Council of Great City Schools. It was her hope that the program will one day be established nationally.

Siebert continued to oversee the day to day operations at the seven branches of her firm until her death, ensuring that her contributions as a businesswoman and philanthropist will shape our nation for years to come.

Beverly Sills
1929–2007

Beverly Sills, from her professional debut at the age of three as Bubbles Silverman on Uncle Bob's Rainbow House radio show, made the performing arts accessible to generations of Americans. With her brilliant runs and trills, she became one of the most beloved and respected sopranos in the 20th century.

Sills delighted audiences around the world with her talent and charisma. A member of the New York City Opera from 1955 to 1980, she performed in the world's leading opera houses, recorded 18 full-length operas and numerous solo collections, and appeared in hundreds of television programs. In addition to the many awards for her albums, Sills received four Emmys for her weekly television program, *Lifestyles with Beverly Sills*. Her autobiography, *Bubbles: A Self -Portrait*, became a bestseller.

Under her leadership at the New York City Opera, opera became accessible to the masses when she introduced to American audiences the use of subtitles for all foreign language productions – a method soon adopted in opera houses around the world.

After retirement from performing, Sills served as General Director and then President of the New York City Opera. In 1993, she became the first woman, the first performing artist and the first former head of an arts company to become chair of the Lincoln Center for the Performing Arts, which encompasses 11 world-renowned institutions, including the Metropolitan Opera, the New York Philharmonic and the New York City Ballet. Sills also was actively involved in a myriad of charities and organizations, including the National Victim Center, the Hebrew Home for the Aged at Riverdale, and the March of Dimes Mother's March on Birth Defects, for which she served as national chair. She was also a member of the boards of several foundations and corporations. Her many major awards included a Grammy, five Emmy nominations, honorary doctorates, other music-related awards as well as charitable and humanitarian awards.

Eleanor Smeal
1939–

As one of the co-founders of The Feminist Majority Foundation, a former president of the National Organization for Women, and publisher of Ms. Magazine, Eleanor Smeal's life and work has been dedicated to the achievement of women's equality and human rights. Known as a political analyst, strategist, and grassroots organizer, Ms. Smeal has played a pivotal role in defining the debate, developing the strategies, and charting the direction of the modern day women's movement. In her more than 40 years as a leader in the United States' women's movement, she has changed the landscape of women's involvement in national life and culture.

One of the modern architects of the drive for women's equality, Ms. Smeal's 1984 book, *How and Why Women Will Elect the Next President*, predicted that women's votes would be decisive in presidential politics. In this writing she was the first to identify the "gender gap", the difference in the way women and men vote, and popularized its usage in election and polling analyses to enhance women's voting clout. Her leading role in state and national campaigns for women's rights legislation, including the Equal Rights Amendment, helped reshape the contours of U.S. politics as politicians could no longer ignore the voices of women, forcing their inclusion as part of the national political discourse. Her efforts led to women's organizations shifting the strategy of targeting only a few select races for women candidates to a philosophy of recruiting women to run for as many elected offices as possible. Recognizing the power of the Internet, she pioneered its use as an organizing and research tool by launching the Feminist Majority Foundation Online in 1995.

At the forefront of nearly every significant women's rights victory, her participation was pivotal in the passage of landmark legislation including the Equal Credit Act, the Pregnancy Discrimination Act, and stronger enforcement of Title IX. She continues to work toward making Social Security and pensions more equitable for women, closure of the wage gap and achievement of pay equity for women who are segregated in low-paying jobs.

Ms. Smeal serves on a number of boards, including the National Council for Research on Women, the National Organization for Women, and the Leadership Circle of CEDAW (the Convention on the Elimination of all Forms of Discrimination Against Women).

*B*essie Smith
1894–1937

At the age of nine, Bessie Smith was singing on the streets of Chattanooga, Tennessee. She joined a traveling vaudeville show as a dancer, but it was soon apparent that her singing talent outshone her dance ability.

Inspired by Gertrude "Ma" Rainey, Bessie found that her deep, soulful voice was ideally suited to the new blues music. She quickly became a favorite entertainer on the theater circuit. In 1923, Columbia Records issued her first recording, *Down-Hearted Blues*, which was a huge success. She was soon the highest paid black entertainer in the country. She composed many of her own songs, and when she sang the blues, she sang of the American Black experience – suffering and joy, betrayal and courage.

An extraordinary talent, Bessie was given the title "Empress of the Blues" by her fans and her peers. Off-stage, Bessie Smith was a volatile personality with a zest for life. She enjoyed her fame, spending freely without thought for the future. In the 1930s, however, the Great Depression and talking movies crippled vaudeville and nearly killed the recording industry. This was a difficult period for her, although she continued to work.

In 1937 Bessie Smith had begun to stage a successful comeback, adapting her powerful voice to the new swing music. While on tour, she was fatally injured in a car accident. The greatest blues singer of her time, she left a musical legacy that grew as her recording inspired later performers.

Margaret Chase Smith
1897–1995

She was the daughter of a barber in Skowhegan, Maine. Unable to afford college, she pursued a career in office work at the telephone company and a weekly newspaper until, at the age of thirty-four, she married Clyde Harold Smith, a prominent Republican politician twenty-one years her senior.

When Smith was elected to the House of Representatives, Margaret served as his secretary. After he suffered a heart attack in 1940, she filed for the primary in his place, intending to withdraw when he recovered. His unexpected death left her heir to the Republican nomination, which nearly guaranteed election in the state of Maine.

Margaret Chase Smith went on to serve well and win repeated reelection in her own right. Her independent views were evident in her very first vote, defying isolationist sentiment in her party to support the draft. In 1948 she went after the newly vacant Senate seat and won a hotly contested Republican primary with a low budget grassroots campaign. She went on to serve four full terms in the "most exclusive men's club in the world," the U.S. Senate becoming the first woman to serve in both houses and the first woman to represent Maine in either house. She was famous for her early challenge of McCarthyism.

In 1950, she and six other Senators issued a "declaration of conscience" denouncing "hate and character assassination," though neglecting to mention Joseph McCarthy by name. She consistently supported a strong national defense and became known as the "Mother of the WAVES" for her efforts to advance the position of women in the Navy. She was a staunch cold warrior, charging that President Kennedy was afraid to stand up to the Communists and voting against the nuclear test ban treaty. In 1970 she issued a second "declaration of conscience," deploring the hatred and extremism of the Vietnam War era.

Sophia Smith
1796–1870

Sophia Smith, born in Hatfield, Massachusetts in 1796, was one of seven children of a prosperous and frugal New England farmer. As a young girl, Sophia strove to achieve the type of education generally closed to women in the early nineteenth century. She attended a local school and, for one term, an academy in Hartford, Connecticut. She then continued her education informally, reading widely throughout her life. Deaf by the age of forty, Sophia spent most of her time at home and involved with her church. By 1861, at the age of sixty-five, Sophia was the last of her immediate family. With careful management and wise investments, her brothers and uncles had increased the family wealth to a small fortune. Determined to do something meaningful with her money, Sophia consulted her pastor and others. Eventually, she decided to endow a woman's college, to be located in Northampton, Massachusetts. The college, she hoped, would provide the highest quality undergraduate education for young women – equal to that provided at the time for young men – thus enabling women to develop their intellects and talents and to participate effectively and fully in all areas of American society.

Upon her death in 1870, Sophia's bequest of nearly $400,000 became the foundation for the establishment of Smith College, which was chartered in 1871 and then opened its doors in 1875 with 14 students. Since it began, Smith College has been one of the most preeminent liberal arts colleges for women in the nation.

Since its humble beginnings in 1871, tens of thousands of women from around the world have attended Smith College. They have gone on to serve as leaders in their communities and their nations. Sophia Smith truly achieved her goal: to establish an institution of higher education for women that would impart an education by which women could "incalculably" enlarge "their power for good" by increasing their role in society and the economy and working to reform "the evils of society…as teachers, as writers, as mothers, [and] as members of society."

Induction Year: 1995

Hannah Greenebaum Solomon
1858–1942

As the visionary founder of the National Council of Jewish Women, Hannah Greenebaum Solomon spent her lifetime organizing communities to work cooperatively for social good. Solomon and her sister, Henriette Frank, were very active in Chicago social clubs and organizations, and were the first Jewish members of the Chicago Women's Club.

In 1890, Solomon was asked to organize a nationwide Jewish Women's Congress as part of the World's Fair. The Congress became the National Council of Jewish Women, to teach all Jewish women their obligations to their faith and to the community. Solomon was the Council's first president, encouraging local chapters to be founded nationwide. She was also involved in creating the Council of Women of the United States.

In 1904, Solomon journeyed to Berlin with her friend and fellow suffragist Susan B. Anthony for a convention of the International Council of Women. Solomon was a lifelong activist in Chicago, working with Jane Addams at Hull House, advocating for reform and improvements in child welfare, reforming the Illinois Industrial School for Girls, and even involving herself in improving the city's waste disposal systems. She established penny lunch stations in the public schools, and placed the first probation officers for juvenile delinquents in the courts.

During World War I, she was chairperson of all Chicago City ward leaders, dealing successfully with the city's forty different nationalities to coordinate war efforts. She also worked for slum clearance, low cost housing, child labor laws, mothers" pensions and public health measures.

Today, the National Council of Jewish Women is the oldest active Jewish women's volunteer organization in America. It stands as a living testimony to the vision of its activist founder, as well as the positive energy organized women can exert for the good of the larger community.

*S*usan Solomon, Ph.D.
1956–

Susan Solomon is widely recognized as a leader in the field of atmospheric science. She is best known for having both pioneered the theory explaining how and why the ozone hole occurs in Antarctica, and obtaining some of the first chemical measurements establishing manmade chlorofluorocarbons (CFCs) as its cause.

Dr. Solomon forged an early interest in science while watching such shows as *The Undersea World of Jacques Cousteau*. By high school, she directed her focus toward atmospheric science after placing in a national science contest. Her project measured the amount of oxygen in various gaseous mixtures. After receiving her bachelor's degree in chemistry from Illinois Institute of Technology, Solomon earned her doctorate at the University of California at Berkeley. In 1981, she began working at the National Oceanic and Atmospheric Administration in Boulder, Colorado. She is now the Ellen Swallow Richards Professor of Atmospheric Chemistry and Climate Science at MIT.

In 1986 and 1987, Dr. Solomon led expeditions to Antarctica, observing that levels of chlorine dioxide were one hundred times greater than predicted. This was the first direct evidence that pointed to chlorine chemistry as the cause of the Antarctic ozone hole. Dr. Solomon received the National Medal of Science in 1999 in chemistry for "her key scientific insights in explaining the cause of the Antarctic ozone hole and for advancing the understanding of the global ozone layer; for changing the direction of ozone research through her findings; and for exemplary service to worldwide public policy decisions and to the American public."

Her current research includes climate change, ozone depletion, and the links between them. She served as co-chair of Working Group 1 of the Intergovernmental Panel on Climate Change (IPCC) from 2002-2008. The IPCC provides comprehensive scientific assessments of climate change for the public and for policy makers. The organization shared the Nobel Peace Prize with Albert Gore, Jr. in 2007.

Dr. Solomon has received numerous other awards in recognition of her work, including the Blue Planet Prize from the Asahi Foundation in Japan, the Carl-Gustaf Rossby Medal from the American Meteorological Society, and the William Bowie Medal from the American Geophysical Union. Antarctica's Solomon Glacier and Solomon Saddle were named in honor of her research.

Elizabeth Cady Stanton
1815–1902

Widely credited as one of the founding geniuses of the women's rights movement, Elizabeth Cady Stanton used her brilliance, insightfulness, and eloquence to advocate for many important issues. In addition to being one of the first women's rights activists, she was also a dedicated abolitionist, and advocated in favor of temperance.

Unlike many of her contemporaries, Stanton enjoyed a formal education at Johnstown Academy, where she worked hard to excel in Greek, Latin, and mathematics. The child of a judge, she went on to obtain the finest education then available to women at Troy Female Seminary. A visit to her cousin, abolitionist Gerrit Smith, in Peterboro, New York, helped foster her strong anti-slavery sentiments.

At her insistence, when she married abolitionist Henry Stanton, the word "obey" was omitted from the ceremony. Their honeymoon journey was to the great World's Anti-Slavery Convention in London in 1840. After the women delegates were denied seats at that convention, Stanton became convinced that women should hold a convention demanding their own rights. This decision was delayed until her move to Seneca Falls, where she was isolated and increasingly exhausted by a growing family. Finally in July, 1848, she met with Lucretia Mott and three other Quaker women in nearby Waterloo, New York. Together they issued the call for the first woman's rights convention.

Stanton drafted the Seneca Falls Convention's Declaration of Sentiments, including the historic words "We hold these truths to be self-evident: that all men and women are created equal," She continued to argue forcefully for the ballot, a radical demand opposed by her husband and even Mrs. Mott. Soon thereafter, she met Susan B. Anthony and they formed what would be a lifelong partnership devoted to the cause. Among their earliest targets were laws that discriminated against married women, denying them the right to hold property, or wages, or guardianship of their children.

A prolific author whose works included *Solitude of Self and The Woman's Bible*, Stanton once wrote that "The prolonged slavery of woman is the darkest page in human history."

Gloria Steinem
1934–

Gloria Steinem has said, "If the shoe doesn't fit, must we change the foot?" This thread runs through her life as an activist and change agent, dedicated to fashioning a world that does fit the needs of its people.

Steinem's lifelong career as a writer and journalist began after college. A co-founder of *New York* magazine in 1968, Steinem was always active in a wide array of political and social causes. She became a major feminist leader in the late 1960s and in 1971 co-founded *Ms.* Magazine, where she serves as contributing editor today.

In 1971 she was a co-convener of the National Women's Political Caucus and in l972 helped found the Ms. Foundation for Women, which raises funds to assist underprivileged girls and women. She is a founding member of the Coalition of Labor Union Women, and her books are often bestsellers.

Steinem's lifelong activism has inspired women of all ages to fight for their rights, to take risks, and to defend the rights of others. Her writings form a lasting legacy of ideas and personal revelation that continues to inspire and inform.

Steinem co-founded the Women's Media Center in 2005 - an organization that works to make women visible and powerful in the media. She has received many awards including the Presidential Medal of Freedom.

Helen Stephens
1918–1994

Helen Stephens was always a woman on the move – from teenaged Olympic track and field champion to becoming the first woman owner/manager of an all-woman semiprofessional ball team to activism as a sports advocate.

Stephens drew the public eye as a brilliant champion in the 1936 Olympics, when the Fulton, Missouri farm girl ran the 100 meters in 11.5 seconds – setting a world record that stood for 24 years. "The Fulton Flash" won a second gold as anchor leg in the 400 meter relay. As an amateur she set world, Olympic, American and Canadian records in running, broad jump and discuss.

Stephens started "The Helen Stephens Olympic Co-Eds," in 1938 – the first woman to create, own and manage a semiprofessional basketball team, which remained active until 1952. Stephens was actively involved in national and state senior games, inspiring teenagers and senior citizens alike to exercise and work for good health. She is honored in the National Track and Field Hall of Fame, the US Track and Field Hall of Fame and the Women's Sports Foundation Hall of Fame.

Nettie Stevens, Ph.D.
1861–1912

A 1905 research paper with a long-winded title – "Studies in Spermatogenesis with Especial Reference to the 'Accessory Chromosome'" – written by Bryn Mawr biologist Nettie Stevens, was one of the 20th century's major scientific breakthroughs, showing that the chromosomes known as "X" and "Y" were responsible for determining the sex of individuals. This ended a longstanding scientific debate as to whether sex was determined by heredity or other factors. Now, once and for all, a relatively obscure research biologist had shown that chromosomes influenced human traits, opening the doors for research in science and medicine that continues to this day.

Nettie Stevens, educated at Stanford University and Bryn Mawr College (Ph.D., 1903), taught throughout her relatively short life, inspiring many students to careers in science. She published more than 38 papers from 1901 to her death, in cytology and experimental physiology.

Photo: Carnegie Institution of Washington

Lucy Stone
1818–1893

As an orator and an editor, Lucy Stone won innumerable converts to the cause of women's rights. Growing up on the family farm, she learned the difficulties women faced. Her mother's hardships distressed her, and her father ridiculed Lucy's desire to attend college.

At the age of twenty-five she entered Oberlin, a pioneering co-educational college. She supported her studies through teaching and housework until her father at last relented and gave her some assistance. Her study of Greek and Hebrew convinced her that crucial passages in the Bible (those declaring woman inferior) had been translated wrongly. When she graduated from Oberlin in 1847, Lucy Stone became the first Massachusetts women to earn a college degree.

She was a gifted public speaker, and a dedicated abolitionist. Soon she was appointed a lecturer for the American Anti-Slavery Society. Her natural eloquence drew large crowds, though she often had to face hostility. In 1850 she helped organize a women's rights convention in Worcester, Massachusetts. There, at the first "national" convention, Lucy Stone delivered a speech on women's rights that converted Susan B. Anthony to the cause.

When she married Henry Blackwell (brother of Elizabeth Blackwell) Lucy Stone kept her own name, thus coining the phrase "Lucy Stoner" to describe a married woman who retains her maiden name. Lucy Stone took the lead in organizing the American Woman Suffrage Association. This group, considered the most moderate wing of the women suffrage movement, conflicted with Stanton and Anthony over policy and tactics.

Lucy Stone and her husband founded and edited the organization's weekly newspaper, *The Woman's Journal,* which was considered "the voice of the woman's movement." Lucy Stone spent her lifetime battling for women's rights and inspiring others to join her cause.

Kate Stoneman, J.D.
1841–1925

The first woman admitted to practice law in the state of New York, Kate Stoneman paved the way for thousands who followed.

She left the family farm for Albany, New York to pursue an education at the New York State Normal College, the only state school training teachers for the public schools. Following her graduation in 1866, she worked as a teacher for forty years. During her early years of teaching, Stoneman began to take an interest in women's suffrage. She and others formed the Woman's Suffrage Society of Albany, lobbying for the extension of school suffrage to women. Her interest in law was piqued when she was designated executrix of her great aunt's estate.

After three years of studying law and clerking for an attorney, Stoneman became the first woman to pass the New York State Bar Examination in 1885. When Stoneman subsequently applied for admission to the bar, she was denied due to her sex. Just prior to her bar application, a bill was introduced removing gender requirements for admittance to the bar; however, the bill had been stuck in the judiciary committee. Stoneman launched a successful lobbying campaign to secure its passage. On May 20, 1886, with the new legislation in hand, Stoneman reapplied for admission to the bar. Her application was accepted and she became New York's first female lawyer.

Stoneman's unquenchable thirst for a legal education continued with her 1896 enrollment at Albany Law School. On June 2, 1898, at age 57, Stoneman became the first woman to graduate from Albany Law School. She was also the first woman to receive a bachelor's degree from any department of Union University. Throughout her lifetime, she continued to play a prominent role in the women's suffrage movement, participating in efforts to secure suffrage legislation in New York State. In 1918, as a poll watcher, Stoneman saw New York women vote for the first time.

Harriet Beecher Stowe
1811–1896

Harriet Beecher Stowe was born into one of America's most prominent religious families. The Beecher family was at the forefront of many reform movements of the 19th century.

After her short teaching career she married Calvin Stowe in 1836. In order to supplement Calvin's teaching salary, she wrote short stories dealing with domestic life. Her royalties helped her hire household help to assist with raising their seven children.

In 1850 when the south threatened to secede, Stowe determined that she would write a serial denouncing the evils of slavery. She began, expecting to write three to four installments, but the novel grew to forty chapters. Meanwhile the nation became absorbed in the story. *Uncle Tom's Cabin*, published in book form in 1852, was a huge success. *Uncle Tom's Cabin* was the first major American novel to feature a black hero. With a fine ear for dialogue, deft humor, and dramatic plot, Stowe made her readers understand that slaves were people who were being made to suffer cruelly. Stowe's novel also insisted that slavery undermined the moral sensibility of whites who tolerated or profited from it. Stowe wrote of the evils of slavery so that others could be free. Hers was one of the most effective pieces of reform literature ever published.

Later her *Pink and White Tyranny* attacked the idea that women should be ornamental and helpless. She wrote many subsequent novels but none of her later works achieved the social impact of *Uncle Tom's Cabin*.

Harriet Williams Strong
1844–1926

Harriet Williams Strong was the primary innovator of dry land irrigation and water conservation techniques in late 19th century southern California. With no formal engineering or business school training, she became a renowned inventor, agricultural entrepreneur, civic leader, philanthropist, and advocate of women's rights and women's higher education.

Born in Buffalo, NY, raised in the mining towns of the California-Nevada border, she was widowed at a young age with four daughters to support. Pioneering new methods of conserving flood waters and irrigating to supply her walnut, olive and pomegranate plantings, she saved her family ranch and provided for her children. She turned her talent for invention into patents, raised fast-growing pampas grass and sold the plumes to the millinery trade. In less than five years, she rescued her family and land from debt, became the leading commercial grower of walnuts in the country and known as the *Walnut Queen*.

She tirelessly advocated for water conservation and new approaches to arid land agriculture, for the education of women, women's independence, and for women's suffrage, traveling across the continent with Susan B. Anthony to promote women's causes. Mrs. Strong became the first women member of the Board of the Los Angeles Chamber of Commerce and the first woman Trustee of the University of Southern California Law School.

Anne Sullivan
1866–1936

Born in 1866, Anne Sullivan (Macy) lost her mother when she was young and her father became an alcoholic. She and her siblings were sent to live with relatives, but in 1876 the family sent Annie and her youngest brother to the Tewksbury, Massachusetts poorhouse. There she lost her sight to trachoma. After four years, she was sent to the Perkins School for the Blind in Boston and eventually received medical treatment that restored her sight.

Upon graduation from Perkins in 1886, she began to teach. The next year, the Headmaster of Perkins wrote to her about the situation of a student who was blind and deaf, unable to communicate and demonstrating violent temper tantrums. No one had been successful in reaching her. Anne Sullivan rose to the challenge and traveled to Alabama to meet Helen Keller. Sullivan had learned the manual alphabet and immediately began to teach Keller by letting her touch things. Sullivan would then spell what the object was in Keller's hand. Sullivan succeeded in teaching Keller to read, write and minimally speak. In 1904, Keller graduated from Radcliffe College, supported by Sullivan's presence. Sullivan and Keller became world famous through Keller's writing, lectures and other public appearances.

Sullivan's dedication and innovative teaching had made it possible for Keller to break through the formidable barriers that challenged people with multiple disabilities. Both became role models for thousands of physically challenged people around the world and raised thousands of dollars for organizations that assisted the blind. Sullivan's focus, persistence, and creativity forged a model that contributed to changing public perceptions regarding the capabilities of people with disabilities. Her insight and dedication contributed to the contemporary expansion of opportunities for people with disabilities and to breaking down myths and stereotypes, furthering social and economic justice.

Kathrine Switzer
1947–

As the first woman to officially enter the Boston Marathon, Kathrine Switzer broke the gender barrier and paved the way for women in running.

Born into a military family stationed in Germany, Switzer later attended Syracuse University, earning a B.A. from the Newhouse School of Journalism (1968).

In 1967, Switzer registered for the Boston Marathon as 'K. V. Switzer'. After the race began, the race director realized Switzer was a woman and attempted to forcibly remove her. However, she continued on and completed the course. Photos of this "Boston Incident" ignited the women's running revolution at a time when popular theory held that women were not strong enough to run the 26.2 mile distance.

Thanks to the efforts of Switzer and others, women were officially allowed into road races in 1971. The next year, she earned her M.A. in public communications from Syracuse University.

In 1977, Switzer founded the Avon International Running Circuit, an initiative that created running programs in 27 countries for over 1 million women. These efforts eventually led to the inclusion of the women's marathon as an official event in the Olympic Games. In 1984, 49 athletes from 28 countries ran the inaugural Women's Olympic Marathon.

Switzer went on to simultaneous careers as a fitness expert, television broadcaster, author and public speaker. She formed her own company, AtAlanta Sports Promotions and is an Emmy Award-winning television commentator who has done broadcast work for ABC, CBS, NBC and ESPN. Switzer's books include *Marathon Woman* and *Running and Walking for Women Over 40*.

Switzer has revolutionized the sport of running for women, while at the same time increasing awareness of healthy lifestyles and the importance of fitness. She once noted that, "Triumph over adversity, that's what the marathon is all about. Nothing in life can't triumph after that."

A member of the inaugural class of the National Distance Running Hall of Fame (1998), Switzer was named one of four "Visionaries of the Century" by *Runner's World Magazine* (2002), and has received the Abebe Bikila Award from the New York Road Runners Club for her global contribution to running (2003).

Still recognized as a leader in the running world, Switzer has completed over thirty-seven marathons and dedicated her career to creating opportunities and equal sport status for women.

Henrietta Szold
1860–1945

Educator and social activist Henrietta Szold is best known as the founder of Hadassah, the Women's Zionist Organization of America, Inc.

Szold was born in Baltimore, Maryland in 1860. The oldest daughter of a well-known rabbi, Henrietta was given a well-rounded education both by her parents and at Western High School. Upon her graduation in 1877, having achieved an outstanding academic record, she began teaching at a Baltimore girls' school. For the next fifteen years she taught a broad range of subjects, including languages, mathematics, and history. Also during this time, she developed a night school program to help newly arrived immigrants learn English and civics. By 1898, more than 5,000 Jewish and non-Jewish immigrants had attended the program, which had been taken over by the city of Baltimore.

In addition, in 1893, Szold became the first full-time secretary of the Jewish Publication Society of America, a position she held for twenty-three years, with duties similar to the position of editor-in-chief.

In 1909, she and her 70-year old mother spent six months traveling around Palestine. This trip became a major turning point in Szold's life. Impressed by the beauty of the countryside, but appalled by the overwhelming conditions of poverty and disease, she returned to the U. S. determined to make a difference in pre-state Israel.

In 1912 she founded Hadassah (from the Biblical name for Queen Esther, one of the greatest Jewish heroines), which has since become one of the largest American women's social action organizations. The organization is credited with having had a profound effect on the establishment of life-changing medical, educational, and social practices in pre-state Israel. The American Zionist Medical Unit, founded by Hadassah in 1916, sent doctors, nurses, and supplies to the area, completely transforming health care in the region.

In 1920, Szold returned to Palestine to help the AZMU and spent most of the next twenty-five years there. During this time, her last significant and possibly most important achievement occurred; Szold directed Youth Aliyah, which brought more than 11,000 young people from the threats of Nazi Europe to pre-state Israel. This effort, as much as anything Szold did in her 84 years of social activism, bore witness to her oft-repeated phrase, "make my eyes look toward the future."

*M*ary Burnett Talbert
1866–1923

Mary Burnett Talbert, civil rights and anti-lynching activist, suffragist, preservationist, international human rights proponent, and educator, was born, raised and educated in Oberlin, Ohio. Upon receiving her college degree from Oberlin, she accepted a position as a high school teacher in Little Rock, Arkansas, where she taught science, history, math, and Latin at the high school and then at Bethel University.

In 1887, she was named assistant principal of Little Rock's Union High School, the only African-American woman to hold such a position and the highest position held by a woman in Arkansas.

Mary Burnett married William Talbert in 1891 and moved with him to Buffalo, NY. She was a founding member of the Phyllis Wheatley Club, the first in Buffalo to affiliate with the National Association of Colored Women's Clubs. The Club established a settlement house and helped organize the first chapter of the NAACP (1910). In 1901, Talbert founded the Christian Culture Club at the Michigan Avenue Baptist Church.

Talbert also protested the exclusion of African Americans from the Planning Committee of the Pan-American Exposition. She was instrumental in the founding of the Niagara Movement, pre-cursor to the NAACP (1905). Mrs. Talbert's club connections were extensive. In her NACW Presidential years, she transformed the association into a truly national institution with structure and organizational procedures. Its first national undertaking was the 1922 purchase and restoration of the Frederick Douglass home in Anacostia, MD. She was elected president for life of the Frederick Douglass Memorial and Historical Association.

On the international scene, she served as a Red Cross nurse during World War I in France, sold thousands of dollars of Liberty Bonds during the war, offered classes to African-American soldiers and was a member of the Women's Committee of National Defense. After the war, she was appointed to the Women's Committee on International Relations, which selected women nominees for position in the League of Nations.

Mrs. Talbert was a pioneer in international organizing efforts, gaining a voice for African-American women and developing black female leadership. With conscious intent, she bridged the generation of 19th century abolitionists and freedom seekers: Tubman, Douglass, Truth, and others, and the developing civil rights leadership of the 20th century. Addressing the Fifth Congress of the International Council of Women, Christiana, Norway, 1920, where she was the first African-American delegate, Talbert said, "the greatness of nations is shown by their strict regard for human rights, rigid enforcement of the law without bias, and just administration of the affairs of life."

Maria Tallchief
1925–2013

One of the premiere American ballerinas of all time, Maria Tallchief has been recognized as one of the greatest dancers in the world. She said of her passion, "A ballerina takes steps given to her and makes them her own. Each individual brings something different to the same role."

Tallchief was born in Fairfax, Oklahoma, on the Osage Indian Reservation, and began ballet and piano lessons at the age of three. Her family soon relocated to California, where she began to devote more of her time to dancing. By the age of 12, she was studying with notable teacher Bronislava Nijinska, and upon her graduation from high school, she joined the Ballet Russe de Monte Carlo. Over the next five years, Tallchief attracted much attention with memorable performances, particularly of the works of choreographer George Balanchine.

After marrying Balanchine in 1946, the couple left the Ballet Russe and moved to Paris, France, where Tallchief became the first American ballerina to debut at the Paris Opera. Soon after, Tallchief and Balanchine formed the Balanchine Ballet Society, now known as the New York City Ballet. At the ballet, Tallchief became the first American dancer to achieve the title of prima ballerina, a title she held for 18 years. Among her most significant roles were *Symphomie Concatenate, Orpheus, The Firebird, Scotch Symphony, Caracole, Swan Lake* and *The Nutcracker*.

Following her retirement from ballet in 1965, Tallchief served as artistic director of the Chicago Lyric Opera Ballet (1975). In 1980, she founded the Chicago City Ballet, where she served as the artistic director until 1987. When the State of Oklahoma honored Tallchief in 1953, she was given the name of Wa-Xthe-Thomba, meaning "Woman of Two Worlds," a name that celebrates her international achievements as a prima ballerina and Native American. Tallchief was presented with a National Medal of the Arts award by the National Endowment for the Arts in 1999.

Tallchief's legendary artistic style and excellence continues to inspire dancers worldwide.

*I*da Tarbell
1857–1944

Ida Tarbell helped transform journalism by introducing what is called today investigative journalism. Through her achievements, she not only helped to expand the role of the newspaper in modern society and stimulate the Progressive reform movement, but she also became a role model for women wishing to become professional journalists.

Born on the oil frontier of western Pennsylvania in 1857, Tarbell was among the first women to graduate from Allegheny College in 1880. After trying her hand at the more traditional women's job of teaching, Tarbell began writing and editing a magazine for the Methodist Church. Then, after studying in France for a few years, she joined S. S. McClure's new reform-minded magazine in 1894. Initially she wrote two popular biographical series – on Napoleon and Abraham Lincoln. In 1902, she embarked on her ground breaking study of John D. Rockefeller's Standard Oil Company, or what was called the Standard Oil Trust. Her *History of the Standard Oil Company*, published in 1904, was a landmark work of exposé journalism that became known as "muckraking." Her exposure of Rockefeller's unfair business methods outraged the public and led the government to prosecute the company for violations of the Sherman Anti-Trust Act. As a result, after years of precedent-setting litigation, the Supreme Court upheld the break-up of Standard Oil.

As the most famous woman journalist of her time, Tarbell founded the *American Magazine* in 1906. She authored biographies of several important businessmen and wrote a series of articles about an extremely controversial issue of her day, the tariff imposed on goods imported from foreign countries. Of this series President Wilson commented, "She has written more good sense, good plain common sense, about the tariff than any man I know of." During World War I, she joined the efforts to improve the plight of working women. In 1922, *The New York Times* named her one of the "Twelve Greatest American Women." It was journalism like hers that inspired Americans of the early twentieth century to seek reform in our government, in our economic structures, and in our urban areas. Along with other muckrakers like Lincoln Steffens, Ray Stannard Baker, and Upton Sinclair, Tarbell ushered in reform journalism. Ever since, newspapers have played a leading role as the watchdogs and consciences of our political, economic, and social lives.

Although Tarbell was not, herself an advocate of women's issues or women's rights, as the most prominent woman active in the muckraking movement and one of the most respected business historians of her generation, Tarbell succeeded in a "male" world – the world of journalism, business analysis, and world affairs, thus helping to open the door to other women seeking careers in journalism and, later, in broadcasting.

Photo: Ida M. Tarbell Collection, Pelletier Library, Allegheny College, Meadville, PA

$\mathscr{H}$elen Brooke Taussig, M.D.
1898–1986

The daughter of a Harvard economics professor, Helen Taussig lost her mother to tuberculosis when she was only eleven. Her father became the most important influence in her early years, and he encouraged her professional goals.

Excluded from Harvard Medical School because of her sex, she went to Johns Hopkins instead and became interested in the field of cardiology. As chief of the heart clinic at Johns Hopkins she regularly saw children born with heart defects. The most pathetic were the cyanotic, or "blue babies," condemned to invalidism and early death. Dr. Taussig began to theorize about the nature of the anatomical defects involved, and to devise possible surgical solutions.

Together with a heart surgeon named Blalock, she pioneered the Blalock-Taussig operation, first performed in 1944. The first patient was a one-year old child who weighed just 10 pounds. Dr. Taussig had the thrill of seeing the child develop a healthy pink color for the first time. The operation soon became widely performed. Her medical breakthrough combined caring and inventiveness, and many infants won the chance for a normal life.

Sojourner Truth
c.1797–1883

She was born a slave named Isabella in Ulster County, New York. After slavery was finally abolished in New York, she found refuge with a Quaker family named Van Wagener and took their name.

Isabella Van Wagener was caught up in the atmosphere of religious excitement then sweeping American Protestantism. She did missionary work among the poor of New York City and was associated briefly with a Christian community headed by a dynamic leader who turned out to be a scoundrel.

In 1843 she set out on her own as a traveling preacher. God, she said, had given her a new name: Sojourner Truth. As was common in that era, religious fervor led her into association with reformers who hoped to create a better world. Tall, gaunt, and commanding, she lent her powerful talents as a speaker to the antislavery movement. When she happened upon a women's rights convention, she made that her cause as well. Illiterate all her life, she spoke more often among whites than her own people. Her homely eloquence and native wit disarmed hostile crowds.

At the Civil War's end she worked as counselor to the newly freed slaves who gathered in Washington. Hoping to aid in their transition to freedom, she circulated a petition for public lands to be set aside in the West for a "Negro state." She continued to speak, proclaiming God's love and the rights of the disadvantaged.

Harriet Tubman
c.1820–1913

Born a slave on the eastern shore of Maryland, Harriet Tubman fled north to freedom. There she joined the secret network of free blacks and white sympathizers who helped runaways – the "Underground Railroad." She became a "conductor" who risked her life to lead her people to freedom.

Tubman returned time after time to her native Maryland, bringing out her relatives and as many as 300 other slaves. The shadowy figure of the conductor "Moses" became so feared that a huge reward was put on "his" head, for slave owners did not at first believe a woman capable of such daring. Cool, resourceful, skilled in the use of disguise and diversions, she is said to have carried a pistol, telling the faint-hearted they must go on or die. Apparently only illness prevented Harriet Tubman from joining John Brown in the raid on Harper's Ferry.

When the Civil War began, she worked among the slaves who fled their masters and flocked to Union lines. She organized many of them into spy and scout networks that operated behind Confederate lines from bases on islands off the coast of the Carolinas. After the war she devoted herself to caring for orphaned and invalid blacks, and worked to promote the establishment of freedmen's schools in the South.

Brigadier General Wilma Vaught, USAF
1930–

Wilma Vaught, Brigadier General, USAF (Ret.), one of the most highly decorated military women in United States history, broke through many of the bureaucratic and gender barriers that faced women in the armed forces during her nearly twenty-nine year military career. The many "firsts" she achieved helped pave the way for thousands of other military women to be judged based on their abilities, and not their gender. In 1967, President Johnson signed into law a measure finally permitting women to be promoted to the level of generals and admirals. That same law also lifted the quotas that had been placed on women in achieving other ranks. Today, due to the efforts of General Vaught and others like her, women have much more equality and respect, although, as Vaught insists, much still needs to be achieved.

After receiving her B.S. degree in Business from the University of Illinois, General Vaught enlisted in the Air Force in 1957. She rose through the ranks in the comptroller area, serving in Europe, Vietnam and various posts in the United States. Along the way, she achieved numerous distinctions. In 1966, she became the first woman to deploy with a Strategic Air Command bombardment wing on an operational deployment. In 1972, she was the first female Air Force officer to attend the Industrial College of the Armed Forces. In 1980, she became the first woman promoted to Brigadier General in the comptroller career field. In 1982, she was appointed Commander, U.S. Military Entrance Processing Command, North Chicago, Illinois, the largest command, geographically, in the military. In addition, she served as Chairperson of the NATO Women in the Allied Forces Committee and was the senior woman military representative to the prestigious Secretary of Defense's Advisory Committee on Women in the Service. When she retired in 1985, she was one of only seven women generals in the Armed Forces, and only one of three in the Air Force. She has received numerous military decorations and other honors, including the Defense and Air Force Distinguished Service Medals, the Air Force Legion of Merit, the Bronze Star, and the Vietnam Service Award with four stars. She is also the first woman to command a unit receiving the Joint Meritorious Unit Award.

But perhaps General Vaught's most lasting contribution will be her successful efforts to establish the Women in Military Service for America Memorial Foundation Inc. and raise funding to build the first major national memorial honoring women who have defended their country. As president of the foundation's board of directors, Vaught spearheaded the campaign that raised over $20 million for the memorial. The memorial, standing at the main gateway to Arlington National Cemetery, is the first major memorial to honor the nearly two million women who have served in our nation's armed forces. It stands as a place where the American people and visitors from around the world can learn of the contributions that thousands of American women have made to the military and to their country.

lorence Wald
1917–2008

Florence Wald, after graduating from Mt. Holyoke College and receiving her nursing degree from Yale University in 1941, devoted her life to caring for others.

During World War II, Wald served in the Signal Corps. After the war, she taught nursing at Yale and eventually became Dean of Yale's prestigious School of Nursing. Her most lasting impact was her work in bringing the hospice movement to the United States from Europe. Learning of the hospice movement, Wald went to Europe, studied the movement, and then, in 1971, returned to the United States to establish the first hospice unit in this country. Since then, the movement has spread rapidly because of the great need it fulfills. Hospice, now a household name, has made it possible for tens of thousands to die at home surrounded by loved ones and friends.

Not satisfied with these achievements, Wald continued to work to ensure that hospice services were available to all. In her 80s, Wald worked on making hospice available in prisons, noting the humanitarian act not only aided the dying but also helped rehabilitate the incarcerated. The "Mother of the American Hospice Movement" received an honorary doctorate from Yale University.

Lillian Wald
1867–1940

Lillian Wald originated the public health nursing service and the Henry Street Settlement to meet the needs of the poor in New York City's Lower East Side.

During the early twentieth century, this outstanding nurse and social activist was a dynamic force for social reform, creating widely-adopted models of public health and social service programs.

Wald's nursing education in New York showed her that tenement residents lacked health care, and so she organized the Henry Street Nurses Settlement (1893), the first public health nursing program in the nation. Wald went on to help organize other public health nursing programs in universities and for organizations, including the American Red Cross.

She was the first president of the National Organization of Public Health Nurses, a professional group she helped to create. Recognizing that the urban poor had great needs beyond health care, Wald expanded Henry Street services to include social services, especially those benefitting children. She led the charge to abolish child labor, and helped secure the creation of the federal Children's Bureau in 1912.

Madam C. J. Walker
1867–1919

Madam C.J . Walker – Sarah Breedlove – was a highly successful entrepreneur, widely considered to be the first African-American millionaire.

Walker was known and respected not only for her business acumen but for her inspirational political and social advocacy and her philanthropy. The daughter of former slaves, Walker worked initially as a washerwoman until she devised a hair care and grooming system to meet the needs of African-American women in 1905. Supervising the manufacture of a variety of products, she also developed an enormous marketing network, headquartered in Indianapolis, that employed thousands of African-American women and was the largest African-American owned business in the nation.

Walker encouraged women's economic independence by training others and by serving as a powerful role model. As the wealthiest African-American woman of her time, Walker used her prominent position to oppose racial discrimination, and her massive wealth to support civic, educational and social institutions to assist African Americans.

Induction Year: 2000

Mary Edwards Walker, M.D.
1832–1919

Mary Edwards Walker, M.D., physician and Civil War field surgeon, was the first woman to receive the Medal of Honor.

Much ahead of her time, Dr. Walker, in 1855, was one of the first women in the United States to earn a medical degree. When the Civil War broke out in 1861, Dr. Walker volunteered to work on the Civil War battlefields caring for the wounded. Denied a commission as a medical officer because she was a woman, she volunteered anyway and eventually was appointed assistant surgeon of the 52nd Ohio Infantry. Captured by the Confederates in 1864, she was exchanged only after she spent four months in a Richmond, Virginia prison.

Dr. Walker lived a controversial life. She lectured throughout the United States and abroad on women's rights, dress reform, health and temperance issues, and sexual and political equality. She tried to vote, but was turned away. She rejected corsets and hoop-skirted dresses for the more practical pantsuits (trousers, jackets, top hats) and found herself arrested in New York City for impersonating a man. She spoke against imperialism, the Spanish-American War, and America's acquisition of colonies abroad. She worked for equal rights in all facets of life, from love and marriage to the workplace. She urged the reform of divorce laws that placed women in deplorable situations. She advocated women retaining their own surnames. Much to the horror of her contemporaries, she foresaw that a time would come when men and women would keep their own names when they married and that the children of these alliances would choose the name they preferred. She also authored two books devoted to her views on feminism.

She struggled on the brink of poverty as she lost work because of her refusal to bow to the will of others or to follow standard operating procedures. She was ridiculed for many of her ideas and assertive manner. Her Medal of Honor was revoked. Today, society recognizes her achievements and her insistence that women be treated with the same respect as men. And in 1977, the Army Board, admitting that Dr. Walker had been a victim of sex discrimination, restored the Medal of Honor to her, citing her for "distinguished gallantry, self-sacrifice, patriotism, dedication and unflinching loyalty to her country."

Emily Howell Warner

1939–

At eighteen, Emily Howell Warner flew on a flight to Gunnison, Colorado and fell in love with flying. Hearing about a Norwegian woman who was hired to fly for SAS, Ms. Warner set her sights on the same goal.

Over the next fifteen years she amassed 7,000 flight hours, numerous FAA certificates and ratings: private pilot, commercial, instrument, multi-engine, instructor and then Airline Transport Pilot. She was a flight instructor from 1961-1967 and by 1973, she had been a chief pilot, air taxi and flight school manager, FAA pilot examiner, and in charge of the United Airlines Contract Training Program for Clinton Aviation.

She persevered through years of training male students who went on to pilot for various airlines, and applied for an airline pilot's position with Frontier Airlines in 1973. After a grueling simulator test, Ms. Warner was offered the opportunity to realize her dreams.

She made aviation history almost every time she climbed aboard an airliner. She was the first female pilot for a scheduled U.S. carrier, the first female captain, and in 1986 commanded the first all-female flight crew in the U.S. She was the first woman member of the Airline Pilots Association, pioneering the way.

As a speaker, she seeks to motivate the next generation with the message that determination and persistence will lead to success.

Mercy Otis Warren
1728–1814

Mercy Otis Warren was a staunch advocate of independence from the tyranny of 18th century English monarchic rule. As poet, dramatist, satirist, and historian, her voice was one of the early calls in America for revolt against the British and their policies as implemented by Governor Thomas Hutchinson.

Born in West Barnstable, MA, the third of thirteen children born to James (elected to the Massachusetts House of Representatives in 1845), and Mary Otis, Mercy Otis Warren had no formal education. She was tutored, along with her older brother James, by a local pastor. James Otis shared her political beliefs and became a leader in the agitation against the Stamp Act of 1865. Mercy Otis read intensively, particularly Shakespeare, Pope and Raleigh and applied her literary background and talent in the service of the patriotic cause. She was a friend of Abigail and John Adams, and corresponded with both throughout her life. Her husband, James Warren, a member of the Massachusetts House of Representatives, was an outspoken revolutionary activist. These connections gave Mercy Otis Warren a political involvement highly unusual for a woman of her time.

From 1765 to 1789, she was near the center of revolutionary political events in Massachusetts. It is believed that her 1788 pamphlet "Observations on the New Constitution..." played a role in the design and adoption of the Bill of Rights. She wrote letters, poems and a series of satirical plays: *The Adulateur, The Defeat*, and *The Group*, regarded as the first plays by an American woman. The plays focused on the Tory government in Massachusetts, particularly that of Governor Hutchinson, accusing him of gross ambition and hypocrisy, simultaneously making an outstanding defense for the revolutionary cause. The plays were printed, not staged. Puritan Boston prohibited staging plays. In 1805, after twenty-five years of research and writing, her three volume *History of the Rise, Progress and Termination of the American Revolution* appeared. Her *History* contains knowledgeable and unique observations concerning the events, leaders and campaigns of the period, and is the only full-scale history of the American Revolution written by a woman of the time.

Warren wrote in her preface: "every domestic enjoyment depends on the unimpaired possession of civil and religious liberty."

Faye Wattleton (Alyce)
1943–

As a nurse, Faye Wattleton saw suffering and the consequences of poor health care – and to help change this, she became one of the nation's most effective advocates as president of the Planned Parenthood Federation of America. Wattleton became president of Planned Parenthood in 1978, a position she held until 1992. As the first woman to serve as the organization's president since its founder, Margaret Sanger, Wattleton was the first African American and the youngest president in the organization's history.

Wattleton is credited with developing the organization's extensive national grassroots advocacy network that became a powerful lobbying force to block efforts to restrict and overturn women's rights to make reproductive choices. Additionally, her powerful and articulate leadership gave the organization visibility that furthered its mission and extended its reach.

During Wattleton's administration, she directed the expansion of reproductive health care services for women and families from 1.1 million to about 5 million in 1990. Her strong leadership has made a powerful difference in the lives of many American women and their families.

Annie Dodge Wauneka
1910–1997

Annie Dodge Wauneka, tribal leader of the Navajo Nation and public health activist, worked tirelessly to improve the health and welfare of the Navajo Tribe and reduce the incidence of tuberculosis nationwide.

Born in 1910 in a traditional Navajo hogan, Wauneka was raised by her father, one of the wealthiest men of the Navajo Tribe. While taught Navajo history and culture, Wauneka also gained a general education. When she was eight, while attending a government-run school on the reservation, a tragic event occurred that helped shape the rest of her life. An influenza epidemic struck. Thousands of Navajos, including many of Wauneka's classmates, died. Wauneka escaped with only a mild case that left her resistant to the disease. Thus she was able to care for those who were too ill to feed themselves. After graduation and her marriage to George Wauneka, Annie continued to travel with her father, observing the poverty and disease that plagued most of the Navajo. She studied public health and then, realizing that the best way to change the standards of health and sanitation among tribal members was from within, Wauneka gained election in 1951 to the Tribal Council, the second woman ever so elected.

During her three terms in office, Wauneka led the fight against tuberculosis. She wrote a dictionary to translate English words into Navajo for modern medical techniques, such as vaccination. Her weekly radio broadcasts, in the Navajo language, explained how modern medicine could help improve health among the Navajo. She also worked on other health problems including better care for pregnant women and new babies, regular eye and ear examinations, and alcoholism. She continued working in her community on health issues until her death in 1997. She helped improve housing and sanitation conditions and convinced her tribe to adopt many modern medical practices and avail themselves of hospital care, when needed. She also served on the advisory boards of the U.S. Surgeon General and the U.S. Public Health Service.

In 1963, Wauneka became the first Native American to receive the Presidential Medal of Freedom. *Ladies' Home Journal* selected her a Woman of the Year in 1976. In 1984, the Navajo Council designated her "The Legendary Mother of the Navajo Nation." All recognize that through her efforts in education and health, the lives of every Navajo, as well as the nation at large, have been improved.

Angelina Grimké Weld
1805–1879

Sarah and Angelina Grimke eloquently fought the injustices of slavery, racism and sexism during the mid-19th century. As daughters of a prominent South Carolina judge and plantation owner, the Grimke sisters witnessed the suffering of slaves.

Determined to speak out, they were eventually forced to move to the North, where they continued to appeal to northerners and southerners to work toward abolition. They also urged white northerners to end racial discrimination.

The Grimke sisters were pioneering women. Among the first female abolitionists, they were the first women to speak publicly against slavery, an important political topic. Faced with criticism from clergy and others that they were threatening "the female character," they continued their crusade.

In 1838, Angelina became the first woman to address a legislative body when she spoke to the Massachusetts State Legislature on women's rights and abolition. Active in the women's movement, they helped set the agenda later followed by Elizabeth Cady Stanton, Susan B. Anthony, Lucretia Mott and others, calling for equal educational opportunities and the vote.

One historian said of Sarah's writings: "[They were] a milestone on the road to the Woman's Rights Convention at Seneca Falls" and "central to the feminist writings in the decades that followed." Sarah was one of the first to compare the restrictions on women and slaves, writing that "woman has no political existence… She is only counted like the slaves of the south, to swell the number of lawmakers."

After the Civil War, they continued to champion the causes of equality and women's rights. Through their examples and their words, the Grimke sisters proved that women could affect the course of political events and have a far-reaching influence on society.

Ida B. Wells-Barnett

1862–1931

Born of slaves, Ida B. Wells-Barnett fought to stop the lynching of Black Americans, carrying her fight to the White House. In 1898 she was part of a delegation to President McKinley demanding government action in the case of a black postmaster who had been lynched in South Carolina.

Wells-Barnett's parents, freed from slavery shortly after her birth, died of malaria when she was 14. To support her brother and sisters, she became a school teacher. While she was traveling to a school in Memphis, Tennessee, a train conductor insisted she move from the parlor car to the smoking car, the one reserved for blacks. She refused; he grabbed her wrist; she bit him, and Wells-Barnett brought a suit against the railroad for their actions, and won. Later, however, the state court overruled the decision of the circuit court.

Her teaching career ended after she wrote a series of articles denouncing the education provided to black children. She then became part owner of the *Memphis Star* newspaper. When three of her friends were lynched on false charges, she wrote searing attacks against the practice of lynching. As a result of these and other articles which challenged the actions of whites against blacks, her newspaper was sacked and destroyed. But Wells-Barnett continued the fight, carrying her message to Europe and throughout the country.

She was one of the founders of the NAACP and was active in the Negro Women's Club movement. She opposed Booker T. Washington's philosophy of accommodation. She, along with other black women, marched in suffrage parades, and she worked with Jane Addams to block the segregation of schools in Chicago. Ida B. Wells-Barnett was fearless and respected, an uncompromising fighter for the rights of all human beings.

*E*udora Welty
1909–2001

Eudora Welty, recipient of the Pulitzer Prize in fiction in 1973, is widely recognized as a preeminent novelist and short-story writer.

Born in Jackson, Mississippi in 1909 and educated at the Mississippi State College for Women (now Mississippi University for Women), the University of Wisconsin, and the Columbia University Graduate School of Business, Welty first worked for newspapers, a radio station, and, during the Great Depression, for the Works Progress Administration in Mississippi.

Welty now ranks as one of the most significant writers of the twentieth century. Her work teaches us about ourselves and about the human spirit. She captures the distinctive southern character, enduring in the midst of change. She helps us understand women's views of both themselves and the men around them. Thus she illuminates the complicated interrelationships between men and women. She teaches us that the search for meaning often proves complex, multiple, and elusive. Her Pulitzer Prize-winning novel, *The Optimist's Daughter*, sees the old civilities of small town Mississippi, along with its snobbishness and sense of privilege, collide with the materialistic values of the modern, outside world. In the novel, Welty analyzes other confrontations and their meaning, such as death and love. She also examines the interdependence of children and their parents.

Her writing has been recognized with numerous awards, including the French Legion of Honor, the Presidential Medal of Freedom, the American Book Award, the National Book Critics Award, the O. Henry Award, the Commonwealth Award for Distinguished Service in Literature from the Modern Language Association of America, along with honorary degrees from many leading universities.

Through her short stories and novels, Welty will have a lasting impact on our lives and our understanding of love between men and women, the fleeting joys of childhood, and the many dimensions and stages of women's lives.

Edith Wharton
1862–1937

Considered one of the major American novelists and short story writers of the 20th century, Edith Wharton was known for her unflinching portrayal of the societal norms of her time.

Wharton was raised in the highly stratified and wealthy society of the urban Northeast. Although she published a volume of poetry at the age of 16, it was not until almost 20 years later that she began her literary career earnest. Following publication of several short stories, her first book, *The Decoration of Houses* (1897), had a pronounced influence on the styles of interior decoration of the day. Her first novel, *The Valley of Decision* (1902), was published when Wharton was 40. From then on, she averaged more than a book a year for the rest of her life.

The majority of Wharton's works provided keen, and sometimes harsh, observations of society's upper strata. Her upbringing provided her with insights on the upper class, while her sense of humor and polished prose made the reading interesting to a wide audience. Her attention to the physical contexts in which her characters lived led Edmund Wilson to describe Wharton not only as "the pioneer, but the poet, of interior decoration." In the early 1900's, Wharton changed her focus and created the memorable and eerie *Ethan Frome* (1911) and *Summer* (1917). These were followed by *The Age of Innocence* (1920), a Pulitzer Prize winner that explored social hypocrisy and convention with sharp irony.

Wharton was a member of the National Institute of Arts and Letters and the American Academy of Arts and Letters. She also was the first woman to receive an honorary doctorate from Yale University. During World War I, the writer aided refugees and the wounded. At one time she fed and housed 600 war orphans at her own expense. The French and Belgian governments officially honored her wartime service.

Photo: Edith Wharton Restoration, The Mount

$\mathcal{S}$heila E. Widnall, Ph.D.
1938–

Dr. Sheila E. Widnall, a woman of outstanding scientific achievement, dedicated citizen, and skilled administrator, was Secretary of the United States Air Force from 1993-1997, the first woman to head a branch of the U.S. military.

Master pilot, astrophysicist, educator on the faculty of the Massachusetts Institute of Technology for over 30 years, her engineering accomplishments recognized by election to the National Academy of Engineering, Widnall is internationally known for her work in fluid dynamics, specifically in the areas of aircraft turbulence and the spiraling air flows called vortices created by helicopters.

Before her appointment as Secretary of the Air Force, Widnall served on the USAF Academy Board of Visitors, and on advisory committees to Military Airlift Command and Wright-Patterson Air force Base, Ohio. She was appointed a member of the Columbia Accident Investigation Board in February 2003.

A native of Tacoma, Washington, Widnall came east to attend Massachusetts Institute of Technology at a time when women students in science and technology were few. She was one of twenty-three women in the freshman class of nine hundred thirty-six. She earned her B.Sc. in 1960, her M.S. in 1961, and her Sc.D. in 1964 in aeronautics and astronautics at the Institute, and was appointed Assistant Professor in 1964. She was appointed Abby Rockefeller Mauze Professor of Aeronautics and Astronautics in 1986 and Institute Professor in 1998. She served as Associate Provost 1992-1993. Known for her accomplishments in education and training, her people first attitude, her prolific writing and research, and ability to spur technological and scientific development,

Widnall has been a major role model and trailblazer for women in the military and in science. Prior to her appointment as Secretary of the Air Force, she was the first MIT alumna appointed to the faculty of the School of Engineering and the first woman to serve as chair of the faculty (1979-1980).

Emma Hart Willard
1787–1870

A pioneer in women's education, Emma Hart Willard founded Troy Female Seminary, the first school for young women in the United States.

Emma Hart was the sixteenth of seventeen children, born in Berlin, Connecticut, to a family that valued education. Her mother was literate at a time when very few women in New England could read and write, and her father believed in educating his daughters as well as his sons. Hart attended local schools and began her teaching career in 1804. In 1807, she moved to Middlebury, Vermont to manage a women's academy.

Two years later, she married John Willard and, as was customary, she retired from teaching for a period of time. In 1814, Willard returned to her profession and opened a girls' school in her home. Struck by the contrast between the education she could offer her students and the curriculum provided to young men at a nearby college, she wrote *A Plan for Improving Female Education*. The document advocated equal education for young women through the academy level.

At the encouragement of Governor DeWitt Clinton, Willard moved to New York in 1819 and opened a school in Waterford. In 1821, she relocated again, to Troy, and opened Troy Female Seminary. Renamed the Emma Willard School in her honor in 1895, the school saw thousands of young women pass through its doors during Willard's lifetime.

In 1838, Willard left daily management of the school to her son and daughter-in-law and spent the last 30 years of her life traveling and writing. She returned often to the school, entertaining students in her house at the edge of the grounds, or even filling the role of principal as needed.

At the time of her death in 1870, Willard was proclaimed the best known woman in America. Since its founding, the Emma Willard School has been one of the nation's leading schools for young women.

*F*rances *Willard*
1839–1898

Frances Willard, founder of the World's Woman's Christian Temperance Union, influenced the history of reform and helped transform the role of women in nineteenth-century America.

After graduating from North Western Female College in 1859, Willard became a leading educator, teaching at a number of schools in Illinois, Pennsylvania, and New York before becoming, in 1871, the first female president of a college granting degrees to women – the newly-formed Evanston College for Ladies. After the college merged with Northwestern University, Willard became the first Dean of Women and Professor of Aesthetics. In 1873, she helped found the Association for the Advancement of Women.

Willard left education for work in temperance in 1874. In that year, the Woman's Christian Temperance Union (WCTU) was founded with Willard as the first corresponding secretary. In 1879, she would become its second president. For Willard, the WCTU was an effective school for women, giving them a chance to achieve identities beyond those of wives and mothers. The WCTU, with Willard was president, became the largest organization of women in the United States. At WCTU meetings, women followed parliamentary procedures; they assumed leadership roles and learned to use their skills to achieve many different goals. Willard, herself, traveled throughout the nation, lectured, wrote books, and edited WCTU publications. In 1883, Willard helped found the World's Woman's Christian Temperance Union.

Willard also influenced the suffrage movement. She urged suffragists to work on the local level to achieve the vote rather than focus all their energies on a constitutional amendment. Such a strategy won numerous gains. Moreover, Willard convinced many reluctant women to support the suffrage movement, so they could use the power of the vote to make and keep their towns dry and improve the moral fiber of America.

In addition to temperance and suffrage, under Willard's leadership the WCTU supported broad social reforms such as equal pay for equal work, the eight-hour work day, Armenian relief, world peace, the protection of women and children in the workplace, kindergartens, mothers' clubs (the forerunner of the PTA), dress reform, jail reform, uniform marriage and divorce laws, and physical education in grade schools. The WCTU established homes for working girls, shelters for abused women and children, and free kindergartens. In addition, Willard was a founding member of the Illinois Woman's Press Association, one of the first five women elected to the Methodist General Conference, and a founder and first president of the National Council of Women.

For nineteen years as WCTU president, Willard promoted unlimited aspirations for women: higher education, choice of vocation, and equality of opportunity along with suffrage and temperance.

Oprah Winfrey
1954–

At the heart of everything Oprah Winfrey does, there is a consistent message – that individuals should take personal responsibility for their lives, and to improve the world.

Winfrey is the first African-American woman to own her own production company; a talented actress nominated for an Academy Award in her first movie; television's highest-paid entertainer; producer and actress in her own television specials; and the successful host of a syndicated television talk show that reached 15 million people a day.

She does all that she can to eradicate child abuse. As a victim herself, Winfrey knows the damage abuse does to young lives, and she was a major force in the drafting, lobbying and passage of the National Child Protection Act, signed into law by President Clinton in 1994. The Act establishes a national registry of child abusers to help employers and those working with children to screen out dangerous people.

Winfrey is also a committed philanthropist, providing significant assistance to schools (Morehouse College, Tennessee State University, Chicago Academy of Arts) as well as to the Chicago Public Schools. She also funds battered women's shelters and campaigns to catch child abusers.

Sarah Winnemucca
c.1842–1891

Born the daughter of Chief Winnemucca of the Paiutes, a tribe in Nevada and California, Sarah Winnemucca lost family members in the Paiute War of 1860.

She tried to operate as a peacemaker, using her language skills learned in convent school to work as an interpreter in an Army camp. She went with her tribe to the Malheur reservation in 1872, and when the Bannock War broke out in 1878 she offered her services to the Army. She volunteered to enter Bannock territory when she learned that her father and other tribesmen had been taken hostage by the Bannocks. She freed her father and other captives and served as an army scout in the war against the Bannocks.

She spoke out, describing the plight of her people, exiled from their homelands, and the treachery of dishonest Indian agents. She drew much attention, and was able to speak with President Hayes and Interior Secretary Carl Schurz; promises to return her tribe to the Malheur Reservation were never honored.

She wrote *Life Among the Piutes [sic]: Their Wrongs and Claims*, published in 1883. Despite passage of Congressional legislation enabling the return of the Paiute land, the legislation was never enacted.

Victoria Woodhull
1838–1927

Victoria Woodhull was a passionate campaigner for social justice who combined deep belief in Spiritualism, radical views on achieving equal rights for women, advocacy of divorce law changes, birth control, working people's rights, and tax reform as her platform for change. She was the first American woman to address Congress and the first to run for the office of President of the United States.

Overcoming childhood poverty, abuse and exploitation, Woodhull supported her family by working as a medium and fortuneteller. Her success as a clairvoyant connected her with Cornelius Vanderbilt. His backing made it possible for Mrs. Woodhull and her sister Tennessee Claflin to own and operate a brokerage firm and publish the highly successful *Woodhull & Claflin's Weekly*.

Woodhull's charisma, sense of mission, incisiveness, wealth, and independence made it possible for her to briefly reinvigorate the women's movement. Many of Woodhull's views and themes were prophetic of issues and debates of the twentieth century. Stanton and Anthony at first embraced Woodhull but drew back as her extreme critiques of marriage and America's class disparities, involvement in flamboyant scandals, and "free love" doctrines made her increasingly controversial.

After years of speeches before packed houses, the adulation of thousands, and acceptance in the wealthiest circles of the nation, Woodhull lost support because of her embroilment in scandal and manipulation, her scathing critiques and unveiling of hypocrisies. She and her sister moved to England in 1877, married wealthy men and lived comfortable, conventional lives.

Fanny Wright
1795–1852

The first American woman to speak publicly against slavery and for the equality of women, Fanny Wright was a rebel who pursued equality for all. She lived according to her own ideals rather than society's dictates.

Wright was an inspiration to Susan B. Anthony and Elizabeth Cady Stanton. She was a friend to the Marquis de Lafayette, and with him visited Jefferson and Madison. In 1852 she published a treatise setting forth a plan for the gradual emancipation of all American slaves, and in 1825 created Nashoba, a settlement in Tennessee to train slaves for freedom. For a variety of reasons the project failed, and Wright then moved to New Harmony, where Robert Owen had created his Utopian community.

She helped edit the *New Harmony Gazette* and gave public lectures – considered scandalous in society of the time. She supported the free-thinkers, publishing the *Free Enquirer* with Robert Owen, calling for birth control, liberalized divorce laws and more.

Courageous throughout her life, her tombstone in Cincinnati reads, "I have wedded the cause of human improvement, staked on it my fortune, my reputation and my life."

Martha Coffin Pelham Wright
1806–1875

Martha Coffin Pelham Wright's life as an activist was influenced by her Nantucket Quaker heritage. With a strong female role model in her mother, Anna Folger Coffin, and the Quaker tenets of individualism, pacifism, equality of the sexes, and opposition to slavery, young Martha was well prepared for her future role as an abolitionist and suffragist.

Martha Coffin was the youngest of eight children, born in Boston on Christmas Day, 1806. The Coffin family moved to Philadelphia when she was three. Following the death of her father in 1815, Martha's mother opened a boarding house. Martha attended a Philadelphia day school and eventually transferred to a Quaker boarding school outside the city.

In 1822, Peter Pelham, a wounded soldier from the War of 1812, came to Philadelphia for medical care and boarded at the Coffin home. Martha, then 16, and Peter, 37, fell in love and wished to marry but Peter was not a Quaker and Martha's mother refused to give consent. He left for a Florida military posting, but maintained correspondence during his time away. Upon his return to Philadelphia in 1824, Mrs. Coffin finally gave consent for the couple to marry. The Quaker community, however, refused to accept the marriage and Martha was expelled from the group for marrying outside the faith.

Following Peter's early death in 1826, 19-year old Martha and her year old child, Marianna, joined Martha's mother in Aurora, New York. Here she taught with her mother at a Quaker girls" school and in 1829 married David Wright, a young law student. As David's law practice grew, the family moved to nearby Auburn, the county seat.

In the summer of 1848, Wright, by then six months pregnant with her 7th child, joined her older sister, Lucretia Coffin Mott, at a meeting with Elizabeth Cady Stanton, Jane Hunt, and Mary Ann McClintock in Waterloo, NY. These five women planned and led the first women's rights convention, held in Seneca Falls, NY on July 19th and 20th, 1848 – an event of worldwide historic importance.

Thus began Wright's twenty plus years of dedication and commitment to women's rights and the abolition of slavery. She traveled extensively on behalf of the American Anti-Slavery Society and the National Woman Suffrage Association, which she served as president in 1874. Minutes from the 1874 NWSA meeting in New York City read in part, "Martha C. Wright, one of the most judicious and clear-sighted women in the movement," a fitting tribute to one of the major 19th century reform leaders of New York State.

Chien-Shiung Wu, Ph.D.
1912–1997

Dr. Chien-Shiung Wu, a pioneering physicist, radically altered modern physical theory and changed our accepted view of the structure of the universe.

Born and educated in China, Wu received her bachelor's degree in physics from National Central University in 1934. In 1936, she moved to the United States, where she pursued a doctorate in physics from the University of California, Berkeley (1940). Dr. Wu taught briefly at Smith College before being hired as Princeton University's first female instructor.

A year later, Dr. Wu accepted a post at Columbia University, where she became involved in the Manhattan Project, designing and building the world's first atomic bombs. She held various positions with the university until her retirement in 1981, but is best known for her experiments on beta decay in 1957. For six months, Dr. Wu tested the theory presented by Drs. Tsung-Dao Lee and Chen Ning Yang, that parity – a theory that the laws of nature are not biased in any particular direction – was not conserved in certain types of nuclear reactions. Dr. Wu's groundbreaking experiments proved Drs. Lee and Yang's theory right; the longstanding belief that parity was conserved in weak subatomic interactions was shattered, altering the way in which scientists viewed the structure of the universe. In late 1957, Drs. Lee and Yang were awarded the Nobel Prize in physics for their theoretical contributions to the project, while Dr. Wu's experimental proof of the theory was overlooked.

Dr. Wu received numerous awards for her work, including eight honorary degrees, the National Medal of Science (1975), the first Wolf Prize in Physics awarded by the state of Israel (1978), the first Research Corporation Award given to a woman (1959), and the first Comstock Award given to a woman from the National Academy of Sciences (1964). She was elected as a member of the National Academy of Sciences in 1958, and in 1990, Dr. Wu became the first living scientist with an asteroid named after her.

As one of the world's foremost nuclear physicists, Dr. Wu's work was instrumental in shaping modern physical theory and blazing a trail for women in science.

Rosalyn S. Yalow, Ph.D.
1921–2011

Rosalyn Yalow was one of the nation's premier medical physicists, the first American woman to win the Nobel Prize for Medicine (1977) and the first woman to win the Lasker Prize (1976).

Yalow's Lasker Prize and Nobel Prize were awarded for one of the century's most significant scientific discoveries. Working in radioisotopes, she and her colleague, Dr. Solomon Berson, refined a new approach – called radioimmunoassay (RIA) – using radioisotopes to analyze physiological systems. The technique used radioisotopes to "tag" certain hormones or proteins, making detailed measurements possible of previously undetected concentrations of hormones. RIA opened many doors in the study of disease and chemical responses.

Rosalyn Yalow, wife and mother of two children, believed women could balance career and family life. On receiving her Nobel Prize, Yalow spoke about women in science careers: "We must believe in ourselves or no one else will believe in us…we must feel a personal responsibility to ease the path for those who come after us. The world cannot afford the loss of the talents of half its people if we are to solve the many problems that beset us."

Gloria Yerkovich
1942–

Gloria Yerkovich discovered the absence of a national system for locating missing/abducted children when her daughter was abducted by her natural father in 1974. Yerkovich didn't see her daughter again until 1984.

Yerkovich searched for years, and realized the heart of the problem of many abducted and missing children lay in the absence of a way for such children to find help. Yerkovich started Child Find in 1981, and built the organization with volunteer labor, donated equipment and skillful appeals to the media for help and support. Since more than 150,000 children a year are considered missing or abducted, a national registry of missing children was developed, as was a photographic directory of such children, and implementation of a toll-free number for children trying to find their parents.

Child Find was the prototype for the National Center for Missing and Exploited Children, and Yerkovich's efforts contributed greatly to national awareness of the problem. Awareness led to the 1982 Omnibus Victims Protection Act and the Missing Children Act, the signing of which Yerkovich witnessed at the invitation of the President of the United States.

ildred "Babe" Didrikson Zaharias
1911–1956

Babe Didrikson, the female athletic phenomenon of the century, was the child of Norwegian immigrants. Reared in poverty in South Texas, she began her extraordinarily versatile athletic career in high school basketball. She soon found that few sports opportunities were open to women. In fact, in the 1920s the trend was toward the elimination of interscholastic competition for girls, because of its "undue stress" and "morbid social influences." In many high schools all but intramural sports disappeared, and not until the 1970s would girls' high school competition be restored.

After Babe switched to track and field and collected gold medals at the 1932 Olympics, her fame enabled her to barnstorm the country with a team called "Babe Didrikson's All Americans." She excelled at every sport she tried, but she combined her natural talent with hard work. When she first took up golf she hit over a thousand balls a day, eight to ten hours a day. Drives of two hundred and fifty yards were not unusual for her.

She began to win the major ladies' golf tournaments but was quickly ruled a pro and disqualified. There was then no pro golf tour for women. Only after 1938, when she met and married George Zaharias, a professional wrestler, could she afford to refuse endorsements and reestablish amateur status. Babe went on to sweep the major ladies' titles.

In 1949 she became one of the founding members of the Ladies' Professional Golf Association. A fierce competitor with a free-wheeling style, she closed her career with a courageous, losing battle against cancer.

Category Index

Arts
Alcott, Louisa May
Anderson, Marian
Angelou, Maya
Ball, Lucille
Nellie Bly (Cochran, Elizabeth Jane)
Bourgeois, Louise
Bourke-White, Margaret
Brooks, Gwendolyn
Buck, Pearl S.
Cassatt, Mary
Cather, Willa
Child, Julia
Cooney, Joan Ganz
Croly, Jane Cunningham
de Forest, Marian
Dickinson, Emily
Fitzgerald, Ella
Fuller, Margaret
Gilman, Charlotte Perkins
Graham, Katharine
Hayes, Helen
Holdridge, Barbara
Holiday, Billie
Holladay, Wilhelmina Cole
Hurston, Zora Neale
Lange, Dorothea
Lazarus, Emma
Lin, Maya Y.
Lindbergh, Anne Morrow
Millett, Kate
Oakley, Annie
O'Keeffe, Georgia
Saubel, Katherine Siva
Shouse, Catherine Filene
Sills, Beverly
Smith, Bessie
Stowe, Harriet Beecher
Tallchief, Maria
Tarbell, Ida
Warren, Mercy Otis
Wells-Barnett, Ida B.
Welty, Eudora
Wharton, Edith
Winfrey, Oprah

Athletics
de Varona, Donna
Ederle, Gertrude "Trudy"
Gibson, Althea
King, Billie Jean
Krone, Julie
Rudolph, Wilma
Stephens, Helen
Switzer, Kathrine
Zaharias, Mildred "Babe" Didrikson

Business
Alvarado, Linda G.
Bradley, Lydia Moss
Cooney, Joan Ganz
Graham, Katharine
Harper, Martha Matilda
Holdridge, Barbara
Holladay, Wilhelmina Cole
Perkins, Rebecca Talbot
Schwartz, Anna Jacobsen
Schwartz, Felice N.
Siebert, Muriel
Strong, Harriet Williams Russell
Walker, Madam C.J.
Winfrey, Oprah

Education
Bancroft, Ann
Baum, Eleanor K.
Bethune, Mary McLeod
Bunch, Charlotte Anne
Calderone, Mary Steichen
Colvin, Ruth
Cooney, Joan Ganz
Height, Dorothy
Jackson, Shirley Ann
Keller, Helen
Keohane, Nannerl O.
Locke, Patricia A.
Lyon, Mary
Pipher, Judith L.
Sandler, Bernice Resnick
Saubel, Katherine Siva
Shalala, Donna E.
Smith, Sophia

Sullivan, Anne (Sullivan Macy)
Widnall, Sheila
Willard, Emma Hart

Government
Abzug, Bella
Albright, Madeleine Korbel
Allen, Florence Ellinwood
Bradwell, Myra
Chisholm, Shirley
Clinton, Hillary Rodham
DeCrow, Karen
Dole, Elizabeth Hanford
Ferraro, Geraldine
Ginsburg, Ruth Bader
Grasso, Ella
Griffiths, Martha Wright
Hallaren, Mary A.
Harris, Patricia Roberts
Hobby, Oveta Culp
Holm, Jeanne
Jordan, Barbara
Latimer, Allie B.
Lockwood, Belva
Mikulski, Barbara A.
Mink, Patsy Takemoto
Motley, Constance Baker
Novello, Antonia
O'Connor, Sandra Day
Pelosi, Nancy
Perkins, Frances
Rankin, Jeannette
Reno, Janet
Ridgway, Rozanne L.
Rogers, Edith Nourse
Schroeder, Patricia
Shalala, Donna E.
Smith, Margaret Chase
Stoneman, Kate
Vaught, Wilma L.
Widnall, Sheila

Humanities
Adams, Abigail
Addams, Jane
Andrus, Ethel Percy
Anthony, Susan B.
Baker, Ella

Blackwell, Antoinette
Bloomer, Amelia
Bumpers, Betty
Bunch, Charlotte Anne
Cabrini, St. Frances Xavier
Calderone, Mary Steichen
Carter, Eleanor Rosalynn Smith
Cary, Mary Ann Shadd
Catt, Carrie Chapman
Child, Lydia Maria
Cope, Mother Marianne
Davis, Paulina Kellogg Wright
Day, Dorothy
De Forest, Marian
DeCrow, Karen
DeVoe, Emma Smith
Dix, Dorothea
Dole, Elizabeth Hanford
Drexel, St. Katharine
Dudley, Anne Dallas
Dyer, Mary Barret
East, Catherine
Eastman, Crystal
Eddy, Mary Baker
Edelman, Marian Wright
Ford, Betty
Foster, Abby Kelley
Friedan, Betty
Gage, Matilda Joslyn
Grimké, Sarah
Hamer, Fannie Lou
Height, Dorothy
Holt, Bertha
Howe, Julia Ward
Huerta, Dolores
Hutchinson, Anne
Jones, Mary "Mother" Harris
Kelly, Leontine T.C.
Kelly-Dreiss, Susan
King, Coretta Scott
Kuhn, Maggie
La Flesche, Susette
LaDuke, Winona
Ledbetter, Lilly
Low, Juliette Gordon
Mankiller, Wilma
McCormick, Katharine Dexter
Millett, Kate

Mott, Lucretia
Mullany, Kate
Parks, Rosa
Paul, Alice
Peterson, Esther
Rogers, MM, Mother Mary Joseph
Roosevelt, Eleanor
Rose, Ernestine Louise Potowski
Roulet, Elaine
Ruffin, Josephine St. Pierre
Sacagawea
Sandler, Bernice Resnick
Sanger, Margaret
Saubel, Katherine Siva
Schiess, Betty Bone
Seton, St. Elizabeth Bayley
Shaw, Anna Howard
Shriver, Eunice Kennedy
Solomon, Hannah Greenebaum
Stanton, Elizabeth Cady
Steinem, Gloria
Stone, Lucy
Szold, Henrietta
Talbert, Mary Burnett
Truth, Sojourner
Tubman, Harriet
Wattleton, Faye (Alyce)
Weld, Angeline Grimké
Wells-Barnett, Ida B.
Willard, Frances E.
Winnemucca, Sarah
Woodhull, Victoria
Wright, Fanny
Wright, Martha Coffin Pelham
Yerkovich, Gloria

Philanthropy
Bradley, Lydia Moss
Eustis, Dorothy Harrison
Hunt, Helen LaKelly
Hunt, Swanee
Jacobs, Frances Wisebart
Leet, Mildred Robbins
McCormick, Katharine Dexter
Shouse, Catherine Filene
Smith, Sophia
Walker, Mary Edwards
Winfrey, Oprah

Science
Abdellah, Faye Glenn
Andersen, Dorothy H.
Apgar, Virginia
Bancroft, Ann
Barton, Clara
Baum, Eleanor K.
Benedict, Ruth Fulton
Blackwell, Elizabeth
Blackwell, Emily
Breckinridge, Mary
Cannon, Annie Jump
Carson, Rachel
Cochran, Jacqueline
Cohn, Mildred
Coleman, Bessie,
Collins, Eileen
Colwell, Rita Rossi
Cori, Gerty Theresa Radnitz
Douglas, Marjory Stoneman
Earhart, Amelia
Earle, Sylvia A.
Elion, Gertrude Belle
Evans, Alice
Ford, Loretta C.
Free, Helen Murray
Gaskin, Ina May
Gilbreth, Lillian Moller
Goeppert-Mayer, Maria
Hamilton, Alice
Hicks, Beatrice A.
Hopper, Grace Murray
Jackson, Shirley Ann
Jacobi, Mary Putnam
Jemison, Mae C.
Kelsey, Frances Oldham
Kubler-Ross, Elisabeth
Kwolek, Stephanie L.
Lindbergh, Anne Morrow
Lucid, Shannon W.
Mahoney, Mary
McClintock, Barbara
McManus, Louise
Mead, Margaret
Mitchell, Maria
Novello, Antonia
Patrick, Ruth
Pennington, Mary Engle

Pipher, Judith L.
Richards, Ellen Swallow
Richards, Linda
Ride, Sally
Sabin, Florence
Scott, Blanche Stuart
Seibert, Florence B.
Solomon, Susan
Stevens, Nettie
Taussig, Helen Brooke
Wald, Florence
Wald, Lillian
Walker, Mary Edwards
Warner, Emily Howell
Wauneka, Annie Dodge
Widnall, Sheila
Wu, Chien-Shiung
Yalow, Rosalyn

Date of Induction Index

1973
Addams, Jane
Anderson, Marian
Anthony, Susan B.
Barton, Clara
Bethune, Mary McLeod
Blackwell, Elizabeth
Buck, Pearl S.
Carlson, Rachel
Cassatt, Mary
Dickinson, Emily
Earhart, Amelia
Hamilton, Alice
Hayes, Helen
Keller, Helen
Roosevelt, Eleanor
Sabin, Florence
Smith, Margaret Chase
Stanton, Elizabeth Cady
Taussig, Helen Brooke
Tubman, Harriet

1976
Adams, Abigail
Mead, Margaret
Zaharias, Mildred "Babe" Didrikson

1979
Dix, Dorothea
Low, Juliette Gordon
Paul, Alice
Seton, St. Elizabeth Bayley

1981
Sanger, Margaret
Truth, Sojourner

1982
Catt, Carrie Chapman
Perkins, Frances

1983
Lockwood, Belva
Mott, Lucretia

1984
Jones, Mary "Mother" Harris
Smith, Bessie

1986
McClintock, Barbara
Stone, Lucy
Stowe, Harriet Beecher

1988
Brooks, Gwendolyn
Cather, Willa
Ride, Sally
Wells-Barnett, Ida B.

1990
Bourke-White, Margaret
Jordan, Barbara
King, Billie Jean
Seibert, Florence B.

1991
Elion, Gertrude

1993
Andrus, Ethel Percy
Blackwell, Antoinette
Blackwell, Emily
Chisholm, Shirley
Cochran, Jacqueline
Colvin, Ruth
Edelman, Marian Wright
Evans, Alice
Friedan, Betty
Grasso, Ella
Griffiths, Martha Wright
Hamer, Fannie Lou
Height, Dorothy
Huerta, Dolores
Jacobi, Mary Putnam
Jemison, Mae C.
Lyon, Mary
Mahoney, Mary
Mankiller, Wilma
Motley, Constance Baker
Oakley, Annie

O'Keeffe, Georgia
Parks, Rosa
Peterson, Esther
Rankin, Jeannette
Richards, Ellen Swallow
Roulet, Elaine
Saubel, Katherine Siva
Steinem, Gloria
Stephens, Helen
Wald, Lillian
Walker, Madam C.J.
Wattleton, Faye (Alyce)
Yalow, Rosalyn S.
Yerkovich, Gloria

1994
Abzug, Bella
Baker, Ella
Bradwell, Myra
Cannon, Annie Jump
Croly, Jane Cunningham
East, Catherine
Ferraro, Geraldine
Gilman, Charlotte Perkins
Hopper, Grace Murray
Hunt, Helen LaKelly
Hurston, Zora Neale
Hutchinson, Anne
Jacobs, Frances Wisebart
LaFlesche, Susette
McManus, Louise
Mitchell, Maria
Novello, Antonia
Richards, Linda
Rudolph, Wilma
Schiess, Betty Bone
Siebert, Muriel
Stevens, Nettie
Winfrey, Oprah
Winnemucca, Sarah
Wright, Fanny

1995
Apgar, Virginia
Bancroft, Ann
Bloomer, Amelia
Breckinridge, Mary
Collins, Eileen

Dole, Elizabeth Hanford
Dudley, Anne Dallas
Eddy, Mary Baker
Fitzgerald, Ella
Fuller, Margaret
Gage, Matilda Joslyn
Gilbreth, Lillian Moller
Keohane, Nannerl O.
Kuhn, Maggie
O'Connor, Sandra Day
Ruffin, Josephine St. Pierre
Schroeder, Patricia
Solomon, Hannah Greenebaum

1996
Alcott, Louisa May
Bunch, Charlotte Anne
Cabrini, St. Frances Xavier
Goeppert-Mayer, Maria
Hallaren, Mary A.
Hobby, Oveta Culp
Holladay, Wilhelmina Cole
Lindbergh, Anne Morrow
Rose, Ernestine Louise Potowski
Tallchief, Maria
Wharton, Edith

1998
Albright, Madeleine Korbel
Angelou, Maya
Bradley, Lydia Moss
Calderone, Mary Steichen
Cary, Mary Ann Shadd
Cochran, Elizabeth Jane (Nellie Bly)
Cooney, Joan Ganz
Cori, Gerty Theresa Radnitz
Grimké, Sarah
Howe, Julia Ward
Jackson, Shirley Ann
Lucid, Shannon W.
McCormick, Katharine Dexter
Ridgway, Rozanne L.
Rogers, Edith Nourse
Schwartz, Felice N.
Shriver, Eunice Kennedy
Sills, Beverly
Wald, Florence
Weld, Angelina Grimké
Wu. Chien-Shiung

2000

Abdellah, Faye Glenn
DeVoe, Emma Smith
Douglas, Marjory Stoneman
Dyer, Mary Barret
Earle, Sylvia A.
Eastman, Crystal
Holm, Jeanne
Kelly, Leontine T.C.
Kelsey, Frances Oldham
Mullany, Kate
Reno, Janet
Shaw, Anna Howard
Smith, Sophia
Tarbell, Ida
Vaught, Wilma L.
Walker, Mary Edwards
Wauneka, Annie Dodge
Welty, Eudora
Willard, Frances E.

2001

Andersen, Dorothy H.
Ball, Lucille
Carter, Eleanor Rosalynn Smith
Child, Lydia Maria
Coleman, Bessie
Day, Dorothy
de Forest, Marian
Gibson, Althea
Hicks, Beatrice A.
Holdridge, Barbara
Strong, Harriet Williams Russell
Warner, Emily Howell
Woodhull, Victoria

2002

Davis, Paulina Kellogg Wright
Ginsburg, Ruth Bader
Graham, Katharine
Holt, Bertha
Pennington, Mary Engle
Warren, Mercy Otis

2003

Alvarado, Linda G.
de Varona, Donna
Ederle, Gertrude "Trudy"
Harper, Martha Matilda

Harris, Patricia Roberts
Kwolek, Stephanie L.
Lange, Dorothea
Leet, Mildred Robbins
Mink, Patsy Takemoto
Sacagawea
Sullivan Anne (Sullivan Macy)
Widnall, Sheila

2005

Allen, Florence Ellinwood
Benedict, Ruth Fulton
Bumpers, Betty
Clinton, Hillary Rodham
Colwell, Rita Rossi
Cope, St. Marianne
Lin, Maya Y.
Locke, Patricia
Scott, Blanche Stuart
Talbert, Mary Burnett

2007

Baum, Eleanor K.
Child, Julia
Hunt, Swanee
Kubler-Ross, Elisabeth
LaDuke, Winona
Pipher, Judith L.
Shouse, Catherine Filene
Szold, Henrietta
Wright, Martha Coffin Pelham

2009

Bourgeois, Louise
Cohn, Mildred
DeCrow, Karen
Kelly-Dreiss, Susan
Latimer, Allie B.
Lazarus, Emma
Patrick, Ruth
Perkins, Rebecca Talbot
Solomon, Susan
Stoneman, Kate

2011
Drexel, St. Katharine
Eustis, Dorothy Harrison
Ford, Loretta C.
Foster, Abby Kelley
Free, Helen Murray
Holiday, Billie
King, Coretta Scott
Ledbetter, Lilly
Mikulski, Barbara A.
Shalala, Donna E.
Switzer, Kathrine

2013
Ford, Betty
Gaskin, Ina May
Krone, Julie
Millett, Kate
Pelosi, Nancy
Rogers, MM, Mother Mary Joseph
Sandler, Bernice Resnick
Schwartz, Anna Jacobsen
Willard, Emma Hart

2015
Albright, Tenley
Brinker, Nancy
Graham, Martha
Greenberger, Marcia
Iglewski, Barbara
Kilbourne, Jean
LaNier, Carlotta Walls
Marrack, Philippa
Rumsey, Mary Harriman
Smeal, Eleanor

Professions Index

Abolitionist
Cary, Mary Ann Shadd
Child, Lydia Maria
Davis, Paulina Kellogg Wright
Foster, Abby Kelley
Grimké, Sarah
Mott, Lucretia
Ruffin, Josephine St. Pierre
Stowe, Harriet Beecher
Truth, Sojourner
Tubman, Harriet
Weld, Angelina Grimké
Wright, Fanny
Wright, Martha Coffin Pelham

Academic
Abdellah, Faye Glenn
Baum, Eleanor K.
Cohn, Mildred
Ford, Loretta C.
Hamilton, Alice
Harris, Patricia Roberts
Hopper, Grace Murray
Hunt, Swanee
Jackson, Shirley Ann
Jordan, Barbara
Keohane, Nannerl O.
Kübler-Ross, Elisabeth
Locke, Patricia
Mitchell, Maria
Sabin, Florence
Shalala, Donna E.
Stevens, Nettie
Widnall, Sheila
See also Educator

Activist
Andrus, Ethel Percy
Baker, Ella
Bethune, Mary McLeod
Bumpers, Betty
Bunch, Charlotte Anne
Carter, Rosalynn Smith
Croly, Jane Cunningham
de Forest, Marian
Edelman, Marian Wright
Friedan, Betty
Hamer, Fannie Lou
Huerta, Dolores
Kelly, Bishop Leontine
Kuhn, Maggie
La Flesche, Susette
LaDuke, Winona
Ledbetter, Lilly
Locke, Patricia
Mankiller, Wilma
McCormick, Katharine Dexter
Mikulski, Barbara
Millett, Kate
Oakley, Annie
Parks, Rosa
Paul, Alice
Peterson, Esther
Rankin, Jeannette
Roulet, Elaine
Sandler, Bernice Resnick
Sanger, Margaret
Saubel, Katherine Siva
Schwartz, Felice N.
Stanton, Elizabeth Cady
Steinem, Gloria
Strong, Harriet Williams Russell
Szold, Henrietta
Talbert, Mary Burnett
Walker, Mary Edwards
Wauneka, Annie Dodge
Wells-Barnett, Ida B
Willard, Frances
Winnemucca, Sarah
Wright, Fanny

See also specific cause

Actor
Ball, Lucille
Hayes, Helen
Winfrey, Oprah

Adventurer
Bancroft, Ann
Oakley, Annie
Sacagawea
Scott, Blanche Stuart

Ambassador
Hunt, Swanee
Ridgway, Rozanne L.

Anthropologist
Benedict, Ruth Fulton
Hurston, Zora Neale
Mead, Margaret
Saubel, Katherine Siva

Architect
Lin, Maya Y.

Artist, *See* Visual Artist

Astronaut
Collins, Eileen
Jemison, Mae C.
Lucid, Shannon W.
Ride, Sally

Astronomer
Cannon, Annie Jump
Mitchell, Maria
Pipher, Judith L.

Athlete
de Varona, Donna
Ederle, Gertrude "Trudy"
Gibson, Althea
King, Billie Jean
Krone, Julie
Rudolph, Wilma
Stephens, Helen
Switzer, Kathrine
Zaharias, Mildred "Babe" Didrikson

Attorney, *See* Lawyer

Aviator
Cochran, Jacqueline
Coleman, Bessie
Collins, Eileen
Earhart, Amelia
Lindbergh, Anne Morrow
Scott, Blanche Stuart
Warner, Emily Howell

Biologist
Carson, Rachel
Earle, Sylvia
Evans, Alice
Stevens, Nettie

Business Professional. *See* Corporate
Executive; Entrepreneur

Cabinet Member
Albright, Madeleine Korbel
Clinton, Hillary Rodham
Dole, Elizabeth Hanford
Harris, Patricia Roberts
Hobby, Oveta Culp
Perkins, Frances
Reno, Janet
Shalala, Donna E.
Widnall, Sheila

Chef
Child, Julia

Chemist
Cori, Gerty Theresa Radnitz
Free, Helen Murray
Kwolek, Stephanie L.
Pennington, Mary Engle
Richards, Ellen Swallow
Solomon, Susan

Choreographer, *See* Dancer and
Choreographer

Civic Leader
Barton, Clara
Ruffin, Josephine St. Pierre
Sanger, Margaret
Szold, Henrietta

See also Public Servants; Social Reformers

Civil Rights Advocate
Baker, Ella
Coleman, Bessie
Hamer, Fannie Lou
Height, Dorothy
King, Coretta Scott
LaNier, Carlotta Walls
Latimer, Allie B.
Motley, Constance Baker

Parks, Rosa
Ruffin, Josephine St. Pierre
Talbert, Mary Burnett
Wells-Barnett, Ida B

Civil War Personality
Howe, Julia Ward
Walker, Mary Edwards

Colonial Era Personality
Dyer, Mary Barret
Hutchinson, Anne
Warren, Mercy Otis

Computer Science and Industry Leader
Hopper, Grace Murray

Congressional Member. *See* Legislator;
Senator

Corporate Executive
Cochran, Elizabeth Jane (Nellie Bly)
Graham, Katharine
Hicks, Beatrice A.
Perkins, Rebecca Talbot
Siebert, Muriel
Walker, Madam C.J.
Winfrey, Oprah

See also Entrepreneur

Dancer and Choreographer
Graham, Martha
Tallchief, Maria

Diplomat
Albright, Madeleine Korbel
Clinton, Hillary Rodham
Hunt, Swanee
Ridgway, Rozanne L.

Disability Advocate
Ederle, Gertrude "Trudy"
Eustis, Dorothy Harrison
Holt, Bertha
Keller, Helen
Shriver, Eunice Kennedy
Sullivan, Anne (Sullivan Macy)

Doctor. *See* Physician

Economist
Schwartz, Anna Jacobson

Editor
Cary, Mary Ann Shadd
Child, Lydia Maria
Fuller, Margaret
Graham, Katharine
Steinem, Gloria
Stone, Lucy

Educator
Abdellah, Faye Glenn
Andrus, Ethel Percy
Baum, Eleanor K.
Bethune, Mary McLeod
Blackwell, Emily
Cary, Mary Ann Shadd
Cohn, Mildred
Colvin, Ruth
Davis, Paulina Kellogg Wright
Drexel, St. Katharine
Ford, Loretta C.
Hunt, Swanee
Jackson, Shirley Ann
Keohane, Nannerl O.
Kübler-Ross, Elisabeth
Locke, Patricia
Lyon, Mary
McManus, Louise
Mitchell, Maria
Perkins, Frances
Richards, Ellen Swallow
Richards, Linda
Sabin, Florence
Seton, St. Elizabeth Bayley
Shalala, Donna E.
Sullivan, Anne (Sullivan Macy)
Talbert, Mary Burnett
Willard, Emma Hart

Engineer
Baum, Eleanor K.
Gilbreth, Lillian Moller
Hicks, Beatrice A.
Widnall, Sheila

Entertainer
Oakley, Annie

See also Actor; Musician; Television and Radio Personality; Singer

Entrepreneur
Alvarado, Linda G.
Ball, Lucille
Bloomer, Amelia
Bradley, Lydia Moss
Harper, Martha Matilda
Holdridge, Barbara
Siebert, Muriel
Strong, Harriet Williams Russell
Walker, Madam C.J.
Winfrey, Oprah

Environmentalist
Carson, Rachel
Douglas, Marjory Stoneman
Earle, Sylvia
LaDuke, Winona
Patrick, Ruth
Richards, Ellen Swallow

Fashion Designer and Innovator
Bloomer, Amelia

Financial Services
Siebert, Muriel

First Lady
Adams, Abigail
Carter, Rosalynn Smith
Clinton, Hillary Rodham
Ford, Betty
Roosevelt, Eleanor

Governor
Grasso, Ella

Historian
Warren, Mercy Otis

Humanitarian
Addams, Jane
Barton, Clara
Brinker, Nancy
Bumpers, Betty

Carter, Rosalynn Smith
Cope, St. Marianne,
Dix, Dorothea
Drexel, St. Katharine
Eustis, Dorothy Harrison
Holt, Bertha
Jacobs, Frances Wisebart
Kelly-Dreiss, Susan
King, Coretta Scott
Latimer, Allie B.
Perkins, Rebecca Talbot
Rogers, Mother Mary Joseph, MM
Roosevelt, Eleanor
Roulet, Elaine
Shriver, Eunice Kennedy
Solomon, Hannah Greenebaum
Wauneka, Annie Dodge
Yerkovich, Gloria

Inventor
Elion, Gertrude
Hicks, Beatrice A.
Kwolek, Stephanie L.
Pennington, Mary Engle
Strong, Harriet Williams Russell

Journalist
Bloomer, Amelia
Bourke-White, Margaret
Bunch, Charlotte Anne
Cary, Mary Ann Shadd
Cochran, Elizabeth Jane (Nellie Bly)
Croly, Jane Cunningham
Davis, Paulina Kellogg Wright
Day, Dorothy
de Forest, Marian
Fuller, Margaret
Graham, Katharine
Tarbell, Ida

Judge and Supreme Court Associate Justice
Allen, Florence Ellinwood
Ginsburg, Ruth Bader
Griffiths, Martha Wright
Motley, Constance Baker
O'Connor, Sandra Day

Labor Leader
Huerta, Dolores
Jones, Mary "Mother" Harris
Mullany, Kate
Perkins, Frances
Peterson, Esther

Lawyer
Abzug, Bella
Allen, Florence
Bradwell, Myra
Cary, Mary Ann Shadd
Clinton, Hillary Rodham
DeCrow, Karen
Eastman, Crystal
Edelman, Marian Wright
Ginsburg, Ruth Bader
Griffiths, Martha Wright
Harris, Patricia Roberts
Jordan, Barbara
Latimer, Allie B.
Lockwood, Belva
Mink, Patsy Takemoto
Motley, Constance Baker
O'Connor, Sandra Day
Reno, Janet
Stoneman, Kate

Lecturer
Anthony, Susan B
Foster, Abby Kelley
Gilman, Charlotte Perkins
Keller, Helen
La Flesche, Susette
Roosevelt, Eleanor
Rose, Ernestine Louise Potowski
Sanger, Margaret
Shaw, Anna Howard
Stone, Lucy
Truth, Sojourner

Legislator
Abzug, Bella
Chisholm, Shirley
Grasso, Ella
Griffiths, Martha Wright
Jordan, Barbara
Mikulski, Barbara
Mink, Patsy Takemoto

Pelosi, Nancy
Rankin, Jeannette
Rogers, Edith Nourse
Schroeder, Patricia
Smith, Margaret Chase

See also Senator

Mathematician
Hopper, Grace Murray

Medical Professional. See Nurse; Physician

Midwife
Gaskin, Ina May

Military Personnel
Hallaren, Mary A.
Hobby, Oveta Culp
Holm, Jeanne
Hopper, Grace Murray
Vaught, Wilma

Museum Founder
Holladay, Wilhelmina Cole
Saubel, Katherine Siva

Nobel Laureate
Addams, Jane
Buck, Pearl S.
Cori, Gerty Theresa Radnitz
Elion, Gertrude
Goeppert-Mayer, Maria
McClintock, Barbara
Yalow, Rosalyn S.

Non-Profit Organization Executive
Brinker, Nancy
Calderone, Mary Steichen
Dole, Elizabeth Hanford
Edelman, Marian Wright
Holt, Bertha
Jacobs, Frances Wisebart
Kuhn, Maggie
Leet, Mildred Robbins
Low, Juliette Gordon
Roulet, Elaine
Schwartz, Felice N.
Solomon, Hannah Greenebaum
Wattleton, Faye (Alyce)

Nurse
Abdellah, Faye Glenn
Barton, Clara
Breckinridge, Mary
Ford, Loretta C.
Mahoney, Mary
McManus, Louise
Richards, Linda
Wald, Florence
Wald, Lillian
Wattleton, Faye (Alyce)

Painter
Cassatt, Mary
O'Keeffe, Georgia

Philanthropist
Hunt, Helen LaKelly
Hunt, Swanee
Leet, Mildred Robbins
McCormick, Katharine Dexter
Perkins, Rebecca Talbot
Shouse, Catherine Filene
Siebert, Muriel
Smith, Sophia
Walker, Madam C.J.
Winfrey, Oprah

Photographer
Bourke-White, Margaret
Lange, Dorothea

Physician
Andersen, Dorothy H.
Apgar, Virginia
Blackwell, Elizabeth
Blackwell, Emily
Calderone, Mary Steichen
Cori, Gerty Theresa Radnitz
Hamilton, Alice
Jacobi, Mary Putnam
Jemison, Mae C.
Kelsey, Frances Kathleen Oldham
Kübler-Ross, Elisabeth
Novello, Antonia
Sabin, Florence
Seibert, Florence B.
Taussig, Helen Brooke
Walker, Mary Edwards

Physicist
Goeppert-Mayer, Maria
Jackson, Shirley Ann
Ride, Sally
Wu, Chien Shiung
Yalow, Rosalyn S.

Playwright
Warren, Mercy Otis

Poet
Brooks, Gwendolyn
Dickinson, Emily
Howe, Julia Ward
Lazarus, Emma
Warren, Mercy Otis

Politician
Abzug, Bella
Chisholm, Shirley
Clinton, Hillary Rodham
Ferraro, Geraldine
Grasso, Ella
Jordan, Barbara
LaDuke, Winona
Lockwood, Belva
Pelosi, Nancy
Rankin, Jeannette
Rogers, Edith Nourse
Schroeder, Patricia
Smith, Margaret Chase

Psychologist
Gilbreth, Lillian Moller

Public Servant
Albright, Madeleine Korbel
Allen, Florence Ellinwood
Colwell, Rita Rossi
Earle, Sylvia
East, Catherine
Edelman, Marian Wright
Ginsburg, Ruth Bader
Grasso, Ella
Griffiths, Martha Wright
Harris, Patricia Roberts
Hobby, Oveta Culp,
Kelsey, Frances Kathleen Oldham
Latimer, Allie B.

Mankiller, Wilma
Motley, Constance Baker
Novello, Antonia
O'Connor, Sandra Day
Parks, Rosa
Pelosi, Nancy
Perkins, Frances
Peterson, Esther
Reno, Janet
Ridgway, Rozanne L.
Sandler, Bernice Resnick
Shalala, Donna E.
Siebert, Muriel
Solomon, Susan
Widnall, Sheila

See also Civic Leaders; Diplomats; Politicians

Public Speaker. *See* Lecturer

Publisher
Bradwell, Myra
Gilman, Charlotte Perkins
Graham, Katharine
Holdridge, Barbara
Woodhull, Victoria

Religious Leader
Blackwell, Antoinette
Cabrini, St. Frances Xavier
Cope, St. Marianne
Drexel, St. Katharine
Dyer, Mary Barret
Eddy, Mary Baker
Hutchinson, Anne
Kelly, Bishop Leontine
Rogers, Mother Mary Joseph, MM
Schiess, Betty Bone
Seton, St. Elizabeth Bayley
Shaw, Anna Howard

Representative. *See* Legislator

Revolutionary War Personality
Adams, Abigail
Warren, Mercy Otis

Scientist
Andersen, Dorothy H.
Cannon, Annie Jump

Carson, Rachel
Cohn, Mildred
Colwell, Rita Rossi
Cori, Gerty Theresa Radnitz
Earle, Sylvia
Elion, Gertrude
Evans, Alice
Free, Helen Murray
Goeppert-Mayer, Maria
Iglewski, Barbara
Jackson, Shirley Ann
Kwolek, Stephanie L.
Marrack, Philippa
McClintock, Barbara
Mitchell, Maria
Patrick, Ruth
Pennington, Mary Engle
Pipher, Judith L.
Richards, Ellen Swallow
Ride, Sally
Sabin, Florence
Seibert, Florence B.
Solomon, Susan
Stevens, Nettie
Taussig, Helen Brooke
Wu, Chien Shiung
Yalow, Rosalyn S.

Sculptor
Bourgeois, Louise
Lin Maya Y.

Senator
Clinton, Hillary Rodham
Dole, Elizabeth Hanford
Mikulski, Barbara
Smith, Margaret Chase

Singer
Anderson, Marian
Fitzgerald, Ella
Holiday, Billie
Sills, Beverly
Smith, Bessie

Social Reformer
Addams, Jane
Davis, Paulina Kellogg Wright
Day, Dorothy

Dix, Dorothea
Eastman, Crystal
Eustis, Dorothy Harrison
Foster, Abby Kelley
Keller, Helen
Mott, Lucretia
Rose, Ernestine Louise Potowski
Talbert, Mary Burnett
Wald, Lillian
Willard, Frances

See also Civil Rights Activist; Humanitarian; Suffragist

Sports Executives
Alvarado, Linda
Stephens, Helen

Sports Figure. *See* Athlete

Suffragist
Allen, Florence Ellinwood
Anthony, Susan B.
Blackwell, Antoinette
Bloomer, Amelia
Catt, Carrie Chapman,
Davis, Paulina Kellogg Wright
DeVoe, Emma Smith
Dudley, Anne Dallas
Foster, Abby Kelley
Gage, Matilda Joslyn
Howe, Julia Ward
Mahoney, Mary
McCormick, Katharine Dexter
Mott, Lucretia
Paul, Alice
Rose, Ernestine Louise Potowski
Ruffin, Josephine St. Pierre
Shaw, Anna Howard
Stanton, Elizabeth Cady
Stone, Lucy
Stoneman, Kate
Strong, Harriet Williams Russell
Talbert, Mary Burnett
Truth, Sojourner
Wells-Barnett, Ida B.
Wright, Fanny
Wright, Martha Coffin Pelham

Surgeon General
Abdellah, Faye Glenn
Novello, Antonia

Television and Radio Executives
Ball, Lucille
Cooney, Joan Ganz
Winfrey, Oprah

Television and Radio Personalities
Ball, Lucille
Child, Julia
de Varona, Donna
Winfrey, Oprah

Visual Artist
Bourgeois, Louise

Women's Rights Activist
DeCrow, Karen
East, Catherine
Friedan, Betty

Writer
Alcott, Louisa May
Angelou, Maya
Anthony, Susan B.
Brooks, Gwendolyn
Buck, Pearl S.
Cather, Willa
Child, Lydia Maria,
Dickinson, Emily
Friedan, Betty
Fuller, Margaret
Gilman, Charlotte Perkins
Howe, Julia Ward
Hurston, Zora Neale
Keller, Helen
Kübler-Ross, Elisabeth,
La Flesche, Susette
Lazarus, Emma
Lindbergh, Anne Morrow
Millett, Kate
Schwartz, Felice N.
Stanton, Elizabeth Cady
Stowe, Harriet Beecher
Tarbell, Ida
Warren, Mercy Otis
Welty, Eudora
Wharton, Edith

Youth Group Founder
Low, Juliette Gordon

Author Bios

Jill S. Tietjen, P.E., CEO of the National Women's Hall of Fame, has a long affiliation with the Hall. An electrical engineer by profession, Tietjen brings a depth of knowledge about women's history to the position through her years of service in the non-profit arena and as the co-author of the best-selling and award-winning book *Her Story: A Timeline of the Women Who Changed America*. She currently blogs for the *Huffington Post*, speaks nationally on the contributions of women and nominates women for national awards. She has successfully nominated women into the National Women's Hall of Fame and has twice seen her recipients receive the National Medal of Technology and Innovation. Her life mission is to tell the stories of great women. She is a graduate of the University of Virginia and the University of North Carolina at Charlotte.

A native of northern New York, **Jillaine Newman** joined the National Women's Hall of Fame as an administrative assistant in 2014. Along with nearly 15 years' administrative support experience in diverse industries, Jillaine has extensive experience copyediting journal articles, conference submissions, grant proposals and course syllabi for academics speaking English as a second language. She previously taught English to adults in Kamakura, Japan. Jillaine received a bachelor of arts in professional and technical communication from SUNY Polytechnic Institute.

Merrill Amos, M.A. is the Curator and Educator at the National Women's Hall of Fame. A graduate of the University of San Francisco and Hobart and William Smith Colleges, she holds degrees in Museum Studies and Women's Studies, respectively, and is also an accomplished singer/songwriter. She has curated exhibitions ranging in topic from Mexican folk art to Catholic women's education and remains in constant pursuit of her passion for achieving social justice through education. She has lived many places throughout the U.S. but calls Cazenovia, New York home. Merrill Amos once trespassed at Harriet Tubman's house with a suffragette's great-great-granddaughter and a congresswoman, during which time she learned first-hand what it means to not be a well-behaved woman.

Acknowledgements

The authors wish to thank The Jacobs Press,
particularly Marsha Costello, Laura Posecznick and Mike Trapani.

We also acknowledge Irene Kelly, Marilyn Bero and Pat Alnes
who suggested putting this information together.

72 of our 266 Inductees pictured: Left to right by rows:

First Row: Allie Latimer, Ann Bancroft, Eileen Collins, Kate Millett, Betty Bumpers, Charlotte Bunch, Coretta Scott King, Sandra Day O'Connor

Second Row: Maya Lin, Joan Ganz Cooney, Donna de Varona, Eleanor Smeal, Rosalynn Carter, Loretta Ford, Susan B. Anthony, Wilma Vaught

Third Row: Nancy Pelosi, Elizabeth Cady Stanton, Antonia Novello, Eleanor Baum, Marcia Greenberger, Helen Hunt, Swanee Hunt, Lucille Ball

Fourth Row: Ella Fitzgerald, Philippa Marrack, Marian Wright Edelman, Rozanne Ridgway, Shannon Lucid, Ruth Colvin, Nannerl Koehane, Dolores Huerta

Fifth Row: Eunice Shriver, Betty Schiess, Susan Solomon, Wilhelmina Holladay, Elaine Roulet, Winona LaDuke, Helen Murray Free, Kathrine Switzer

Sixth Row: Julia Child, Madeleine Albright, Harriet Tubman, Faye Wattleton, Janet Reno, Alice Paul, Faye Abdellah, Patsy Mink

Seventh Row: Mae Jemison, Lucretia Mott, Barbara Mikulski, Jean Kilbourne, Oprah Winfrey, Sheila Widnall, Carrie Chapman Catt, Judy Pipher

Eighth Row: Sally Ride, Rita Colwell, Pat Schroeder, Gloria Yerkovich, Annie Dodge Wauneka, Gloria Steinem, Sylvia Earle, Maria Tallchief

Ninth Row: Shirley Jackson, Barbara Holdridge, Elizabeth Dole, Ina May Gaskin, Amelia Earhart, Susan Kelly-Dreiss, Wilma Mankiller, Carlotta Walls LaNier